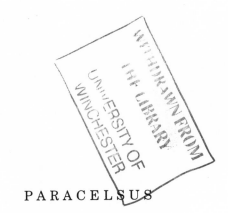

2

PARACELSUS

ALTERIVS NONSIT QVI SVVS ESSE POTEST

EFIGIES AVREOLI THEOPHRASTI AB HOHEN:
HEIM SVE ÆTATIS 47
    OMNE DONVM PERFECTVM A DEO
INPERFECTVM A DIABOLO

1 SA╪ 40

PARACELSUS

Speculative Theory and the Crisis of the Early Reformation

Andrew Weeks

SUNY Series in
Western Esoteric Traditions

David Appelbaum, Editor

STATE UNIVERSITY OF NEW YORK PRESS

August Hirschvogel's contemporaneous engravings of Paracelsus in the cover and frontispiece designs are reproduced with the permission of the Albertina, Vienna.

Production by Ruth Fisher
Marketing by Nancy Farrell

Published by
State University of New York Press

For information, address the State University of New York Press, State University Plaza, Albany, NY 12246

Library of Congress Cataloging-in-Publication Data
Weeks, Andrew.
    Paracelsus : speculative theory and the crisis of the early Reformation / Andrew Weeks.
        p.   cm. — (SUNY series in Western esoteric traditions)
    Includes bibliographical references and index.
    ISBN 0-7914-3147-9 (alk. paper). — ISBN 0-7914-3148-7 (pbk. : alk. paper)
    1. Paracelsus, 1493–1541. 2. Reformation—Europe. German -speaking. 3. Renaissance—Europe, German-speaking. 4. Europe, German-speaking—Intellectual life—16th century. I. Title. II. Series.
B785.P24W35   1997
199'.494—dc20   96-16616
                                                                                CIP

10 9 8 7 6 5 4 3 2 1

To my infant daughter Hannah Rose,
her mother Veronika Weeks-Strotzka,
her grandmother Mary Fern Weeks, and
her greatgrandmother Rosa Hannah Winks

Te digo que la rosa es eterna y que sólo su apariencia puede cambiar.
—Jorge Luis Borges, *La rosa de Paracelso*

Contents

Preface _____

Paracelsus is an errant star in the firmament of sixteenth-century aspirations. Born roughly 500 years ago in 1493 or 1494 at Einsiedeln in Switzerland, he appears to have been destined for the life of a restless wanderer whose travels and stations in mature years would be concentrated in South Germany, Switzerland, and Austria. As a medical theorist and philosopher of nature, Paracelsus met with many setbacks and few successes in life, but soon after his death in 1541, his few printed tracts and myriad scattered manuscripts would make him one of the most famous and controversial figures of his age. In character, language, and scope, the writings of Paracelsus are certainly among the most formidable documents of early German literature. However, their content often rambles toward uncertain ends, dissipating between the elaborations of a physician and those of a philosopher and mystic.

This uncategorizable thought and writing can be fittingly characterized by means of a term used by Paracelsus himself, a word resonant with current preoccupations. *Theory* fills a large portion of his books, tracts, and fragments. What his writings convey most often and most spectacularly is neither practice nor empirical observation, but rather a speculative and contemplative thought that roams among disciplines and subjects as freely as Paracelsus wandered between cities. Despite the vast differences between his mentality and ours, theory is an apt characterization for a writing that can alternate in a single fragment between the projects of explaining nature, healing human life, interpreting the meanings of things, and imagining their cosmic, metaphysical, and divine contexts.

Paracelsian theory is a strange creation. Already during his own century, conjectures were made regarding its origins and kinships. Even knowledgeable modern commentators have differed greatly on the issue of his key influences, finding his religious sources among the medieval, Lutheran, or dissenting Spiritualist tendencies of his period, or associating him with Neoplatonistic, Hermetic, or Gnostic elements in Renaissance philosophy. Though the suggestions are diverse, they fall into two chief categories: either his work is seen as affiliated with the religious culture of his time, or it is linked to the philosophical and scientific currents of the Renaissance. During his own century, his name was connected with the two figures who were to become emblematic for the affinities accorded him: Luther and Faust, the reformer and the charlatan—as some would have it, the medieval bigot or the forward-looking humanist. Aptly or not, the alternative of Luther or Faust has often stood for reaction versus progress.

Because of these dichotomies, the study of Paracelsus has frequently been subdivided by the orientations of science and religion. The scientific-historical approach to Paracelsus has been represented by Karl Sudhoff, Walter Pagel, and, most recently, Allen G. Debus; and the theological viewpoint most ably in this century by Wilhelm Matthießen, Franz Strunz, and, above all, Kurt Goldammer. If in recent times the scientific-historical interpretation has endeavored to incorporate an awareness of Paracelsus's "mysticism," the two approaches have not surmounted the duality of Renaissance and Reformation frames of reference. To some extent, however, the duality of resultant perspectives can be surmounted by our term *theory*. To be sure, Paracelsus's *theorica* is a usage of the medical or philosophical writings. Yet, in them, the term is employed neutrally with regard to the modern dichotomization of scientific and religious speculation. Theory-*theorica* can characterize metaphysical elements in the scientific division of his complete writings without implying a *contradictio in adjecto*. No other term is broad enough to surmount the false dichotomy that relegates religious themes to a sociological context extraneous to intellectual history.

Paracelsian theory was born of the crisis of the 1520s, in an era when many of the intellectual strains and conflicts of the preceding decades and centuries were being revived with a frenzied vitality that brought forth new creations of intellect, imagination, and faith. My argument in this monograph is that Paracelsus's seminal writings originated during a much briefer interval than has commonly been maintained, during a span of several decisive years, and that they arose, not in isolation of the events accompanying the early Reformation, but rather as an immediate outgrowth of these events. In relating Paracelsian theory to the crises of the early Reformation, my purpose is not to uphold or disclaim his putative allegiances to Lutheranism, Neoplatonism, Spiritualism, Catholicism, or any other doctrine, confession, or group of the time. Such allegiances have often been exaggerated. My intention is rather to demonstrate that his work originated in a crisis of authority which motivated other doctrinal, philosophical, and political disputes occurring in his surroundings. Issues will be discussed that should offer insight into intellectual sources of his theories. However, surely the most profound source of Paracelsian theory has to be sought in a critical transformation of thinking, in an explosion, collapse, and reconstruction of traditional authority, an event from which we can retrieve only shards and pieces in the form of declamations, doctrines, or theories.

My objective is not to argue for the present-day relevance of Paracelsian theory. His ideas presuppose conditions of life and knowledge quite remote from ours. Although it is an error to assume that his more peculiar notions were widely believed in his time, little is learned by measuring him against an anachronistic standard of progress or reaction. Coherence and incoherence are the poles between which his thought struggles for expression and therefore can best be evaluated. This is not said in order to relativize the truth claims of his work. Because Paracelsus did consider his formulations true, he might indeed have considered our search for influences misguided. A correct formula is, after all, true in its coherent entirety; the miscalculation has a source that can be traced to some precise point of introduction. What attracted assent in the discourse of Paracelsus rang true for him by virtue of its inner cohesion and its resonance with a context remote from our own but present to him and his fellows. This wellspring of validity is only obfuscated by representing him and his notions as exemplary or relevant to our own values and purposes.

I will argue for a text-centered historicism that approaches the writings of Paracelsus as writings, not as collections of sayings by an oracular genius and not as grist for a postmodern theoretical mill. In-depth perspective should mean letting his writings speak for themselves and allowing the voices that speak through his work to evoke their own historical context. No doubt the theme of this book, Paracelsus and the crisis of the early Reformation, is in many respects a remote one for modern readers. But neither the theme nor the reader would be served by claiming him as an unrecognized prophet and man for our time, much less by browbeating his obscurity with the anachronisms of contemporary critical theory. The *prima facie* remoteness of his writings calls for a text-centered historicism, for an approach that, without losing itself in tangential details, allows Paracelsus to mean what he says, without requiring us to accept at face value what is insupportable or contradictory.

In interpreting Paracelsus, I am indebted to the many path-forging researchers of the past and present who have devoted much of their lifetimes to editing and analyzing his work, and whose first-hand knowledge of the manuscript sources I lack. Assuredly, much of what is right in this book derives from their efforts, while much of what is wrong results from the absence of their experience and involvement. Nevertheless, the outsider to the field of Paracelsus studies can enjoy one advantage: that of an interested but uncommitted skepticism.

Introduction

ich bin nit Lutherus, ich bin Theophrastus,
und bin der Theophrastus, den ir zu Basel
Cacophrastum hießen. . . . und bin ich euch
Cacophrastus nit genug gewachsen, ich sag
euch, meine schuchriemen wissen mer dan ir
und alle euer schulmeister, Galenus und
Avicenna, und all eure hohenschul. wolt ir
das nicht lassen war sein, legent curam
utramque auf die wag und secht wie die wag
ausschlage.

I am not Luther, I am Theophrastus, the
Theophrastus you called 'Cacophrastus' in
Basel. . . . And if I am not match enough
for you as Cacophrastus, I tell you, my
shoestrings know more than you and all your
schoolmasters, Galen and Avicenna, and all
your high schools. If you can't accept that
as true, lay both cures on the scales and
see how they tip.[1]

Theophrastus was of course not Luther. But the two men were
contemporaries, and no one but Luther is so appositely other for the
medical reformer Theophrastus Bombastus von Hohenheim, who is
known as Paracelsus. This sixteenth-century physician, medical
theorist, philosopher of nature, writer on theology, and mystic, who
was also an antiauthoritarian and a rebel against traditions and
institutions, rivalled Luther in resolve, if not in results. The gestures and cadences of the medical reformer are those of an age of
religious war. The challenge hurled at his opponents to weigh their
cures on the scales of justice recalls a Reformation engraving in
which Holy Scripture alone tips the balance against the crushing

1

pomp and luxury of the Roman Church. Similarly, the symbolic gauntlet cast down in defiance: just as Luther and his students had burned the canon law and bull of excommunication in Wittenberg, Paracelsus publicly cast into the flames a medieval medical compendium at the University of Basel. Instinctively aware of the symbolic form of his actions, Hohenheim flaunted the intransigence of a man beholden to none. Through his actions and writings, he made the agony of his uncompromising determination, made the apodictic certainty of his intuitions and the sweeping scope of his theories, into distinctive marks of the life and legend of Paracelsus.

At a critical moment of his career, Paracelsus signaled his sense of mission by distinguishing himself from, and by the same token comparing himself with, the supreme reformer of his time: the "humble monk" who had defied the pope, breaching the legal fortifications of Rome; who stood his ground even before Emperor Charles V, thereby awakening new conscience in people of all estates throughout the German lands and beyond. For a Paracelsus whose writings and actions were perforce concerned nearly as much with rhetorical and propagandistic self-legitimation as with medical practices or clearly enunciated religious doctrines, the preeminence of Luther as the sovereign reformer of the world could exert an influence that did not entail creedal conformity.

No one is more appositely other than Luther. When the name is invoked, it is as if kingdoms were being defined by a boundary which the physician deigns to suffer: "You well know that I let Luther answer for his affairs; I shall answer for my own. . ." (*du weißt wol, ich laß Lutherum sein ding verantworten; ich will das mein selbst verantworten. . . .*) The statement seems to echo Luther's own pledge, in the *Letter to the German Nobility* (1520), to let the medical field reform its own university faculties and leave theology and law to him. The wary respect expressed by Paracelsus does not entail doctrinal adherence. The point is that he and Luther are up against the same treachery. Nothing more than a coarse word of nonaggression is therefore in order: "for [Luther] shall not unbind a lace of my shoes" (*dan er sol mir nicht ein rinken auftun in meinen schuhen*). By no means does the physician, who calls himself in the same passage the *Monarcha medicorum*, wish to be deemed less than his counterpart in Wittenberg.

Paracelsus was not a Lutheran, nor a Humanist, nor a member of any religious sect of the day. He was certainly not a loyal Catholic during his lifetime, though he was buried in this faith in Salzburg. He stands as an anomaly. The very name conveys a mixture of exaltation and antithesis, a lofty but rather cryptic flourish of sovereignty. Generally, the Humanistic nomenclature of sixteenth-century Germany either translated a German surname into Latin or Greek (thus Bauer, "peasant," became *Agricola*; and Schwarzerd, "black earth," became *Melanchthon*), or the Humanistic name offered a motto (Luther as *Eleutherius*, "the free man"). By contrast, the root intention of the name *Paracelsus*—a name that appeared on tracts ushered into print in the author's lifetime—has not been resolved to the agreement of scholars. It is either an oblique rendering of Hohenheim, or perhaps a boast that the so-named exceeds the ancient medical authority Celsus, or that the bearer is the author of works of a paradoxical, antithetical character. Several of Paracelsus's posthumously published works bear mysterious but resonant titles containing the prefix *para-* (*Opus Paramirum de Medica Industria*, *Opus Paragranum*, and the versions of *Opus Paramirum*). A distinctive trademark is conveyed by the combination of the name with the titles of these books.

Despite numerous imitations, the authenticated writings of Paracelsus, which have been gathered and evaluated in a process of edition centuries in duration, bear the vivid stamp of their author's personality. They address the modern reader in a voice that is reckless yet also unaffected and unpolished, in a tone ranging from the personal, almost confessional, admission, to the coarse fury of the self-proclaimed "monarch of physicians," who, like a harried beast, threatens to sweep aside the horde of vile detractors hounding his path.

If this voice has no equal in early German literature, the tone of his productions was largely unfiltered by a reflective and studied process of composition of the kind that characterized most thoughtful literature then or thereafter. We learn from the contemporary account of Johannes Oporinus, and from Paracelsus's own hint, that he dictated many of his works to "secretaries."[2] Beginning in Basel, Oporinus served him for several years in this capacity, during what would prove to be the zenith and debacle of the master's career. In 1555, Oporinus recalled in a letter to Johann Weyer (an anti-Paracelsian, but also an independent-minded critic of witchcraft persecutions) how the master, who had been dignified by a dual position at the university and as an official physician to the city, was in the habit of returning home late after garrulous nocturnal drinking bouts. Sometimes Paracelsus would fall into bed fully clothed and then wake up in a fit of rage, terrifying young Oporinus by banging against the wall the sword he carried with him at all times and claimed to have received from an executioner. But it could also happen that the master would arouse himself and his amanuensis from sleep, and, though still inebriated, dictate forth his philosophy with such fluidity and clear sense that, as Oporinus recollected, a sober person might not have improved upon it.

The unflattering frankness of Oporinus's recollections has elicited censure from German Paracelsus scholars.[3] However, the context of the letter is by no means one-sidedly hostile; and the details actually tally with Paracelsus's own writings in point of his bouts of rage and knowledge of wine. At the very least, the memoir of Oporinus confirms what is implicit in the known facts of Paracelsus's biography: he was a man perpetually on the move, driven by passions and ideas. His motto was that of the self-made independent: "Let no one belong to another who can belong to himself" (*alterius non sit qui suus esse potest*).[4] Lacking stable ties and long-term associations, he produced his works, even in the best of years, unharbored by a scholar's study and library. In this, Paracelsus would appear to have been the very antithesis of Luther, the sedentary Wittenberger and unflinching center of the Reformation. However, he resembles Luther in that what he wrote, and what he in writing became, was conceived and carried out in large part in the heat of furious controversies.

Paracelsus may be said to have created himself *ex nihilo*, by uttering and enacting into being the great congeries of theories, legends, and deeds that became associated with his name. Though much has been written about his broad background of experience, far less is evident in his work than scholars favorably disposed to him have cared to acknowledge. What we know about his past, prior to his first record of himself as a writer and polemicist, is vague. There is no reason to doubt that the elder Hohenheim, a physician of Swabian origin, imparted to his son a love of medicine, nor that his father and others in the mining regions of Carinthia and Tirol furnished the pupil and young man with a practical knowledge of alchemy that would become a key ingredient in the Parcelsian medicine and philosophy. His writings give evidence of filial loyalty and trust. They display a wealth of practical-alchemical lore, and document his informed interest in the occupational diseases of miners, all of which may be read as tokens of an early vocation inherited from a physician father in a mining region in the South of Austria.

It is especially striking that in his claims of originality, he also acknowledges his debt to his father, as in this boast of a peculiar knowledge of mathematic art: "For I am different. I give thanks to the school into which I came, [and] boast of no other man than of him who gave birth to me and instructed me early" (*dan anderst bin ich. ich bedank mich der schul in die ich komen bin, berüme mich keines menschen als alein des, der mich geboren hat und mich jung aufgeweist hat*—I,12:205). Actually, no branch of learning is less in evidence in his writings than mathematics; but even this overbearing confidence in all fields must have owed something to the encouragement of his elders. Another passage in his late writings expands his filial gratitude with reference to an early instruction in *philosophia adepta*:

From childhood on, I pursued these things and learned from good instructors, who had the firmest knowledge of the *adepta philosophia* and energetically researched the arts in the most thorough way. First of all, Wilhelm von Hohenheim, my father, who has never forsaken me, and then, with him, a great number whose names cannot easily all be mentioned, with many writings of the ancients and moderns from various sources, who expended much effort . . .

von kintheit auf hab ich die ding getriben und von guten under- richtern gelernet, die in der adepta philosophia die ergründesten warent und den künsten mechtig nach gründeten. erstlich Wilhelmus von Hohenheim, meinen vatter, der mich nie verlassen hat, demnach und mit sampt im ein große zal, die nit wol zu nennen ist, mit sampt vilerlei geschriften der alten und der neuen von etlichen herkomen, die sich groß gemühet habent . . . . (I,10:354)

He goes on to give several names of Carinthian churchmen to whom he considers himself indebted. This acknowledgment late in life of having been influenced or educated by clericals who pursued alchemistic studies takes on some further credibility from the indications found throughout his writings of a casual knowledge of a kind that might have been readily acquired by someone who had attended monastery schools (but not sufficient to demonstrate that he had studied theology). References to religious figures abound. These include the twelfth-century visionary mystic and medical writer,

Hildegard of Bingen (I,13:334), who is a possible precursor of his own medicine and nature philosophy, with its study of microcosm, macrocosm, and its divine signs borne by the created things of nature.

However, there is no certainty regarding Hohenheim's study at the University of Ferrara, where he is supposed to have earned a doctorate,[5] nor regarding his attendance at the other Italian, German, and French universities where, years later, he claimed to have sought to learn the true "ground in medicine" (*den grunt in der arznei*—I,10:19). In one treatise, he refers to Ficino as the "best of Italian physicians" (*Italorum vero Marsilius medicorum optimus fuit*—I,4:71). But he could easily have known of Ficino, Leoniceno, or Manardo of Ferrara without having studied there or anywhere else in Italy.

The same must be said of the great migratory period of the young man. His reportedly far-ranging wanderings fulfill several functions in Paracelsus scholarship: biographically, they cap his uncertain years of study in Ferrara; historically and culturally, his travels qualify him as an intrepid seeker-discoverer of the Renaissance type; methodologically for his work, the journeyman years appear to bear out his preference for fresh experience over stale academic doctrine. With regard to the multifariousness of his observations, the awareness of many countries is put forward by him as a rationale for his distinct findings. On the last two points, caution is in order: if we were to suppose that Paracelsus had never departed from German lands, or, conversely, if we had a sure documentation of his itinerary, the problem of interpreting his writing and thought would remain much the same.

There is, however, no compelling reason to exclude an early peregrination of Paracelsus, whether or nor it acquainted him with nearly all regions of Europe, from Portugal and Spain to Sweden, Poland, Croatia, Rhodes, and Muscovy. Paracelsus was a lifelong wanderer. A clue to the specifics of an itinerary is his claim of having served in Venetian, Danish, and Dutch wars, where he gained his knowledge of fevers and wounds (I,7:374). These engagements would point to the years 1516–1517, 1520, and 1519, respectively. Scholars have speculated about the specific stations and events of his travels. But here again, nothing can be established with certainty.

Nor did Paracelsus, who was otherwise anything but reticent about connections and achievements, detail the specifics of his informal attendance of other universities in Italy, Germany, and France (aside from lambasting all these insititutions in the most sweeping terms). Characteristically, he writes that everywhere he went, he not only asked questions of the professors, but also, he asserts, of other learned and nonlearned healing practitioners of whatever kind. Besides the barber surgeons and the bathhouse officials (who were organized in guilds and often entrusted with minor medical duties) and the educated physicians, the itinerant seeker had inquired about the medicine of "women, necromantic artists concerned with such things, of alchemists, of cloisters, of noble and commoner, of the clever and the simple" (*weibern, schwarzkünstlern so sich des pflegen, bei den alchimisten, bei den klöstern, bei edlen und unedlen, bei den gescheiden und einfeltigen*—I,10:20). The egalitarian openness to an unlearned medicine agrees with other accounts of Paracelsus's predilection for the company of the common people. Bullinger, who knew him in Zurich, thought him more like a drayman-laborer than a doctor.[6]

Even during the early 1520s, Paracelsus could scarcely have evaded the tidings of the Reformation, which were spreading even beyond German lands and into other countries, some of which were caught up in similar turmoils of their own. In mid-decade, by the time of the earliest documentation of Paracelsus's encounter with such events, the enthusiasm of the popular reformation was building to the tragic climax of the Peasant War of 1525.

In 1524–1525, the author Paracelsus openly challenged the ecclesiastic authorities in Salzburg during the revolutionary events that coincided with the Peasant War. The polemical and theological tracts he penned and circulated by hand before he was compelled to flee the city are among his very earliest writings. A dedicatory letter accompanying one of these early writings was respectfully addressed to Luther, Melanchthon, and Bugenhagen in Wittenberg.[7] If authentic, the letter indicates that Paracelsus was endeavoring to ingratiate himself at this juncture with the leaders of the Reformation. Not much later, he is known to have been accompanied by a learned assistant named Ulrich Geyger, who had studied at the University of Wittenberg.[8] However, this was precisely the juncture during which Luther was vehemently distancing himself from erstwhile supporters among the radical peasants and reformers, calling for their violent suppression. It is unlikely that he would have reacted favorably to Paracelsus's overtures.

After the great massacres of peasants in 1525, there began a gradual but continual curtailment of doctrinal individualism and mass utopian fervor. Paracelsus migrated toward the cities of the Upper Rhine, where a civic reform spirit and a greater degree of doctrinal openness persisted. The greatest breakthrough and central episode of his life occurred early in the year 1527. Summoned to Basel by reform-minded burghers and clergy, he was asked to fulfill a dual position as official city physician and university professor or instructor. Basel was a cosmopolitan center of learning, momentarily caught up in the throes of reformation, a city with cultural ties to much of Europe. Here Paracelsus was suddenly catapulted to precarious heights. He enjoyed the good will of Oecolampadius, the reformer of Basel, of the Amerbach brothers, illustrious Humanists, and of the famous printer Froben, who was his patient. Unfortunately, he was also at the mercy of the Basel medical professors, students, and the city's apothecaries who eschewed his new theories and mocked his German lectures. After incurring considerable open hostility in the city, a quarrel with a patient over payment led to scandals that put an abrupt end to his year of greatest opportunity.

Paracelsus fled headlong in order to avoid punishment and to seek new opportunities. Outwardly, the remaining years of his life consisted of a series of rearguard actions undertaken during an extended retreat. Some of his efforts met with modest success. Most ended in failure. His flight from the Upper Rhine also coincided with the continuing suppression of Anabaptists and unauthorized preachers (*Winkelprediger*). City governments were beginning to warn their citizens against quarrels and disputes that could easily give rise to blasphemies and heresies. Such ordinances and warnings could only have made Paracelsus all the more troublesome and suspicious in the eyes of the governing powers.[9] At the end of the decade, he sought to gain a foothold in Nuremberg, a city which, in consultation with the magisterial reformers Luther and Brenz, had been purging itself of dissenting elements; and which soon, under consultation with the University of Leipzig, implemented a ban on the printing of Paracelsus's works. This was around the time of the crisis following the Diet of Speyer in 1529, when a general war against Protestant cities and territories seemed imminent.

For Paracelsus, the end of the decade was again something of a turning point, an ebbtide and reevalutaion of beliefs. An air of gloom and hysteria pervades certain of his writings from this period. By 1531, little hope remained for the restoration of his lost position or the realization of his overriding ambitions. He spent the early 1530s wandering in Alpine regions, perhaps among outcasts and like-minded souls. Prof. Goldammer suspects that he preached and wrote religious tracts, while continuing to pursue his medical-theoretical projects. As evidence of his pressing sense of religious mission during this period, Paracelsus in 1534 responded to a humiliating rebuff by the Protestant and Catholic clergy of the Alpine town of Sterzing (Vipiteno), by professing not only expertise in all categories of medicine but credentials as a "doctor of Holy Scripture" as well.

The years 1534–1535 coincided with the spectacular demise of militant Protestant dissent exemplified by the millenarian "Kingdom of God" at the North German city of Münster. For Paracelsus's religious orientation, the midpoint of the decade appears to have effected a reversal in his public stance. After 1535, he again sought official recognition with some tentative success. The latter half of the 1530s even brought a mild improvement in his fortunes. His work on surgery was published; and the estates of his native Carinthia promised to subsidize publication of three tracts (the pledge, however, was honored only in 1955). With increasing fame, he became more desirable as a medical consultant and court adornment of nobles. The duke of Bavaria, who later conserved many of his writings, may have intended to bring him to his court. However, before matters could be so happily resolved, Paracelsus died in Salzburg in 1541.

In his writings, the epithet *Lutherus medicorum* occurs only once and it is attributed to detractors (I,8:63). Yet extensive parallels justify it. An early nineteenth-century philosophical historian of medicine, Dietrich Georg Kieser, observed that only the simultaneous epoch of the Lutheran Reformation could account for the emergence of Paracelsus.[10] If one compares a medical man and lay theologian with one of the great theological geniuses of all time, the comparison tends to produce glaring contrasts or slavish imitations. But if one regards their relationship in the context of their experienced crises, their provenance in the same catastrophic epoch is readily apparent.

The adventurous career of Paracelsus is certainly outwardly unlike that of Luther, who remained always the professor of Holy Scripture, even while the world around him fell apart and formed itself again. Just as Luther lived much of his life in or near Wittenberg, his massive corpus of writings was firmly centered. If his writings and person invite questions as a whole, his style and language are almost invariably direct and intelligible. By contrast, Paracelsus's writings, both as a whole and in countless details, can be as opaque as Luther's are transparent. Where the thinking of Luther perpetually circles around and returns to the word of God, that of Paracelsus seems to take up every sphere of investigation that impinges on his interests: medicine, surgery, alchemy, psychology, botany, astrology, meteorology, philosophy, prophecy, theology, and biblical exegesis. Within his writings, Paracelsus often meanders and abruptly shifts topics, in contrast to the unflinching purposefulness of Luther. Paracelsus is drawn to natural magic as Luther certainly is not.

It would be utterly misleading to call Paracelsus a *medicus lutheranus*; however, there are very sound reasons for calling him the *Lutherus medicorum*. Several generations of researchers have gradually revealed that a major portion of Paracelsus's writings were on religion, and of these perhaps half devoted to biblical exegesis; the five printed works found in his estate consisted of one medical work, a Bible, a New Testament, a concordance, and a gospel commentary by Hieronymous.[11] His lengthiest extant writing is his *Commentary on Psalms*.[12] The second division of the complete writings edited by Kurt Goldammer reveals him to have been nearly as preoccupied with speculative theology and biblical exegesis as with medicine and philosophy. In 1953, Goldammer observed that, "The connection between the Christian personality and the scientist, between the theological and the naturalistic work is extraordinarily close in Hohenheim" (*Der Zusammenhang der christlichen Persönlichkeit und des Wissenschaftlers, des theologischen und naturforschenden Werkes ist bei Hohenheim außerordentlich eng*).[13] The medical and natural-scientific work contains countless theological observations, and the theological writings stand on the foundation of his scientific research and thought, according to Goldammer.[14] The wandering theorist wrote extensively on the Eucharist and other sacraments and doctrines, as well as on the Virgin Mary and the saints in a manner that distinguishes him from most Protestants. If his theological writings often differ from Lutheran teachings, it is nevertheless significant that he composed them at all; and that they express his spirit of radical protest and stand in an important relation to his medical reform. His religious writings are indeed among his earliest, dominating the seminal phase of his career as an author. Moreover, even the earliest medical or philosophical works reflect his preoccupation with religious themes.[15]

Like Luther, Paracelsus rose from humble beginnings and aspired to a reform that would have exalted a kind of divinely sanctioned immediate certainty above hierarchically vested traditional authority. The advance of the print medium, the fame and influence of the Humanists, and above all the lightninglike success of Luther's writings in the early 1520s had set the stage for his emergence as an author. Hans J. Hillerbrand summarized the early propagation of the Reformation debate through the print medium: "The number of Protestant publications was legion. By 1523 some thirteen hundred different editions of tracts by Luther alone had been published; assuming that each edition involved between seven hundred and fifty and eight hundred copies, we reach a total of about one million copies. The first truly popular tract from Luther's pen, the *Sermon on Indulgence and Grace* written in German and printed in 1518, was reprinted fourteen times in 1518, five times in 1519, and four times in 1520."[16] By the early 1520s, there were other and more topical tracts to be printed and read: Luther's three great works of that year, *On the Freedom of a Christian*, which according to Oberman inspired more people than any other work by Luther,[17] *On the Babylonian Captivity of the Church*, with its strong metaphor of a victorious breaching of fortifications, and the *Letter to the Christian Nobility*, which held out the prospect of a sweeping reformation of social and academic life, including even a reform of medicine— though Luther disavowed expertise in that area.

As Hillerbrand observes, one has to look beyond the most famous reformers and consider the authorial output of those in the second and third ranks of prominence to gauge the immense mental energies liberated by the Reformation. The effectiveness of this output can be measured by the responses, for and against. We can only look back in horror at the persecution of simple men such as Sebastian Lotzer, author of the *Twelve Articles* of the revolutionary peasants, or Johannes Hergot, the Nuremberg printer executed in Leipzig in 1527 for publishing a programmatic appeal for a reformation in the interests of the poor. But for all the crushing injustice of these repressive measures, they reacted to the potential power of ideas expressed in the tract or sermon.[18]

During the 1520s, one bold figure after another attempted to seize the initiative in this multifaceted transformation of power and beliefs in order to realize the potentials that seemed within grasp under the conditions of rapid change. At the beginning of the decade, Andreas von Bodenstein, known as Karlstadt (ca. 1480–1541), hastened the pace of the reforms in Wittenberg in Luther's absence and, after being forced aside, turned even more radical and populistic. The Humanist knight, Ulrich von Hutten (1488–1523), learned to write effective appeals to the people in German and attempted to forge a national alliance between the rebelling knights and the Wittenberg theologians. Failing to attain any of his goals, Hutten died of syphilis on the island of Ufenau near Zurich. There, after being turned away by Erasmus in Basel, he was granted asylum by this city that stood under the leadership of Huldreich Zwingli (1484–1531). A reformer and priest to the people, Zwingli was another doer and thinker in one: he became a reformer through his intensive studies, dominating the affairs of his city. He died in battle against the forces of the Catholic cantons at Kappel. Certainly, the most spectacular example of a speculative mind hurtling itself through the opened door of the early Reformation into revolutionary action is the case of Thomas Müntzer (1490–1525). More than any of the magisterial reformers, this intellectual pastor turned chiliastic prophet attempted to translate his inner vision directly into reality by preaching and leading the peasants in their great revolutionary uprising. Men such as these dominated in the unstable regions of Switzerland, South Germany, and Austria during the period of Paracelsus's wanderings there.

Like the Wittenberg reformer addressing the German people from his seat in the north, Paracelsus wrote and lectured in the vernacular. In adopting German over Latin, Luther, according to Heiko Oberman, was acting as "pastor to the nation":

> His opting for the German language is based on the conscious decision to serve the common folk rather than the sodalities of *eruditi*. . . . Primarily it is related to the discovery of the dimension of *experientia, Erfahrung*, which is to become thematic in Luther's tracts and sermons in the coming years, the experience of God and death which does not know social boundaries.[19]

The same ethos of service to the people, sometimes heightened to an apostolic duty and service of Christian love, is expressed in many of

Paracelsus's writings. Disavowing a separate spiritual estate, Luther upgraded every activity as a service to God; he spoke of the universal priesthood of the laity. For Paracelsus, the activity of the physician has a priestlike import that goes far beyond what Luther might have accorded it. For either of the two, writing in the vernacular and serving the common folk were understood as part of a Christian ethos or mission.

There are other important similarities in their respective outlooks: Luther and Paracelsus both rejected the nonscriptural foundations of Scholasticism, objecting strongly to Aristotelian philosophy. Luther rejected it in favor of a Bible open to every lay believer, and in favor of the experienced inner faith that alone justified the believer. Paracelsus cast the Aristotelian philosophy of medieval Scholasticism aside in favor of a nature that he viewed almost as a second bible, complementary to the written one; and in favor of what he called *experientia*—a usage that, I will contend, owes as much to the inner experience of religious faith as to observation in modern scientific method.

Luther's doctrine of the universal priesthood of the laity and his emphasis on inner faith led to an individualization of sin and salvation. There is a parallel to this in Paracelsus's rejection of a Galenic medicine that, in its generalized form, considered all diseases as variants of humoral imbalances. The traditional recourses of the Galenists were as discredited for Paracelsus as the commerce in indulgences for the Lutherans: either recourse, Galenic prescriptions no less than indulgences, was thought to be motivated by greed and venality. In rejecting humoral medicine, Paracelsus individualized disease and health by emphasizing specific external causes of illness and by enlarging the repertoire of cures to incorporate prescriptions derived from alchemical lore.

By turning away from the universals as the ultimate reality, nominalistic philosophy had broken ground for Luther's new sense of reality, meaning, and experience, emphasizing the particular and the individual. Alchemy, with its sense of the particularity and multiple transformability of substances, might be regarded as the nominalism of the Paracelsian medicine. On the foundation of an "experience" that included alchemy, Paracelsus could claim to understand not only the real substances of disease, but also the true signs or signatures of things that revealed their inner God-given powers to heal. Paracelsus as well as Luther understood human experience as a perilous encounter of eternal and temporal powers. To both men, there are invisible and visible aspects of experience. Paracelsus as well as Luther saw ubiquitous strife in the world: a mixture of the good with the poisonous in nature; or the struggle of the warring kingdoms of Satan and Christ. Both Luther and Paracelsus believed in the omnipresence of a divine power in the world. For either, this power was associated with faith in a real divine presence in the Eucharist and with the substantially transforming power vested in the sacraments. Paracelsus of course went beyond Luther in developing a medical philosophy that recognized the manifestations of the divine power operating in arcane forces and inner virtues within nature.

On the question of divine ubiquity, the teaching of Luther arose from a doctrinal dispute and rested its case on a literal reading of Scripture: this seems to militate against comparisons with Paracelsus's occult pantheism. But, here again, the point is not that the physician held to an orthodox Lutheran explanation of the Eucharist; the point is that the transformation of the bread and wine is apposite to the transforming processes in the body and in nature; and that the transformation and the healthy functioning of the body are effected by ubiquitous divine powers. Galenic medicine could make do with an immanent and essentially materialistic explanation, based on the humoral imbalances. By contrast, the omnipresence of divine virtues and arcane forces is every bit as important in the medical theory of Paracelsus as is the ubiquitarian-eucharistic doctrine in Luther's theology.[20]

Paracelsus the philosopher-physician was concerned with the secrets of nature, a theoretical preoccupation that cannot be ascribed to Luther. Nevertheless, both men undoubtedly partook of a sense of things that was common enough, if not universal, in their time. They also merit comparison with respect to the mentalities that contextualized and informed their respective doctrines. Just as Paracelsus saw the light of nature as a complement to scriptural revelation, Luther could only understand his doctrines by way of an intelligibility informed by perceptions of nature, by a common sense or reason that is much in evidence in his work. Luther was of course not speaking as a scientist in likening the eucharistic *Abendmahl* to the miracle that causes plant life to spring forth out of dead earth, but he was speaking his mind and expressing an experience of nature, for him bound up with the understanding of the divine omnipresence.

The mentality of their age is expressed when, in his *Letter to the Christian Nobility*, Luther argues that a potter knows more about physics than can be learned from the books of the "heathen" Aristotle—presumably because the potter recognizes the world as the handiwork of a creator, as Aristotle's thesis of an uncreated universe did not. The same mentality is evident when Paracelsus, always contemptuous of Aristotle, characterizes the processes of digestion as the work of an agent, acting as an alchemist in the body: creation or transformation are the work of an artisan. The more intricately constructed and abstractly conceived universes of Scholasticism or Renaissance Neoplatonism are gone. Despite a number of conceptual or terminological remnants, the thinking of Paracelsus is informed as much as that of Luther by a common, palpable, and immediate experience—be it of objects touched and seen or be it of those feared, imagined, or believed in.

Just as there is an inner realm of nature, essential to the healing powers of herbs or the transforming power of sacraments, there is a similar power in the human spirit: this inner power is faith to Luther; it is faith, as well as a magical potency of the imagination, for Paracelsus. To be sure, Paracelsus does not go so far as to equate the imagination with faith altogether, yet in some contexts, these terms signify a single power. Paracelsus's successors went beyond him to interpret faith and imagination conjointly, so that at times the transforming power of religious faith could appear virtually identical with a higher power of the inspired imagination.

In part because of its origin in the immediate, the writing of Paracelsus is in a particular sense time-bound. It has been said that his travels vouch for his universality. But this can hardly be the case. Knowledge of other countries is remarkably vague for this world-traveller. What he has seen confirms that lands are different and Germany is as good as or better than others; or it allows him to draw figural comparisons between the globe and the human body. But he has learned nothing that could not have been gleaned from hearsay. Even his references to the parts of the globe still adhere to the old threesome of Europe, Asia, and Africa.[21] Over four decades after Columbus's discoveries, and two decades after the great wanderer Paracelsus claims to have visited Portugal, Spain, and sundry other maritime nations—when even some who had never left Germany were reading and writing of the New World—Paracelsus's map of the earth remains the medieval one. In 1537, his *Astronomia*

Magna at last registers a report of "concealed islands" (*die verbor-genen insulen*). But news of human inhabitants excites no anthro-pological or geographical curiosity. It arouses suspicious increduli-ty that the inhabitants could be his flesh-and-blood relatives by the same Adam (I,12:35).

His sense of time is equally vague and restricted. Luther admit-ted to knowing little of prior history. His sense of the present and the past was molded by eschatological suppositions. Similarly, his-tory to Paracelsus is a flat slate inscribed with a smattering of names unreferenced to year, century, or historical context; history is overshadowed by prophetic and eschatological perspectives. His rough and perspectivally flattened picture of the past is evident in his *Kärntner Chronik*, a brief chronicle of his "second fatherland," the South Austrian land of Carinthia. The chronicle is addressed to the Carinthian estates who had promised to publish this and other works in 1537 (the promise that was made good by the modern Carinthian government in 1955). According to the chronicle, Carinthia was settled by descendants of the biblical Japhet, as well as by an influx from the tribe of the Philistines. The chronicle enu-merates the illustrious men who have been linked in some way to the Carinthian past. They include Julius Caesar, Carolus Magnus, and Attila the Hun, as well as the apocalyptically renowned medieval German king and Holy Roman Emperor, Frederick I, "Barbarossa." As for him (the chronicle embarks here on an odd digression): he once founded a monastery and outfitted it with reli-gious objects. One of the images depicted a monk, shown beneath a portentous caption with the barely legible letters: "LUTHERUS." Paracelsus may have written this at a time when his own opposition to Luther had already been voiced; but one can only wonder how the bishops and prelates to whom the Carinthian writings were addressed took this curious portent, served up by the author with much solemnity but without further explanation. One wonders if their bewilderment might have had something to do with the 400-year delay in publication.

Except for the biblical past, which is so pertinent as to appear almost present, the history of knowledge is disdainfully marked *swindel* and *bunk*. As for the future, despite occasional flights of hero-ic optimism, the outlook is as confining as the vault that encloses the earth "as a yolk in an egg," "as a shell an egg" (*als ein dotter im ei*— I,8:162; *wie ein schal ein ei*—I,1:184). The yolk is the earth, the shell the firmament upon which he based the astrological prognostications that were his most successful publications to appear during his lifetime. The human or external cosmos is rounded by time, as it is enclosed by the encircling vault of the heavens. This closeness of things in space and time is essential to the understanding of microcosm and macrocosm, as well as to the correlations of stars and life and of astrology and disease.

Present time looms large for Paracelsus, overshadowing and encompassing darkly what was and is yet to be, absorbing the past as a legendary lore that is credulously accepted as experienced fact, and projecting the future in catastrophic premonitions that are the shadows cast by current events. A threateningly urgent immediacy underlies and informs the hastily composed or dictated treatises. In expressing relationships, his language is homely and cumbersome; but it waxes inventive in heaping ridicule on his opponents.[22] The inventiveness of his invective can appear as blunt and pointed as a doctrinal broadside condemning satanic heresy or as a peasant's scythe hammered into a lance for improvised combat. A preface of the Carinthian writings recounts how his opponents contended hotly with him from streetcorner to streetcorner in Vienna, and how they sought to forge the "iron" of his own theory into a pike to wield against him (*mit meinem eisen ein spieß wider mich zu machen*—I,11:4). Paracelsus's diatribes endeavor to turn the weapons of his opponents against them. He often deflects accusations that were presumably first launched against him: all critics, all those with whom he quarrels, beginning with the foolish Aristotle, are possessed of a wild imagination. He alone bases his statements on "experience." Turnabout is not only fair play for Paracelsus; it appears to be the preferred strategy, shaping his arguments in many writings. Admiring commentators have tended to ignore this or offset it by credulously accepting his polemics as justified by the errors and abuses of his opponents. This overlooks the extent to which an agitated spell of the moment informs, vivifies, and at the same time obscures his work. In stripping away everything conditioned by responses to immediate disputes, one effaces the meaning of his work.

What is of potential relevance to nonspecialized readers of Paracelsus is best brought to light by recognizing that his very real obscurities are to some extent a function of perspective, a product of implicit perceptions of time. Barbara Tuchman wrote of fourteenth-century Europe as "a distant mirror" of twentieth-century catastrophes. Whether or not the sixteenth century is more deserving than other periods to be dredged for revealing parallels to the geopolitical and intellectual realignments of our own time, the search for such parallels, or, more generally, the interest in historical or theoretical models for describing life, meaning, and change, should offer a privileged vantage for regarding the intellectual culture to be explored in this study.

In the view of a traditional, still popular historiography, sixteenth-century Germany—the venerable and crisis-racked Holy Roman Empire of the German Nation in the age of Martin Luther and Emperor Charles V—conjures up a complex image, a sort of trick picture or *Vexierbild* of overlapping perspectives, each of which, taken in itself, superimposes its contours on the central figures and upon the pattern of the whole. It was the age of Copernicus, Dürer, Hutten, and Erasmus, as well as of Luther. Sixteenth-century Germany can be viewed in the light of the Renaissance or the Reformation; as medievalism or incipient modernity; in terms of German specialism or its European context; as continuity, regression, or epochal transformation.

German intellectual historians have underscored the epochal significance of the sixteenth century by referring to everything after 1500 as *die Neuzeit*. *Die Neuzeit* is the complement of *das Altertum* and *das Mittelalter*; it is the "new time" that follows upon antiquity and the Middle Ages. Professors of German used to specialize either in the study of literature before 1500 or in *neuere deutsche Literatur*, everything after that date. The idea of *Neuzeit* highlights Luther and his age by framing them with the aura of a dawn horizon. The antecedent periods are circumscribed in antecrepuscular time zones. It seems that, previously, culture had devolved from distinct presuppositions. Literature had been composed mainly in Latin, and thought bound by centuries-old traditions and restrictions. The dawn of the *Neuzeit* broadens, reinterprets, and deepens the medieval world; the orb is widened geographically to include the New World; the cosmos reinterpreted by the astronomy of Copernicus and other innovations in the sciences. In the *Neuzeit*, thought and culture are deepened by the recovery of ancient learning. Human existence is magnified and intensified by philosophical or doctrinal legitimations of the knowledge and faith of the individual. No one would seem to exemplify the term *Neuzeit* more powerfully and ambiguously than the idiosyncratic Paracelsus, who rejected most prior learning as ludicrous. A dawn halo effect therefore frames his perceived figure. Figures on any horizon appear to loom larger than life, to rise up out of nowhere and move directly toward the beholder.

There can be little doubt that to a greater or lesser degree the developments of the sixteenth century bore a cumulative force that, sooner or later, brought home to contemporaries the sense of a dawning new time glowing with chiliastic overtones; or that the events of that century decisively transformed the world. But was it one transformation or many? Was the transformation unique in more than the obvious sense? To what extent is the nature of the change conditioned by later perception? We know that renaissances and chiliastic fervors are a recurrent mark of European cultural history. Even present-day culture is sufficiently taken with its own mood of *Neuzeit* that it looks forward by looking back at looking forward in embracing for itself the sobriquet of postmodernity. Whether sixteenth-century Germany can serve as an adequate mirror of the outgoing twentieth century, it does offer us a *Vexierbild* of conflicting perspectives, a puzzle suited to arouse an awareness of current ambiguities. Peering into the distant mirror of sixteenth-century Germany, we should expect to discover—a figure peering into a mirror.

In another respect, the *Vexierbild* or puzzle of overlaid images is an appropriate point of departure for this study. I will show that Paracelsus's confusing congeries of concepts and theories derives its coherence and meaning from the underlying notion of the *image* as the pattern of creation and the focus of recognition. "Image" (*bilt* or *biltnus*), "figure" (*figur*), and "imagination" (*fantasei* or *imagination*) are terms that guide his thinking. Paracelsus's concepts of *microcosm* and *macrocosm* are rooted in his peculiar theory of generation as image-formation, a notion that reflects biblical precepts. Moreover, his emphasis on what he calls *theorica*—remote as it may be from our usage—can serve as a valuable reminder that much of what he writes is neither medicine, nor philosophy, nor theology, nor science, but a kind of speculation that floats freely and assimilates all of these. Taken as a heuristic keynote, his *theorica* offers us a pretext for drawing comparisons and contrasts with contemporary intellectual preoccupations. Parallel to contemporary critical theory, Paracelsus extended relationships of signification beyond all spoken or written systems of signs in order to pursue something on the order of a general theory of things: what we might refer to as a semantics or iconology of life and nature. Admittedly, this comparison incorporates an anachronistic bias of the sort this study professes to overcome. However, if scholarly biases are inevitable, they are certainly not well disposed of by being left unspoken.

1 ▪ The Ambiguities of Paracelsus

Despite the tremendous advances in the scholarly knowledge of Hohenheim of the last hundred years, the myth of Paracelsus has proven remarkably resilient against adverse evidence. Before examining the beginnings of Paracelsian theory in the context of the early Reformation, I want to suggest that his received image has been greatly affected by perspectival distortions, wrought by his Faustian and Renaissance associations, by certain categorical prejudgments that induced scholars to look for and perceive what was required to sustain the myth, and by a scholarly division of labor that tends to exaggerate the distinction between the scientific and religious components of his thought and even to skew the dating of his work. Other factors rendering the Paracelsus myth impervious to outside challenges include the relative inaccessibility of his remaining unedited writings and the role of patriotisms, national as well as local, in setting the agenda for the journals and congresses devoted to his study.

Much Paracelsus scholarship has followed from an overriding fixed certainty, by way of a subordinate and variable procedure. The certainty is that the aim of scholarship is to discover what makes him great. The variable procedure is represented by the many divergent approaches, by the great variety of *Paracelsuses*—Humanistic, scientific, occultist, proto-Jungian, Fascist, devout, or dissenting—that have been proposed in order to flesh out his presumed stature. Moreover, because the ideological shifts in the reception of Paracelsus have come and gone with no decisive endeavor to reassess him as a whole, hardly any other author or oeuvre of German literature has remained more shaped and colored in presentation by ideologies than Paracelsus. During the last hundred years, the period in which the scholarly understanding of his person and work has been elaborated, his image has reflected several very distinct ideologies: scientific positivism, *völkisch* biologistic racism,

21

and Christian social ethics, as well as other religious or occult beliefs. Throughout these transformations, a number of characteristics have remained widespread: the tendency to identify Paracelsus with the Renaissance, the underestimation of his religious point of departure, and the undiscriminating impulse either to embrace or discount him as a whole—always the charlatan or the persecuted saintly genius. Before investigating the coherence of his ideas, it is therefore essential to examine some of the assumptions that have generated the Paracelsus myth.

The received notions of Luther and Paracelsus contrast as Reformationist single-mindedness and spirituality contrast with Renaissance universality and openness to natural experience. The portrait of Paracelsus as Faust has been retouched from era to era, yet it has persisted in nearly every era from Paracelsus's own down to the twentieth century. In the late sixteenth century, the Humanist Conrad Gesner compared the wandering philosopher-physician to the wayward magician Faust,[23] thereby associating Paracelsus with the same powers of illicit magic that incited Luther's hatred of the nefarious scholar. Gesner also remarked on the reputation of Paracelsus as a physician and alchemistic innovator with efficacious cures. We have no means of assessing either the true similarity with the shadowy Faust or the degree of success of Paracelsus's medicine; what is certain is that his reputation remained largely dependent upon a variable relation of transgression and knowledge, dominated always by the same extreme alternatives of charlatanism versus idealistic truth-seeking.

Again and again, the association of Paracelsus with the Renaissance spirit and with Faust has been reasserted. In 1789, Johann Christoph Adelung assigned Paracelsus along with Faust to a rogues' gallery of charlatans. Only a year later, Goethe's *Urfaust* appeared, reflecting, according to scholars, its author's early interest in Paracelsus. Goethe, Wieland, and the Romantics defended Paracelsus against the aspersions of charlatanism and thereby reinforced the extreme options governing his reputation as mountebank or misunderstood genius.[24]

The rehabilitated Faust would be perceived as a vindication of a belated German Renaissance suppressed by Luther. Faust was to become an emblem of progress and enlightenment for the German *Bildungsbürgertum*. Karl Sudhoff, the great medical historian who edited the writings of Paracelsus, subtitled his 1936 biography, *Ein deutsches Lebensbild aus den Tagen der Renaissance.* With a different idea of genius, Jung's discussion of Paracelsus adhered to much the same concept of progress—though recognizing that, in addition to his "revolutionary" status in the history of science, he was a "conservative" with respect to Church doctrine.[25] Even in scholarship not obsessed with Faust, the Renaissance portrait of the anti-Luther continued to prevail. Walter Pagel's classic study, *Paracelsus: An Introduction to Philosophical Medicine in the Era of the Renaissance,* conceded superficial resemblances to Luther, but nonetheless insisted that Paracelsus was a man of the Renaissance, who could not have been more strictly opposed to the "religious dogmatism" and "mystical belief" of Luther.[26] Though Pagel could also argue the mysticism of Paracelsus, he meant by this a syncretic, Renaissance mysticism, decisively influenced by Neoplatonism.[27] The fine recent survey by Allen G. Debus of *The French Paracelsians* presents Hohenheim in much the same light, as a representative of Renaissance "Hermeticism and natural magic." Debus relegates the "religious issues" accompanying Paracelsian chemistry and medicine to a "sociological study," extraneous to "intellectual history."[28]

In the history of Paracelsus reception, the turning point that proved most prodigious and far-reaching in its consequences came toward the end of the nineteenth century, at around the time of the four-hundredth anniversary of his birth. Though scholars in the nineteenth century had already investigated the status of Paracelsus in medical and scientific history, a broader interest was now kindled by the stimulating and controversial appraisals of Friedrich Mook, Karl Sudhoff, Eduard Schubert, and others.[29] After 1900, the era of fervent interest in Paracelsus began to unfold, climaxing in the veritable mania of the 1930s and 1940s.

Certainly, the climate of the times shaped the perceptions of the Faustian and Renaissance giant. In the late nineteenth century, Jacob Burckhardt's celebrated study of the Renaissance had encouraged enthusiasm for a heroic founding epoch of the modern individual and the modern state. Some Germans aspired to recoup a glorious medieval past after founding the Hohenzollern *Reich.* In the same vein, Richard Wagner's operas were reviving and reinterpreting Germanic mythology. Perhaps the heroic world was not a myth after all. If the scene of the great Homeric poem known to the graduates of humanistic *Gymnasien* could be unearthed when Schliemann undertook the remarkable step of digging in Asia Minor in order to discover the historic Troy—perhaps one could unearth a true historical prototype for Goethe's Faust as well.

In 1911, the Germanist Agnes Bartscherer published a study of Goethe's *Faust* as a work inspired by the life and writings of Paracelsus. She based her arguments on Goethe's account of his alchemical avocation during his early convalescence in Frankfurt and on a close examination of the writings of Paracelsus. Though she was not the first to draw such connections, Bartscherer drew them more specifically than any scholar before her. Interpreting *Faust* in the light of Paracelsus's writings, she in fact *improved* the image of the fictional character, as others were resurrecting that of his real prototype. Thus, citing an alchemical work *De Spiritibus Metallorum*, she attempted to upgrade the understanding of the fictional father of Faust by what amounts to a vindication of progress. According to Goethe's poem, father and son poisoned more people in treating the plague with alchemistic remedies than the plague itself killed. Bartscherer made much of a clue to the good intentions of Faust father and son, when Goethe hints of the alchemistic symbol of "the young queen":

> Since Faust's father in time of plague is only concerned with helping against the Black Death, not with making gold, it is understandable that he makes do with the queen, instead of transforming her through a further drawn out process of heating, into the king who produces golden treasures, and about whom the book of *Alchimia* speaks further.

> *Da es sich für den Vater Fausts in der Pestzeit nur um Hilfe gegen den schwarzen Tod, nicht um Goldmachen handelt, ist es verständlich, daß er sich mit der Königin begnügt, statt sie durch weitere langwierige Erhitzung in den König zu verwandeln, der goldene Schätze verschafft und von dem die Schrift Alchimia weiter redet.*[30]

In killing their patients, father and son rose above base intent. Bartscherer recognized in Faust's reference to his father an echo of the filial piety of Paracelsus. Neither the idealizations of Faust and Paracelsus, nor the filial trust that stirred the heart of more than one generation of Paracelsus admirers, nor the lofty ideals of service to humanity and progress (superimposed upon the poison kitchen of

Faust *père*, as on his presumed prototype) were compatible with Goethe's knowing cynicism regarding the misguided trust of the common folk in their revered benefactors, father and son: well-intentioned betrayers of the people and perpetrators of a deadly mass malpractice.[31]

More significant in the present context than the influence of Paracelsus on Goethe's *Faust* is the erosion of the boundary between fiction and historical fact in German attitudes toward Paracelsus. The breakdown has roots in *Geistesgeschichte*, in its recognition that forms or archetypes are cultural forces, virtual actors in history. Thus, for Friedrich Gundolf, Paracelsus was a figure of "macrocosmic zeal" (*makrokosmischen Eifer*), who knew no match in Georg Agricola, Kepler, Leibniz, or any other scientific mind prior to—and here Gundolf leaps from history into literature—the Goethe of the first *Faust* poem (*Urfaust*).[32]

In the aftermath of the defeat of 1918, the intellectual historian and *Kulturpessimist* Oswald Spengler (*Der Untergang des Abendlandes*) presented what he characterized as "Faustian Man": the archetypal "culture soul of Western man" (*die abendländische Kulturseele*). Faustian man was a generalized archetype that bore as much resemblance to the refurbished stylizations of Paracelsus as to Goethe's Faust, or to the obscure sixteenth-century Faust. Rising above the horizon of *Neuzeit*, Faustian Man represented an underlying quest for infinite knowledge and experience in Western culture after the Middle Ages. *Kultur*, to the extent that it had not yet been corrupted by the *Zivilisation* of England or America, was centered in Germany. In this light, the German proto-heroes, Faust or Paracelsus, seemed harbingers of something far greater and more fateful that had yet to yield its full consequences.

Vague intimations were offered in the Paracelsus trilogy of Erwin Guido Kolbenheyer, of which the first part (*Die Kindheit des Paracelsus*) was published in 1917, the second (*Das Gestirn des Paracelsus*) in 1921, and the third, with its ominous title, *The Third Reich of Paracelsus* (*Das dritte Reich des Paracelsus*), in 1925.[33] Kolbenheyer was not only an imaginative writer. He was an assiduous researcher of Paracelsus who copied the language and followed the outline of the known biography, though with much unavoidable embellishment. What was more problematical than mere imaginative license was Kolbenheyer's attempt to incorporate the hysterias and anxieties of the post-war period into a sixteenth-century life and, at the same time, to arrange the whole panorama of Paracelsus beneath the pantheon of his German cultural idols. In the age of trench warfare, Kolbenheyer recreates hand-to-hand front-line combat in the Swiss-Swabian battles of Paracelsus's century; and he exploits the *Heimkehrer*-motif of the returning warrior. Moral decadence and racial degeneracy are coupled in the person of Cursetta, courtesan to a papal legate who cavorts with a homosexual African. Paracelsus is Nordic Man. Wagner's Wotan and Luther's Christ augur and contend for the German soul. The North Wind is "the Hater of Pestilence." Remaining in step with the times, Kolbenheyer subsequently explicated the socio-biological racism of his so-called *Bauhüttenphilosophie*. In the trilogy, the Nordic hatred of pestilence is embodied in Paracelsus's steadfast struggle to halt a plague epidemic in Ferrara. It is here that the Nordic hero develops his alchemical medicine and breaks with Galenism.[34] Entranced by premonitions of an eternal German *Kulturseele*, Kolbenheyer adorned the final novel of his trilogy with a phrase popularized by Moeller van den Bruck's fatal title: *Das dritte Reich des Paracelsus*.

Kolbenheyer was an independent theorist of *Deutschtum* and a philosopher of race and folk. He was midwife to the Paracelsus cult of the Nazi era that yielded an enormous progeny of novels, poems, dramas, operas, studies, dissertations, and journalistic or propagandistic articles championing the German and "European" facets of the incomparable German folk genius.[35] A typical (and for its period, by no means ideologically extremist) expression of this cult can be found in Franz Spunda's biography, published in the banner year of Paracelsus writings, 1941. It begins with this characterization:

> The Faustian Man, in the final form acquired through Goethe, is the outcome of a spiritual struggle (*eines Geisteskampfes*) that has extended over many millenia. The German soul of the Middle Ages, threatened and frightened by images of terror, almost expiring under the burden of its religious duties, sought peace and calm in fervent devotion to God without in the process being hemmed in by church dogma.

> *Der Faustische Mensch, wie er durch Goethe seine endgültige Gestalt gewann, ist das Ergebnis eines Geisteskampfes, der sich über viele Jahrhunderte erstreckt hat. Die deutsche Seele des*

Mittelalters, die unter der Last ihrer religiösen Verpflichtungen fast erlag, von Schreckbildern umdroht und verängstigt, suchte Ruhe in einer inbrünstigen Hingabe an Gott, ohne dabei vom kirchlichen Dogma eingeengt zu sein.[36]

As if in order to break out of such encirclements by initiating a second military front, the German soul recognizes with the aid of the concepts of macrocosm and microcosm that it is able to have an impact upon the external world: "Such a worldview explains the essence of the Faustian Man" (*Ein solches Weltbild erklärt das Wesen des faustischen Menschen*).[37] The Faustian Paracelsus prevails over the medieval contempt for the flesh, according to Spunda. For Paracelsian medicine, the body is sacred. As one who dwells in the twilight between ages, the figure of Paracelsus remains ambiguous in a way that that of Luther or Faust does not, writes Spunda. Faust represents striving; Paracelsus, experience and observation. What distinguishes him from the other Faustian natures of the late Middle Ages is his view to the future.[38] In an age of strong personalities, strength for him is only a means to the end of assisting his fellows. This echoes the Paracelsus of Bartscherer, Spengler, Kolbenheyer, or Gundolf. The dawn hues of *die Neuzeit* are always glimmering in the background.

It is not difficult to uncover and itemize the ideological myths. What is harder to explain, and rather more disturbing to contemplate, is the extent to which many of the same traits are found in portrayals written before, during, and after the period of extreme German nationalism—written by Nazis, nationalists, or democrats. The Paracelsus myth remains at root much the same: he is the Faustian, the man of the people, the new man, tragically in advance of his time.[39] What, we must ask, are the qualities that make it possible for Paracelsus to attract the interest of politically varied groups? What in general are the allures of the Faustian man of the dawning *Neuzeit*? Does Paracelsus truly possess the qualities of such a figure?

We can best answer these questions by offering a credible presentation of his life and thought. But before turning to the life and times of Paracelsus, it is also necessary to suggest to the reader that historians of science and medicine have often engaged in circular demonstrations of his status as an initiator of a new science and medicine, a preordained fulfillment of the Faustian-Renaissance image of Paracelsus that renders the image virtually impervious to counter-demonstration.

This is not to deny Paracelsus's innovations or his sense of a reforming mission. It is generally agreed that he effectively challenged the hegemony of Galenic medicine; that he inaugurated an alternative school of iatrochemical medicine; and that his example encouraged others to search for healing powers in herbs and substances and to experiment in what would become chemistry. From the nineteenth century to the recent work of Debus, chemistry has had the least difficulty acknowledging a debt to his work. Though many claims for his achievements have proven exaggerated,[40] occupational pathology, toxicology, and dietetics are among several specific fields in which he is regarded as a pioneer. Historians of science and medicine have investigated Paracelsus's work for evidence of discoveries. This study will not undertake an inexpert revision of their specific claims.

The unresolved problem attending all such assessments is that the assertion of his advances is not accompanied by any attempt to demonstrate just how he arrived at his conclusions. Among his edited works, there are many drafts and repeated treatments of the same theme. Yet almost no attempt has been made to establish from these drafts that the emergence of his results was an outcome based on experience, logic, or gradual reflection on a rationally conceived problem.[41] It would be difficult to imagine scholars failing to analyze the papers of a Newton or Kepler in order to ascertain their paths to discovery. What are we to make of Pagel's puzzling judgment that Paracelsus was not a scientist—yet he "produced scientific results from a non-scientific world of motives and thoughts"?[42] What does it mean to say that non-scientific thoughts produce scientific results? Are such results perhaps comparable to the explorations encouraged in Paracelsus's time by late medieval writings on the legendary Kingdom of Prester John? No one would place the legend of Prester John in the history of scientific navigation on a level with the invention of the compass or the improvement of cartography—just because the lore of the priest-king's fabled realm obliquely reflected an awareness of Abyssinia and the East. The writings on Prester John pertain to the world of medieval legend; the stimulation they provided to geographical exploration derived from their religious-political agenda.

How should we regard the supposed "scientific results" found in Paracelsus's work, if for every valid precept there are dozens of credulities—for every existent Abyssinia countless chimerical monsters? There has been no consistent attempt at separating the wheat from the chaff in Paracelsus's work, no general comparison of the relative weights of either. It is a circular argument to suggest that what we now regard as his advances were the basis of his sixteenth-century reputation, as if he and his supporters had been prescient. It would be more accurate to say that much of what we now see as progressive insight was the by-product of a garrulous propaganda aimed at inflating his fame. Modern natural science can no more provide an adequate retrospective on the experienced world of Paracelsus than modern mathematics might reconstruct out of itself the beliefs of an ancient Pythagorean mystery cult. What seems to render Paracelsus so keenly modern is the belief, his as well as ours, that he stood at the dawn of a new age.

Because of its circularity and status as a modern article of faith, the Paracelsus legend has proven resistant to reversals in evidence. Thus, in 1911, the Viennese medical historian J. K. Proksch offered a knowledgeably documented, balanced though still devastating, rebuttal to what he criticized as blind hero worship in Sudhoff. Contrary to Sudhoff's views, Proksch demonstrated that Paracelsus was considerably less original and less guided by practical medical experience than his self-praises would lead us to expect. Indeed, Proksch made a compelling case that, even by sixteenth-century standards of progress, Paracelsus was much less progressive and rather more given to credulous superstitions than Sudhoff had allowed.[43]

The last point is crucial, since in defense of Paracelsus's scientific leanings, one might think that the rules and devices of empiricism were altogether unknown in the sixteenth century. This would be a misleading defense. A century before Paracelsus, Nicholas of Cusa called for quantitative research in medicine—empirical experience in our sense. Paracelsus's contemporary Georg Agricola was a man who shared his medical and alchemical interests, along with some of his superstitions and prejudices. Though a Galenist and a Humanist who gleaned the writings of the ancients for naturalistic information, Agricola accumulated and ordered a wealth of information on mining, mineralogy, and the composition of streams and waters. He also composed a work on weights and measures, and a plague tract[44] that, though guided by humoral theory, is less phantasmagorical than Paracelsus's theory of epidemics. Hieronymus Brunschwig, a barber-surgeon and older contemporary of Paracelsus, had already applied antiseptic procedures to wounds, and argued that the surgeon should possess the knowledge of the physician.[45] Medieval alchemists had long since taken the first steps toward chemical therapy. True, their thinking was rife with mystical beliefs. But should one suppose that the thinking of Paracelsus is less so? A thirteenth-century physician, Nicholas of Poland, had long before denounced medieval medical tradition and broken ranks with the medical establishment at the University of Montpellier, to champion specific remedies.

Nancy Siraisi has summarized his Paracelsus-like opposition to scholastic authority and advocacy of a natural medicine utilizing latent healing virtues:

> As a result of his experiences there, Friar Nicholas wrote a poem denouncing the characteristic features of university medical training—reliance on ancient authorities, scholasticism, and rationalism. In his native Poland he tried to develop his own "natural" alternative medicine; it consisted of the idea that God had implanted special healing virtues in revolting things and led him to urge his patients to eat snakes, lizards, and frogs.[46]

This sounds like and unlike Paracelsus: unlike him in appearing to embody medieval contentions rather than Renaissance openness to true naturalistic experience. We might assume that Paracelsus is in a very different category from Nicholas of Poland; that when he proposes strange and seemingly worthless diagnoses and remedies, he is at least doing so on the basis of empirical experience; that he has at least gotten onto the right bus, even if he gets off it at the wrong stop. This assumption is as incorrect for Paracelsus as it is for Nicholas of Poland.[47]

All claims made with respect to his status in the history of science rest in the final analysis on the pivotal assertion that he was, as he himself often proclaimed, an advocate of experience over tradition. Paracelsus's announcement of his lectures in Basel promised a program based on *experientia ac ratio*. It can be argued that if, and only if, this "experience" was on the side of naturalistic observation, are the successes attributed to him recognizable as scientific advances. However, when one compares the experiential findings of Paracelsus with those of others in his century, his "experience" appears to fall into a different category, more akin to religious contemplation than to rigorous observation by the senses.

The image of Paracelsus not only overshadows precursors. It eclipses his contemporaries. This is especially evident when one compares Paracelsus with two medical authors who were younger by only one generation: Paré and Servetus. Even a practice-oriented work such as *Die große Wundarznei* (*The Great Wound-Surgery*), which presumably derived from Paracelsus's early activities in ministering to armies, can be searched in vain for the sort of precise clinical findings and fine accounts of wound dressings recounted of military surgery by Ambroise Paré (1510–1590).[48] As a craftsmanlike barber-surgeon who utilized his labors and expended his leisure in the study of anatomy, Paré stood in the forefront of a medicine contrasting with that of Paracelsus (though, like his older German counterpart, Paré wrote in the vernacular, believed in monsters, and knew that nature could heal wounds without drastic interventions by the practitioner).

Another figure of this century was closer to Paracelsus's dual proccupations with religion and medicine: Miguel Servetus (1511–1553). Servetus was the tragic critic of the trinitarian doctrine who was burned at the stake for this heresy in Calvin's Geneva. Denying that a divisibly threefold vital spirit inhabits the human organism, and stimulated also by his awareness that in Hebrew the word for *spirit* also signifies *air*, Servetus arrived at the discovery of the circulation of blood through the lungs, in a work completed around the time of Paracelsus's death bearing the title *Restitutio Christianismi*.[49] Like Paracelsus, Servetus was an individualist who distanced himself from the Catholic and Protestant camps of his time. Like him, he adhered to the belief in Christ's real presence in the Eucharist. But where Paracelsus insisted on the triadic structure of human being and of nature in the image of the triune Creator, Servetus's skeptical critique of trinitarian doctrine went hand in hand with an innovative study of the inner organic workings of life. Like Servetus, Paracelsus was a theologian-physician. Unlike him, theology did not orient the more renowned physician toward the observable structures of the body.

Servetus could only achieve his discovery as an experienced student of dissection. As such, he stood in the most productive current of sixteenth-century medicine, the century that brought forth Vesalius's great anatomical compendium *De Humani Corporis Machina*, published in 1543 by Paracelsus's erstwhile amanuensis Oporinus. The new anatomical studies proceeded from a critical

reediting and revaluation of Galen's ancient writings. It was discovered around this time that these had been based on animal
anatomy. The judgment of Paracelsus is quite as firm in regard to
the close study of the human body as it is in reference to the study
of Galen: he condemns the new approach as folly, but at the same
time he appropriates the term *anatomy*, applying it not to the inte-
rior of the body but to his own theoretical framework of mystical correspondences, reflecting the image of the Creator:

> all things stand in the image. That is, all things are formed. In
> this image [or form] lies anatomy. The human being is formed,
> his image is his anatomy which the physician must know. For
> thus, too, there are the anatomies of diseases.
>
> *alle ding in dem bild stent. das ist alle ding sind gebildet. in
> diser biltnus ligt die anatomei. der mensch ist gebildet; sein bilt-
> nus ist die anatomei, einem arzt voraus notwendig zuwissen. dan
> also seind auch anatomien der krankheiten.* (I,9:62)

Sixteenth-century critics recognized that Paracelsus was opposed to
Renaissance anatomy.[50] His substitution of his own mystical anatomy rendered observational or diagnostic experience at best imprecise and at worst utterly fanciful—indeed, rendered the very term
experience questionable as employed by this ardent adherent of
supernatural phenomena.

As Goldammer has stated, Paracelsus's outlook was in many
respects medieval.[51] The image correspondences of macrocosm and
microcosm are bound up with the medieval understanding of analogy and symbol, derived from a concept of *analogia entis* and closely
intertwined with the spiritual sense of the Bible. The medieval doctrine of the fourfold meaning of Scripture was undermined by the
Lutheran Reformation; Paracelsus reconstructed his symbolic vision
of nature in part with remnants of a medieval biblicistic authority.
Compared to the most advanced cosmologies of the late Middle Ages,
nature in Paracelsus's *Astronomia Magna* represents a *return* to
biblical authority. In this, the physician was not so much an anti-
Luther as a variant Luther, a *Lutherus medicorum*.

The Faustian image of Paracelsus, reiterated throughout so
much of the German literature, not only subordinates him in the

popular conception to a Renaissance which seems to contrast with what we understand by the Reformation; it also affects the way in which his writings are classified, subdivided, and even dated. As a result, the religious components of his writing are perennially segregated and underestimated. A very long, halting process has restored an understanding of his religious profile. In the late sixteenth century, the compiler of the first extensive edition of Paracelsus is said to have excluded his religious writings to avoid risking the sponsorship of the archbishop of Cologne.[52] Manuscripts as well as imitations circulated. The religious influence of Paracelsus survived in the works of Valentin Weigel and Jacob Boehme, in the writings of despised "enthusiasts," or in Pietists, who transmitted a knowledge of his mystical theory to Goethe and the Romantics. During the nineteenth century, the scholarly recovery of the theology of Paracelsus began in 1839 with Preus's collection of his religious pronouncements.[53] The founder of modern Paracelsus scholarship, Karl Sudhoff, stressed the medical side to the detriment of the religious; but, to his lasting credit, he helped initiate the edition of the religious works by collecting them and encouraging scholars of religion to undertake their publication. While Sudhoff was still carrying out the monumental task of examining the writings attributed to Paracelsus in order to publish the medical-naturalistic work, a younger collaborator, Wilhelm Matthießen, was encouraged to begin editing the theological writings. One volume was published in 1923.[54] However, Matthießen's early death and the difficulties of the editing process prevented the continuation of the second division. Publication could not be resumed until Kurt Goldammer took up the effort after World War II. Even today, the division of the religious writings is only about half finished, after nearly a century of attention.

During much of this time, there was no lack of interest in the non-scientific aspect of Paracelsus. The period around the turn of the century brought a wave of fresh curiosity regarding the varieties of mysticism, occultism, and ecstatic experience. This gave rise to the Paracelsus studies of Franz Hartmann and the Anthroposophist Rudolf Steiner, as well as a Paracelsus-inspired revival of mystical nature philosophy by Professor Karl Joël.[55] The so-called Expressionistic decade (1910-1920) intensified the interest in religious mysticism with works such as Martin Buber's dissertation on Boehme or his *Ecstatic Confessions*, dramatizing the experiences of mystics and visionaries. This excitement was undoubtedly a mixed blessing for Paracelsus scholars. Given the rational viewpoint maintained by Sudhoff, the orientation toward the mystical and the occult threatened to undermine the scientific stature of Paracelsus, lowering his status as an object of scholarship.

Against this trend, Matthießen's dissertation on *Die Form des religiösen Verhaltens bei Theophrast von Hohenheim* at the University of Bonn, published in 1917, tried to clear Paracelsus of disagreeable associations with an irrational mysticism.[56] If anything, the character and importance of the religious elements in Paracelsus now became somewhat clouded and marginalized within the interpretations of serious scholars. In 1935, Bodo Sartorius Freiherr von Waltershausen convincingly argued for Paracelsus's affinity with the Protestant Spiritualists who had followed the lead of Luther's rejection of Scholastic authority by rejecting a new Lutheran Scholasticism and authoritarianism founded on the outer "letter" of Scripture: *Mit den Autoritäten verwirft [Paracelsus] nun auch die Tradition; er entwertet sie zur Menschenlehre, zur Lehre des Buchstabens.* Unfamiliar with the scope and importance of the theological writings of Paracelsus, Waltershausen erroneously asserted that their author had viewed them as an "extraneous work" (*Außenwerk*), for which no expertise comparable to that of the philosophical work was claimed.[57] In 1937, the devout Catholic scholar Franz Strunz correctly, if somewhat tendentiously, revised the assessment of Waltershausen by proving that Paracelsus's assertions of natural knowledge rested on faith and divine authority: "Religion is the real and essential principle of natural understanding and action" (*Die Religion ist das eigentliche und wesentliche Prinzip des natürlichen Erkennens und Handelns*).[58] This was a turning point in Paracelsus scholarship: the religious writings were not only important in their own right; they were essential to the work as a whole. Similar in significance were Wilhelm Ganzenmüller's researches into medieval and Paracelsian alchemy, demonstrating that pre-Paracelsian alchemy was in its main currents devout and that his adaptation followed in the pious tradition.[59] In their own different ways, Strunz and Ganzenmüller laid the groundwork for an integrated understanding of Paracelsus: Strunz by showing that the authority of the naturalist and of the religionist was indivisible; Ganzenmüller by establishing that even what seemed an empirical element in Paracelsus's experience, his alchemical experimentation, was, in its theoretical sources, medieval and devout. After the war, dissertations on Paracelsus's religious work were written by Stephan Török and Michael Bunners.[60]

However, by far the most substantial revision has come about through the lifelong work of Prof. Kurt Goldammer in preparing the second division of the complete writings. His contributions to Paracelsus research also include many books and trailblazing articles cited in this study. Among the more recent scholars who have further explored the ground broken by Goldammer, and whose works were of particular interest in considering the theme of this study, are Ernst Wilhelm Kämmerer, who has written on the trichotomous anthropology of Paracelsus; Hartmut Rudolph, on the trinitarian doctrine of Paracelsus, his biblical exegesis, and his relation to other religious doctrines of the period; Arlene Miller-Guinsburg, who has investigated the Matthew commentaries in connection with the magic of Paracelsus; Katharina Biegger, who has examined the mariology of the Salzburg writings, as well as the ambiguous position of Paracelsus between the confessions of his period; and Ute Gause, who has comprehensively considered the theological evolution of the early religious writings. These studies offer the only readily accessible glimpses into the still unedited religious works.

This study has been written without a first-hand knowledge of the manuscript materials awaiting publication in the second division, and hence can claim to be neither comprehensive nor conclusive. Certainly it would have been preferable otherwise. Nevertheless, the view from this distance in examining the great mass of published primary and secondary materials does bring out some questions and inconsistencies that seem to have escaped the notice of those more directly involved. These questions concern the dating of Paracelsus's work, especially the earlier writings, the fragments, and the undated materials in the second division. The problem of dating his writings is especially important here, because, to some extent, a doubtful periodization recapitulates the old divorce between the religious and medical-philosophical Paracelsus.

Notwithstanding the cautionary intimations of Goldammer, Rudolph, Gause, and others—suggesting that Paracelsus was either more religiously engaged, or more "medieval" than had previously been assumed—a vestige of the old scientific/mystical split has been conserved not only by the organization of his works into the two divisions (an organization valid for parts of his work, yet misleading for the whole), but, just as importantly, by the assumption that his life alternated between divergent engagements, between his major medical-philosophical preoccupation and a minor religious one. If one considers the widely accepted progression of his career as an author, it is presumed to have begun around 1520 with a first naturalistic phase. This is followed in 1524–1525 by the relatively brief but intensive religious interlude in Salzburg. After this, he continues as a naturalist, but with a concurrent religious phase of writing in the early 1530s, when he is attracted to the thinking of the religious outcasts of the period. This is followed at last by the ultimate period of the *Astronomia Magna* and the Carinthian writings addressed to Catholic men of influence in Austria. The last years include some of his most conceptually ambitious and programmatic tracts, as well as, again, some religious writing. It is a period concluded by his untimely death in 1541, a death thought by some to have prevented him from articulating the full system of his speculative thought.

This is the biography of a naturalist who merely *reacts* to extraneous concurrent developments in the Reformation. Instead of this biography, with its medical-scientific continuity and its bracketed periods of religion, we should reverse the relation and recognize that the naturalism of Paracelsus turns on a religious center from the very beginning. The brackets are in reality the comprehensive context. First of all, there is no evidence at all to suggest that he really *had* his often-cited early naturalistic phase of writing around 1520, prior to the religious period in Salzburg, which therefore may well have been his seminal period as a writer and thinker. Second, the presupposition that Paracelsus's religious writing was episodic is groundless. And, finally, as I will argue in the main part of this study, no aspect of his work can be understood rationally without considering his religious-theoretical premises, as conditioned by the crisis of the early Reformation. If a complete study of his authorial development is ever undertaken, it will need to evaluate his work by comparing alternate drafts of the same tract and successive treatments of the same theme. On the same grounds, it will be necessary to reassess the temporal beginning of his work, as represented in the above commonplace periodization of his writings.

Based on not much more than the editorial circumstance that Sudhoff chose to place the very approximate date *um 1520*, "around

1520," at the fore of volume one of the first division, published in 1929, Paracelsus scholarship has continued to hold the notion that around that time the young Theophrastus, returning from his journeyman years, initiated his authorial career with works in a medical-philosophical vein. Indeed, the studies that emphasize his scientific profile often stiffen Sudhoff's approximation into a definitive "*of* 1520." This dating suggests that by 1524 the scientific-medical enterprise was well underway even *before* being briefly interrupted by the Salzburg lapse, during which external events involved Paracelsus with religious questions. The thesis of an early period of medical-philosophical writing purports to identify the point of departure of Paracelsus's work. However, the date *1520* is usually simply taken for granted; and not only by those with a scientific approach: even studies of his religious work assume that he began writing around the year 1520, perhaps while still wandering through Europe.[61]

However, this early period of medical-philosophical writing, beginning around 1520 and presumably lasting until 1524, appears to be based on a conjecture to which even the acknowledged master of scientific Paracelsus studies, Sudhoff himself, did not adhere with any precision or consistency. In Julius Pagel's *Geschichte der Medizin*, which Sudhoff reedited and published in 1922, the discussion of Paracelsus envisages a very different time frame:

Full of great conceptions, he began already in the first half of the Twenties, probably already in 1524 in Salzburg, his authorial elaborations, with a great pathological-therapeutic work, which was to treat related groups of diseases in individual sections; only fragments of it have survived. . . . Alongside this, an outline of the great etiology of diseases was composed in one great endeavor, in grandiose conception and compelling enthusiasm.

Großer Konzeptionen voll, hat er schon in der ersten Hälfte der zwanziger Jahre des 16. Jahrhunderts, wohl schon 1524 in Salzburg, seine schriftstellerischen Ausarbeitungen begonnen mit einem großen pathologisch-therapeutischen Werke, das in einzelnen Abschnitten zusammengehörige Krankheitsgruppen behalten sollte; nur Fragmente davon sind uns erhalten. . . . Daneben wurde in einem großen Wurfe ein Abriß der gesamten Krankheitsätiologie verfaßt, in grandioser Konsequenz und drängender Begeisterung.[62]

The pathological-therapeutic work is presumably the one known as the *Eleven Treatises* (which is associated here with other works that Sudhoff later ascribed to a *subsequent* period); the "great" attempt at a "comprehensive etiology" is that of the so-called *Volumen Paramirum* which, judging by its contents, could indeed be one of the very earliest writings. Here, however, this early work is placed *no earlier than Salzburg, 1524*, thus contradicting the date *um 1520* offered in volume one of Sudhoff's own first division. There is in fact a glaring contradiction between the dating in the collected works and the formulations submitted by Sudhoff here and elsewhere.

Sudhoff's *Paracelsus* biography of 1936—a study with the announced purpose of eliminating the romantic accretions to the image of Paracelsus, and in a sense Sudhoff's last testament to Paracelsus studies—states the matter again very differently: the "treatises on the origin, causes, signs, and cures of individual diseases" (the *Eleven Treatises*), are said to belong, together with some pharmacological drafts, to "the very earliest times [!] of Hohenheimian intellectual activity" (*in die allerfrühesten Zeiten Hohenheimscher Geistesarbeit*): all of these undertakings were already alive in mind at the time of the "first *Paramirum*" (the *Volumen Paramirum*); and Sudhoff would perhaps add some "chemical-alchemical preparations." As for the date, Sudhoff concludes: "But I would prefer to put all this writing in the year 1526" (*Besser aber will ich dies ganze Schriftwerk erst ins Jahr 1526 verweisen . . .*). Why? Well, because it was during this period of wandering on the Upper Rhine that Paracelsus was "veritably stormed by such impulses which he willingly accomodated as a man given to the observation and experience of nature" (*denn dort stürmten solche Anregungen förmlich auf ihn ein, denen er als Mann der Naturbeobachtung und -erfahrung willig Raum gab*).[63] What is decisive for us here is that the last word submitted by this great Paracelsus scholar displays no loyalty whatsoever to the period "around 1520." In fact, he expressly disavows the possibility of finding any proof that the contents of volumes one and two were composed *prior to 1526*: "Whether something of the early writing of Hohenheim which is found in volume one or two of my edition was worked out in the time of the first stay in Salzburg, or, as is to be expected, even prior to that, cannot be said with certainty" (*Ob irgend etwas von dem frühen Schriftwerke Hohenheims, das sich im ersten oder zweiten Bande meiner Ausgabe findet, in den Zeiten des ersten Salzburger Aufenthaltes, oder sogar schon vorher, konzipiert oder gar ausgearbeitet wurde, wie zu vermuten steht, läßt sich nicht mit Bestimmtheit behaupten).*[64]

By Sudhoff's final assessment, then, the *Eleven Treatises* belong to the "earliest" period, which it is best to identify with the time on the Upper Rhine, the interval between Salzburg and Basel. The work of "around 1520" has therefore been displaced by half a decade to the year 1526. This is hard to fathom, inasmuch as the Salzburg religious writings bear dates as early as *1524* and *1525*. Sudhoff apparently blotted out the religious tracts that did not fit into his preconceived opinion of Paracelsus as a Renaissance philosopher-physician. Even more perplexing is the fact that one of the *Eleven Treatises*—which Sudhoff, despite his other vacillations, still places at the very beginning of Paracelsus's intellectual labors—contains a passage that almost certainly identifies this writing with the period in or after Basel (1527–28). The passage instructs:

> If one wants to be a city physician, a lecturer, and professor ordinarius, one should have the appropriate abilities. These [people], however, inasmuch as some of them are lazy from pedantry and others puffed up in rhetoric, [and] the other accustomed to [telling] lies in poetry and so on with other philistinism [*schützerei*]; so being that way, they can't be any different than the way the letters make them, which make many a fool more.

> *So einer iedoch wil ein stattarzt, ein lector und professor ordinarius, so sol er können, das im zustat. dise aber, dieweil etliche in schulmeisterei erfault sind, andere in der rhetoric verschwollen, der ander in der poeterei mit liegen gewont und dergleichen mit anderer schützerei; so mügen sie nit anderst sein, dan wie sich die buchstaben machen, die manchen narren mer machen.* (I,1:150)

This passage cannot have been written prior to 1527, for it spells out the job qualifications of Paracelsus's position in Basel, with a jaundiced diatribe against his academic detractors in that city. There was no university in Salzburg or in Strasbourg (where he took rights of citizenship, apparently in anticipation of permanent residence there, before being summoned to Basel). Moreover, this passage reflects the antagonisms that led to his flight from Basel in 1528. As we shall see, this diatribe resembles so closely those of the post-Basel period that it would be farfetched to imagine it as based on some similar, yet unknown and otherwise forgotten episode. The dating of Paracelsus's seminal works is a time-honored shambles.

Now of course one could ask: *does it really matter whether Paracelsus is thought to have begun writing in 1520 or in 1524?* Does it matter whether we imagine him taking this first step as an author in an attempt to evaluate all the information gleaned from countless observations and consultations on his travels in Europe? Or—as harried by sectarian quarrels and struggles in a situation which was compelling him to take sides and define his ideas? *To even ask such a question is to recognize at once that it matters immensely.* It matters, not least of all because the *scenario of 1520* provides us a meager access to the writings in volumes one and two of the first division. (Where *are* all those observations based on his journeys?) The scenario of a beginning in 1524, by contrast, refers us to anomalous characteristics in what is thought to be the earliest medical-philosophical writing: to the disputes of competing medical "sects" in the so-called *Volumen Paramirum*, and to the attempted resolution of the battle of these competing sects through a criterion of divine agency.

Even when the writings in the first two volumes of division one seem to embody allusions to his empirical observations during his travels—for example, in his references to the diversity of diseases and medicinal herbs from country to country: "Each land grows its own disease, its own medicine, its own physician (*einem ieglichen lant wechst sein krankheit selbs, sein arznei selbs, sein arzt selbs*— I,2:4)—the larger context fails to support such a conclusion. For his point here is that people need *not* rely upon herbs and medicines of other countries. The long and short of his familiarity with other lands, diseases, and medicines is that German diseases are different and German medicines as good or better. Arabia, Chaldea, Persia, Greece, Gallia, and, most especially, Italy are trying "to turn us Germans into Latins" (*machen aus uns Teutschen Walen*), doing so for selfish reasons and not from "brotherly love" (I,2:3)—this was a common German sentiment, characteristic of the early Reformation. But its nationalistic stand is anomalous in a work on medicine. What, after all, can the healing powers of herbs have to do with the relative merits of nations? Given the atmosphere of the early Reformation, the association of healing with salvation was an obvious one. In an allegory attributed to Lazarus Spengler of Nuremberg, the power to heal the body was a transparent metaphor for the power to heal the soul: in the *Dialogue at the Apothecary Shop* (1521).[65] The nationalism of Paracelsus's early *Herbarius*-fragment recalls the Salzburg religious polemic of 1525 against Italian opponents ("Valentio und Remigio Italis"), submitted by one "Theophrastis Hohenheimensis Germanus" (II,3:3).

Not only does the pre-Salzburg period of writing lack for evidence, not only are the Salzburg religious writings part of his earliest recorded period; much of the etiological work that Sudhoff took to be the very earliest (the *Eleven Treatises* and the fragments on gout) is of the *late* 1520s: *it is transitional, not initial, work*. Indeed, most of the medical-theoretical work is as much religious as scientific. The *Archidoxa* is a case in point. Sudhoff's edition dates it 1526, and there is internal evidence to support this: as Hooykaas noted, its discussion of the elements contains no reference to the concept of the three primary things, salt, mercury, and sulphur, so constant in many of the writings of the mature philosopher.[66] Nevertheless, although in its main exposé it tersely lists numerous alchemical recipes and their medicinal applications, this work is prefaced and purposed by theological questions: it is concerned with knowledge of God. Nearly all of the early writings, even when they are preoccupied with worldly existence and disease, remain open to a metaphysical perspective that contextualizes everything and entirely overshadows what is known through observation—as in the fragments on gout in volume one of Sudhoff's edition, where Paracelsus's disquisition leaps from the discussion of the disease to the contemplation of the eternal sources of creation.

The mature programmatic writings of the late 1530s merely provide this mixture of nature philosophy and theology a more integrated form. In the *Labyrinthus Medicorum Errantium* (1538), medicine is a gift of divine illumination. In the compendious, late fragment *Astronomia Magna*, it is impossible to separate the medical-philosophical from the theological. The distinction is altogether arbitrary: anthropology and divinity are inextricably mixed throughout. Neither the category of "Renaissance science" nor that of "lay theology" fits. One would do better to employ his own term *theorica* to designate a speculative enterprise which defies such divisions.

Goldammer and the other scholars associated with the second division of Paracelsus's works have made a commendable attempt at establishing the sequence of the undated religious and social or ethical writings, assigning many of them to the early 1530s. But much of the evidence based on similarities of theme and language appears inconclusive. The longest of the works, the commentary on the Psalms, bears the date of July 12, 1530; but as Goldammer has established, this is in the preface to the second part of the work;[67] the first extant part and another, probably lost, could well extend the process of composition years back in time. It is true that Paracelsus after 1530 was an outcast, seeking guidance in faith, who may indeed have felt more kinship with impoverished roaming religious exiles than with the Humanists and magisterial reformers who had shunned him in city after city, but was he less the outcast in 1526 or 1528? In any case, the tendency of newer scholarship has been to find more religious writing throughout his lifetime.[68] *De secretis secretorum theologiae Theophrasti*, which Goldammer regards as a "late work" (II,3:XXIX), states that the author now looks back upon "twenty years" of "Evangelical church wars" (*in diesen euangelischen kirchen kriegen, so in zweinzig jaren geschehen seindt*); the tract also alludes to the author's having begun the work of the treatise "in the 20s" (*in diesem werk, in dem ich nun in die 20 jar angefangen und gearbeitet hab*—II,3:225, 167). Whether *20 jar* means twenty years ago or means during the twenties of his century, it verifies in either event that he exercised a religious authorship at the beginning and end of his authorial career. Even during his Basel sojourn—in which one could suspect an exclusive medical-philosophical engagement—there is some evidence of a religious activity. A medical tract from Colmar (June 1528) recollects the betrayals of Paracelsus by those in Basel who had "received their religion from me" (*ir religion von mir empfangen*—I,6:319).

What is decisive is not the number of religious or social-ethical works written during the early 1530s, but the conception of his authorial career as a whole. Even if there should have been a phase of religious writing in the early 1530s, the premise of this study would remain intact: *Paracelsus's formative period as an author coincided with the turmoils of the early Reformation* (which had begun soon after the publication of Luther's *Ninety-five theses* in 1517). We are confronted with an interval perhaps as brief as six or seven years. It is bounded by the Salzburg writings on the one hand and by the increasingly mature (that is, more clearly composed and more extensive) writings of the 1530s on the other. The denouement of this foundational period is represented by the works of 1530 and 1531, which bear the prefix *Para-* in their titles. Long heralded by his allusions to the coming "paramiran" works, these are the writings that confirmed Theophrastus as Paracelsus. The works of the 1520s and early 1530s reveal the making of the self-made man more clearly than do all the fanciful considerations of travels and collected observations.

The outline of Paracelsus's writings after 1534 is somewhat clearer. Inasmuch as the later theoretical works and the medical books published after 1535 (*The Great Wound-Surgery*) are more deliberately executed, more studied in design and often calmer in tone, there are grounds for regarding his last six or seven years as a mature period, in contrast with the turbulent formative years under consideration in this study. The earlier years are the epoch in which his theories were forged. I will argue that this occurred under the decisive impact of the early Reformation, to which the thirty-year old Theophrastus responded with radical polemical writings during his early, stormy sojourn in Salzburg. Of course, throughout his entire career, the writer and thinker reacted to many distinct situations and stimuli with writings of various kinds. Yet neither the Salzburg religious writings nor those attributed to the early 1530s represent isolated interludes in his career. If the precise dating of some of his early works is inconclusive, his early, formative writing certainly coincided with a religious authorship that was set aside, if at all, only during and right after his official activity in Basel. I will argue as well that the "medical-philosophical" work of the period around 1530 incorporates and interprets iconoclastic religious tenets first expressed in Salzburg. The theories that result from this seminal period are then expressed, a bit more calmly and systematically, in the mature works, where once again the distinction between his medical and religious authorship proves quite illusory. This distinction may be valid to the extent that the writings of the second division are religious or social in theme, and also to the extent that certain of the writings in the first division (such as those on surgery) are almost exclusively medical. But the distinction is quite misleading for many of the characteristic medical-philosophical or naturalistic writings in division one. Many of these works are hardly less religious.

It should of course be admitted in any discussion that no scholar can reasonably claim that we possess a complete inventory of

Paracelsus's religious or nonreligious writings. He alludes to many titles of unknown works or projects. Even after Sudhoff completed his bibliographic and editorial work, many manuscripts have been discovered. Sudhoff reproduced a kind of advertisement of unspecified date, sent out to publicize and presumably create a market. Among the writings advertised is "*Archidoxa*, in which [Paracelsus] teaches how to separate the pure from the impure" (*Archidoxa, in dem er lehret, das rein vom unreinen zu scheiden*); this known book is advertised as the companion piece to an unknown religious work "*Parasarchum*, in which he treats of the highest good in eternity" (*Parasarchum, in welchem er de summo bono in aeternitate tractirt*). Though this is the only patently spiritual book, the advertisement claims, quite astonishingly, that "the great Paracelsus" is author to no less than 230 books on philosophy (a subject which in his time was rarely secular), forty on medicine, twelve "*de republica*," seven on mathematics or astronomy, and sixty-six on the occult or secret arts (*von verborgenen und heimlichen Künsten*). The advertisement avers that there is a young man in Germany without equal in the entire world. Either his gift is a stellar influence or it comes from the Holy Spirit, or—with an intimation Paracelsus would hardly have proffered on his own—it comes from the evil spirits. In all events, the promoter of his books cannot remember ever having read more learned writings; he commends them to the recipient of the letter with the counsel to esteem them more highly than the books of the ancients.[69]

In addition to the periodization of the religious writings, another sort of bracketing prevents an integrated understanding of Paracelsus and his times: the customary tendency to disregard his fierce diatribes, as if these were somehow extraneous to the development of his thinking, a mere function of his personality, or perhaps a justifiable reaction to the hard knocks suffered by a misunderstood genius. I will argue here that these frequent diatribes are quite essential to the evolution of his thinking. His anger exposes the generation of his theories out of conflict, from struggles in which fundamental issues touching his theology as well as his medicine were being debated and fought over.

In the writings on divine and those on natural matters, the author reacts to real and perceived challenges to his authority with desperate flights of rage and vituperation. In tracts of either division, his diatribes and tirades appear to give impetus and direction to his thought by compelling him to hammer down the uniqueness of his concepts. The great tirades of Paracelsus are prodigious feats. They convey a forgotten determinant of his intellectual activity: the raw force that was expressed in the conflicts of his time even in disputes over matters of sublime doctrine. During the years of his emergence as an author, the Reformation was passing through the decisive crises of the Peasant War, and of the debates of Luther with Karlstadt, Müntzer, Erasmus, and Schwenckfeld.

The Lutheran Reformation, with its doctrinal separation of the "two kingdoms," envisaged a new realm of justice, love, and fellowship. Yet even among the ranks of the faithful, disputes could retain the old aspect of a grim trial by combat, resolved by mental and physical prowess and summarily damning by outcome the weakness of the loser or the isolation of the outcast. One can recognize this in Luther's fulminations against rebellious peasants like those who took up arms during Paracelsus's early stay in Salzburg; or one can observe it in the verbal violence of Luther's dispute with Karlstadt, which happened to coincide with Paracelsus's turbulent time in Salzburg, Strasbourg, and Basel.

In a dramatic scene in August 1524, Luther rebukes his senior academic colleague (whose radical "Wittenberg movement" of 1522 had aggressively espoused doctrines subsequently adopted by Luther himself). The indicted miscreant, Luther charges, is on the side of Thomas Müntzer and of the murderous peasants; he has shown vile ingratitude toward their prince and protector.[70] Karlstadt refuses to abandon his positions. Luther challenges him to write his disagreements and then hands his opponent a gold coin, symbolically authorizing him to go forth and take up the challenge. But no sooner does Karlstadt begin to respond thus in writing than he receives an order of banishment from Saxony. Further radicalized by banishment, Karlstadt flees to Basel and Strasbourg. In the latter city, his views soon found favor among leading reformers—sparking a controversy that was still in progress when Paracelsus arrived in the city a few years later. Luther counterattacks in 1525 with his two-part treatise, *Against the Heavenly Prophets*. Even his sympathizers are taken aback by the brutality of his insinuations: "Therefore, I have said that Dr. Karlstadt is not a murderous prophet, but he has a rebellious, murderous, mob spirit in him, that would come out if it had the opportunity" (*Darumb hab ich wol gesagt, D. Carlstad ist nicht eyn mörderischer prophet, Er hat aber eynen auffrürischen, mörderischen, rottischen geyst bey sich, der wol eraus fure, wenn er raum hette*).[71] By May 1525, the dispute has become so notorious that Agrippa von Nettesheim writes from Lyon that he has read the first part of Luther's tract and is eager to get hold of the second.[72] Such disputes, in which argumentation relied on pious intuitions of truth, and defeat could result in exile or death, convey something significant about the social environment, and no doubt also the conceptual purposes, of Paracelsus's writings.

His great haranguing tirades express the violent tensions of his time. His most central and most characteristic theories take shape amidst these harangues. Their heat molds the coherence and infuses the assurance of his writings on all themes. In an earlier disdainful reception of Theophrastus Bombastus von Hohenheim, his name was construed by false etymology as the root of "bombastic." To cleanse him of this undeserved odor of a bombastic mountebank, scholars who should have known better ignored or rationalized his tirades as expressions of temperament. Every harangue against hostile apothecaries, physicians, or vendors of guaiac wood was hailed as a salutary reaction against venality and incompetence. Rarely was any effort made to substantiate the vitriolic charges, and when evidence did indicate that his opponents were not all such reactionary fools (for example, that the Augsburg Fuggers whom Paracelsus accused of profiteering from the import of guiac wood actually stood to profit far more by supplying the mercury cure favored by the enraged accuser[73]), the findings had hardly any impact on the idolization of Paracelsus. Ironically, even his insupportable claim to hold Luther's title of "doctor of Holy Scripture" would be interpreted as a confirmation of Paracelsus's sincere spirituality. On the whole, his most fervent defenders have either ignored dissenting voices, or simply subtracted any negative findings from the tally of merits in order to present the balance with undiminished enthusiasm.

An outsider to the circle of Paracelsus' scholarship cannot help but wonder whether the outrageous boasts and bouts of rage made him an intimidating subject for the German academic scholars who studied him. Could scholars educated at humanistic *Gymnasien* and trained in the cool methods of *wissenschaftliche Arbeit* have relished his execrations to "shit on your Pliny, Aristotle, your Albertus, Thomas, Scotus . . ." (*auf eueren Plinium, Aristotelem scheißen, auf eureren Albertum, Thomam, Scotum etc. scheißen*) . . .—I,8:138)?

Could it suffice to verify that the men Paracelsus claimed as his educated mentors existed in history (or that he was contemporaneous with Paré or Vesalius) in order to reclaim this obdurate nay-sayer for their humanistic tradition? Did such rationalizations vitiate the perception of him as a flesh and blood creature? Have scholarly specialization and tradition prevented Goldammer and his students from demolishing the myth of a secular-empirical Paracelsus, a myth undermined by, yet still required to dignify, their excavations? How complex was his assigned role as the true Renaissance prototype of Goethe's Faustian *Bildungsideal*? Did German intellectuals half-consciously hope to confirm that, no matter how dark things seemed, progress was inevitable? In any such perspective, the obscure figure making his way across the rim of *die Neuzeit* must have towered up larger than life and moved straight toward the observer—as founder, ally, precursor, or disreputable forebear.

2 ■ Plague and Salvation

Most of Paracelsus's writings are fragmentary, difficult to read, and even more difficult to categorize. We should begin by inquiring after the preconditions of these writings which were so confidently composed and dictated in the vernacular, as if their author were in a position to solve all the deep mysteries of God and the universe by means of an impromptu discourse.

The century before Paracelsus had known great speculative constructs that combined mysticism with philosophy and touched on almost every domain of nature and learning including medicine, the Latin works of the cardinal and liberal-minded intellectual, Nicholas Cusanus (1401–1464), a German who was like Paracelsus a man of humble origin, broad interests, and bold concepts. Among his many achievements, Cusanus championed lay knowledge against the scholastically learned and submitted a theoretical rationale for weighing and measuring objects of inquiry. In the philosophy of Cusanus, there are some similarities to Paracelsus in the centrality of the notion of creation and creature as images of the divine Creator, in the dual concepts of macrocosm and microcosm, in the perception that finite things are irreducibly individual, and in the emphasis on the authority of a lay knowledge, which, for Cusanus as well as Paracelsus, has mystical overtones. However, the cardinal's ability to conceptualize and synthesize compares with the physician's as the open architecture of a Renaissance metropolis might compare with some fanciful but inscrutable clustering of huts.

Cusanus was the mathematician-philosopher of the infinite unity. His universe was immeasurably broader and exponentially more abstract than the world egg of Paracelsus. Cusanus was a man comfortable among the great and powerful, erudite, and filled with deep devotion to the unity of Church and Christendom. It is at least possible, if not certain, that Paracelsus knew of him. In any event, their speculative common ground was attained from opposite points of departure. Cusanus came from the heights of the universities and from his private intellectual avocations. His extraordinarily diverse sources were usually acknowledged. By contrast, Paracelsus disavowed the erudition of the past and groped to the common ground he shared with Cusanus by way of the depths, by tapping traditions far more obscure, popular, and difficult to identify. Cusanus's writings convey a serene calm. He knew the conflicts of his time, but exorcised them by means of his speculative construct of the coincidence of opposites in God. For Paracelsus, one suspects, this last great medieval synthesis would have been meaningless. Instead of calm, the atmosphere of his writing bespeaks a teeming anxiety: fear of diseases old and new, fear of the poisons that pervade everything in nature, fear of *succubi, incubi,* and other monsters, fear of war, violence, and false accusation, and not least of all, fear of ridicule.

The possibility of Paracelsus's writings—original treatises in the language of the people, combining medicine, nature, philosophy, and alchemy with religious and social preoccupations—resides in the coincidence of several developments. His work is conceivable because the traditional learned profession of medicine, with its eternal problems of disease and death, met with new circumstances which undermined the distinctions of the lay and the learned, of the medical and the theological. In this chapter, I will attempt to counter the thesis that Paracelsus's theories presuppose a new empirical "experience." I will argue that his authorship can be understood more plausibly as the late outgrowth of a flourishing growth industry of vernacular medical writing—an area in which the hundred-fifty-year-old tradition of the plague treatise had proven particularly fertile. If the intensely cultivated field of plague theory was wide open to popular initiatives, it was also soon to be highlighted and theologically contextualized by crises of faith. The combined impact of the medical tradition and the religious crisis is registered in what appears to be the earliest Paracelsian medical writing, the so-called *Volumen Paramirum.*

The medicine that dominated the Middle Ages was that of the ancient physician and philosopher Galen. As commonly understood, this medicine treated all illnesses as imbalances among the four humors, the sanguine, phlegmatic, choleric, and melancholy. The humors were in turn constituted by the elements of air, water, fire, and earth. Attuned to the balance of elements, Galenic medicine simplified the conception of illness. Guided by the universal humors, it could not address specific diseases as specific, but instead tended to treat a generalized patient who differed from other patients only in the complexion of the universal humors.

To Paracelsus and later sixteenth-century critics, Galenic medicine and its remedies appeared superficial and false. This was so in part because Scholastic philosophy was coming under challenge. In the diatribes of Paracelsus, the name of Galen sometimes occurs along with that of Aristotle. During the early Reformation, Aristotle was under attack from two standpoints—that of Neoplatonism and that of Holy Scripture. Paracelsus rejects the authority of Aristotle with the same categorical insistence with which he exalts biblical authority. It would be difficult to construe his few remarks on Plato as the ground for a studied philosophical anti-Aristotelianism. Though the word of God is not quoted specifically against Aristotle, it is evident that the Bible supported Paracelsus's opinions in their sharpest antischolasticism. Not the heathen philosopher but Holy Writ confirms Paracelsus's profound belief that nature is not eternal, but rather limited by a time imposed by its Creator and Redeemer. The theoretical physician extended his vision of a cosmos, which appears as if bounded by and carried in time, to the elaboration of a new medicine that individualizes life, health, and disease, and even envisages an evolution of diseases.

For the duration of a century and a half before Paracelsus's time, humoral medicine had already faced its gravest challenge in the form of plague epidemics.[74] The plague devastated medieval Europe in the Black Death of 1348–1350, a disaster regarded by some historians as the most catastrophic in European history. It has been said that plague became a driving force in European history. Plague depressed late-medieval agriculture by reducing the urban market populations, thereby compelling peasants to move to cities where wealth became increasingly concentrated in the hands of the survivors. This concentration of wealth and labor is thought to have diversified urban economies.[75] Moreover, plague epidemics undermined Church authority: priests abandoned congregations; all supplications failed; and divine punishment was visited upon the righteous no less than the wicked. By undermining ecclesiastic authority, epidemics set the stage for the Reformation of Luther, whose theological rejection of merits in favor of faith—the sole recourse in a world ruled by Satan—responded more convincingly to the inexorable menace of mass death. A cliché of cultural history portrays the end of the Middle Ages as symbolized by the all-encompassing Dance of Death—the dark backdrop for the bright optimism and energy of the dawning Renaissance.

In fact, the late fifteenth century ushered in a new epoch of epidemic disease.[76] New strains of bubonic plague were joined by the epidemic spread of syphilis, a malady so unprecedented and quick-spreading that Emperor Maximilian presented it as a sign of God's judgment on the world.[77] The growth of urban centers, the increasing size of armies, and the movement of goods, merchants, mercenaries, and other travellers were conducive to the spread of disease. In 1519, as much as a third of the population of Zurich was decimated by a plague epidemic. While convalescing from near death, Zwingli composed a devotional plague song, ascribing all power to the divine will. Upon recovering, he set about guiding his city from the old faith to the new.[78]

In 1525, the Upper Lusatian city of Görlitz was stricken by a plague epidemic. The wealthy ruling burghers fled the city to the safety of the countryside. In their absence, a local priest comforted his abandoned parishioners by preaching the new doctrine of salvation by faith alone, thereby initiating their conversion to the Lutheran creed. The old faith to which the city fathers clung had built shrines and chapels; this was now discredited as the false doctrine of good works. The new faith and its minister consoled the people in their hour of need.[79]

If disease was but one among many terrors of collective and individual existence to which the new faith addressed its winning message of hope, it was one that disclosed existential realities by separating the creditable from the discreditable in the common experience of the individual and community. Luther understood this clearly enough when he laid down the rule that Evangelical pastors were not to desert their flock in times of pestilence.[80] The year before Paracelsus arrived in Basel, the worst epidemic in a quarter of a century raged in the city. Undoubtedly, it aggravated the religious tensions, arraying the reform-minded burghers who supported his position as physician and professor against the Catholic medical faculty that was his bitter foe.

Plague could sorely test the individual's faith, separating the weak from the stalwart. By tending to the stricken populace of Antwerp during a plague epidemic, Agrippa von Nettesheim incurred the hostility of the physicians of that city. Thorndike assumes that this was because Agrippa was a quack.[81] But why should one exclude the possibility that it was his fearlessness that shamed the local physicians—garnering for him the respect of a populace in no position to demand high standards in epidemiology? The self-interested course of action in time of plague was avoidance.

Epidemics could delineate the boundaries between spiritual and physical communities. This could happen when the secular measures of plague prevention and control clashed with clerical injunctions and authority. Shortly after Paracelsus's time in Nuremberg, an epidemic in 1533 decimated more than five thousand souls, a very substantial portion of the population. A controversy broke out between the Lutheran pastor Andreas Osiander and the city's councillors, when their secular authority acted to encourage or compel the citizenry to flee to avoid contact with the afflicted. The resultant callousness in the treatment of the ill and dying led Osiander to preach a sermon against the city's ordinance, on how a Christian ought to behave in time of pestilence (*Wie und wohin ein Christ vor der Plage der Pestilenz fliehen soll?*). It was printed in Königsberg and even translated into English for publication, suggesting that the dilemma was a widespread one.[82] Osiander's sermon summarized what was being theorized at the time about the possible causes of plague:

> And likewise I do not want to quarrel with those who speak of it in the natural manner [saying]: such a scourge comes perchance from the influence of the stars, from the effect of comets, from extraordinary weather conditions and changes of the air, from southerly winds, from stinking waters, or from rotten vapors of the earth.

> *Desgleich will ich mich auch nicht einlassen gegen denen, die auf natürliche weyß darvon reden und sprechen: Solche plag kom etwo aus einfluß des gestirns, aus wirckung der cometen, aus unordenlicher witterung und endrung des luffts, aus mittägischen winden, aus stinckenden wassern oder aus faulen dempfen des erdtrichs.*[83]

These were common theories, entertained also in Paracelsus's earliest medical writing: plague could be caused by the stars, by poison in nature, or by imbalances of elements or humors, as well as by divine will or human wickedness. Osiander did not contest the "natural wisdom." He admonished the Nurembergers to do their Christian duty: officials should not abandon their offices. On pain of arousing God's anger even more severely, people should not shun neighbors or abandon those in need. Salvation of the soul and deliverance from disease were distinct things. Yet the pestilence could draw theology into a critical confrontation with epidemiology.

Epidemic disease not only tested the new faith and disrupted the traditional belief vested in an ecclesiastic hierarchy, which had appeared to mediate between the created world and the eternal one beyond it. Widespread disease could also challenge medieval Galenic medicine and to some extent the cosmological assumptions that had attended it. The name-coining poem on *Syphilis, sive Morbus Gallicus* by Girolamo Fracastoro (1483–1553) was composed during the period of Paracelsus's earliest recorded activities; it was published in 1530, around the time of his concentrated work on the same disease. The unlikely pastoral poem *Syphilis* was highly acclaimed by Emperor Charles V. Fracastoro's patron Cardinal Bembo received the work with enthusiasm but persuaded the poet to include more material promoting the therapeutic benefits of guaiac wood—imported and distributed under the auspices of the Church.[84] *Syphilis* is remembered for its nonhumoral hypothesis that the seeds of contagion are spread through the air. But the poem also engaged in speculations about the nature of the cosmos: *Aere, qui terras circum diffunditur omnes,/ Qui nobis sese insinuat per corpora ubique,/ suetus et has generi viventum inmittere pestes./ Aer quippe pater rerum est, et originis autor.*[85] In accounting for the new disease with the aid of a new theory, it was also necessary to consider the cosmic context of nature as a whole, to entertain the notion, for example, that air is the cosmological *pater rerum et originis autor*. For Paracelsus, speculations about the origin of diseases would also lead to disagreements with received notions of nature.

This is not to suggest that plague and syphilis epidemics were a decisive stimulus to philosophy, any more than they were, properly speaking, the determinant of Reformation theology. The point is that disease held a universal existential interest which could not be divorced from the other questions moving the world in Paracelsus's day. It was therefore not as aberrant then as it appears now, that, in proclaiming his new theories of disease to the public at large, the discourse of Paracelsus should cross the line from pathology into cosmology and theology: he could proceed so without departing from his objective of explaining disease and health. On an earth that lay enclosed by the heavens as an egg by its shell, life was immediately contiguous with the invisible power that made and sustained it. The supercelestial hierarchies of Ficino or Agrippa were not much more attractive to Paracelsus than to Luther: in their writings the palpability of existence is expressed in a German language, which, compared to the conceptual refinements of Humanistic Latin, favors the tangible entities of this world.

Both of these revolutionaries of immediacy, Luther as well as Paracelsus, emerged during a period in which authorship was acquiring a new directness and popularity of appeal and impact. Luther's Bible translation was only the finest and most original of many prior printed German versions. Luther was inspired by the late-medieval tradition of vernacular religious writings, the tradition that had included Tauler and the austere mystical tract that Luther knew as the *Theologia Deutsch*. German mysticism had translated theology into the idiom of the people and sanctioned individual knowledge of God, making it possible for everyone to engage in theology. Similarly in the field of medicine, popular literature during the fifteenth century encouraged not only the academic physicians. Unlearned surgeons and apothecaries were increasingly inclined to compose and sign their names to medical tracts.[86] Theories were competing more publicly. Late medieval surgery had been represented by figures such as Peter of Ulm; and astrological medicine by the late fifteenth-century physician Conrad Heingarter of Zurich, who, despite his academic loyalty to Aristotle, Galen, and Ptolemy, anticipated Paracelsus's interest in the use of images and seals and his concern with the processes of digestion.[87] German vernacular medical writing had indeed begun long before the advances in printing. *Herbaria*, folk almanacs, and handbooks of surgery became common among the incunabula and printed works of the late fifteenth and early sixteenth century.

Printing held out the possibility of new fame. The earliest medical work printed in German was the *Regimen Sanitatis Deutsch (Von der Ordnung der Gesundheit)*. Published in Augsburg in 1472, it would go through approximately 250 printings.[88] Ortolff's popular medical work, *Das Artzneibuch*, was printed in Nuremberg in 1477; his *Frauenbüchlein*, a handbook for expectant mothers, in 1500. Eucharius Röslin's medical *Rosengarten* appeared in Worms in 1513.[89] In addition, the illustrious foreign medical authors were being translated into German.[90] Dennis E. Rhodes indicates the rising trend in popular medical writings prior to 1500: "The years immediately following the invention of printing brought a spate of semi-popular works on medicine, many of which bore astronomical figures or zodiac men. A total of forty-six of these appeared before 1480, and about 100 before the end of the century."[91] In an increasingly open field of medicine, the paths would seem to converge either in a vista of harmonious prospects of the kind envisaged in Paracelsus's early *Volumen Paramirum*, or in the "labyrinth of medical errors" envisaged late in his life. Lorenz Fries was a rival medical controversialist who immediately preceded Paracelsus into the field of competitive opportunity. Fries's career indicates that that of his colleague and soon-to-be acquaintance was not as unique as one might think. Thorndike's characterization captures some of their similarities and differences:

> Fries' *Spiegel der Artznei*, first published in Strasbourg in 1518, is said by Schmidt to be the oldest work on internal medicine in the German language. The author dedicates it "to the poor sick of the common people," but to this preface adds a prayer in Latin to the learned asking pardon for teaching the science of Apollo in the language of the people. He asserts that his only aim is to extirpate errors, and that the glory of true physicians will not suffer from his book. He warns the folk against charlatans and empirics, and states that the only doctors worthy of confidence are rational physicians possessing academic degrees and a knowledge of grammar, logic, astronomy, arithmetic, geometry, music, cosmography, and especially natural science.[92]

Here, with a different resolution, is the typical Paracelsian task of defining who is to be served by medicine, on whose authority it is to serve, and which disciplines it requires in order to be of service.

Among late-medieval medical writings, it is not surprising that one of the most important categories was the plague tract. Every great epidemic wave yielded a crop of new plague writings. Again and again, these tracts repeated old theories, yet failure was so spectacular and so recurrent that it could only have eased open the door, bit by bit, to new theses and original initiatives in medicine. Sudhoff collected and evaluated an extensive German and European plague literature from 1348 to 1500[93], with results indicating the same tendency for this genre as Gerhard Eis could report for other types of late-medieval medical literature. The tendency was toward more works in German and fewer *anonyma*. The treatises increasingly bore the names of authors. Campbell has evaluated the impact of the plague and of the treatises addressed to it upon late-medieval learning.[94] Part of the Paracelsian legend is that he emerged as a heroic fighter against plague in Ferrara. This is certainly conjectural. However, as we shall see, it is significant that the causes of plague common in the late-medieval plague treatises correspond roughly to the five "substances" of disease discussed in Paracelsus's early writing on the five *entia* (*Volumen Paramirum*). More will be said about the connections of plague theory and Paracelsian etiology in the discussion of the *Volumen Paramirum* later in this chapter.

In addition to what one might call the low medical culture of popular handbooks and plague tracts, the writing of Paracelsus reflects the high medical culture of Italian Renaissance medicine as represented by Marsilio Ficino (1433–1499)—a name, we recall, that drew a rare word of praise. Before Paracelsus, Ficino had addressed the cause of epidemic pestilence, explaining its spread by a supernatural power of the imagination. Walter Pagel has maintained that the theory bears an important similarity to some plague explanations of Paracelsus.[95] Beyond specific influences of this kind, Ficino had erected an exemplary model for the role of the physician as the man of sovereign intellect, the man whose medical theory rests on great learning, comprising the divine and the natural in its purview, and whose medical pursuit amounts to a sacerdotal mission. As Pagel stated the matter: "Paracelsus's whole life and work seems to be an attempt at implementing the ideal of Ficino's priest-physician." Pagel indeed went beyond the importance of Ficino as an ethical model: "It is from Ficino as the exponent of Neo-Platonism that Paracelsus derives his inspiration."[96] According to Goldammer, Paracelsus also knew and adapted Ficino's *De triplici vita*, especially its third part (*De vita coelitus comparanda*), in his own early *De vita longa*, though Goldammer notes as well that the latter differed markedly.[97] Paracelsus certainly contrasted sharply with Ficino or Pico della Mirandola in giving short shrift both to classical antiquity and to learned sources in general. When disproportionate emphasis is assigned to illustrious Paracelsian precursors, there may be a tendency to overlook more obscure sources and affinities—a bias which the studies of Gerhard Eis have done much to rectify.[98]

Another form of nonscholastic writing that cleared a ground for the thinking of Paracelsus is the alchemistic tract composed in the vernacular. The names of many medieval alchemists who wrote in Latin occur in Paracelsus's work. When he alludes to Geber, Roger Bacon, Arnald of Villanova, Rupescissa, and others, invariably his references are sweepingly negative; surprisingly so, since Roger Bacon or Arnald of Villanova indeed offered some precedent for his own medical alchemy.[99] Another work—a book not mentioned by Paracelsus, but which nevertheless struck one contemporary as anticipatory of his three principles[100]—is the early fifteenth-century *Book of the Holy Trinity (Das Buch von der heiligen Dreifaltigkeit)*. It had been composed in Constance between 1415 and 1419. This was the exact place and time of Jan Hus's betrayal and execution by the Council of Constance (1415) and of the start of the Bohemian uprising which threatened German power and papal authority. The German *Book of the Holy Trinity* anticipates Paracelsus's extension of an earlier metallurgical diad of mercury and sulphur to his triad of sulphur, mercury, and salt. The work also anticipates the theological import of this extension; for, like Paracelsus, the *Book of the Holy Trinity* endeavors to synthesize the tenets of alchemy, astrology, and meteorology with those of theology, coordinating in parallel patterns alchemistic references, with a mystically understood "medicine.[101]" The book effectively merges various sources of authority, the divine, the political, and the natural, in a manner designed to glorify the *Burggraf* of Nuremberg and Emperor Sigismund, defenders of an order threatened by Hussite heresy and rebellion in Bohemia. Such a work, as well as the Latin tradition of medieval medical alchemy, could have served Paracelsus, in rather the same way that the mystical German treatise of the *Theologia Deutsch* could serve a Luther, who later rejected mysticism after finding his own way. In its divine sanctioning of inspirations, mysticism could assume various forms and serve diverse purposes. A contrastive symmetry distinguishes the inward-turned mysticism of the *Theologia*, whose anonymous author warns against "the light of nature," from the nature-oriented contemplation of *The Book of the Holy Trinity*. For, unlike the reflective mysticism of the *Theologia Deutsch* and of Tauler, the illumination granted to the devout author of *The Book of the Holy Trinity* reveals instead that eternal and natural truths are confirmed by the homologies of the stars, elements, nature, and Scripture.

In summary, though Paracelsus's actual precedents may remain obscure, his potential sources should have been relatively rich and diverse. Moreover, the advancement of printing was rendering authorship more effective in his time, even as the competition of books, theories, and doctrines was rendering it more public and no doubt more hazardous. Almost from the beginning of his work, he appears to compose as if preparing drafts for print. Between the lines of his writings, in the diatribes echoed and returned, in his gestures of parrying the assaults upon his position, or in his references to competing "sects" in medicine, one discerns the background cacophany of a quarrelsome *Zeitgeist*. This background of conflict in his work is rife with competing voices ever on the brink of open conflict with brutal consequences.

Against the teeming forces of confusion and fear, Paracelsus attempted to reconcile the conflicting claims of authority. The material day-to-day circumstances of his authorship can perhaps be surmised from the travel journal Michel de Montaigne dictated to his secretary some fifty years later while travelling through the very same regions of Switzerland, South Germany, Austria, and Northern Italy frequented by Paracelsus. The details may assist us in imagining a life lived in transit in the sixteenth century. The Frenchman was impressed by the quality of the food, wine, and accommodations; however, the sleeping rooms were often filled with several beds, with no bed curtains and, at best, a clapboard that could be folded out to make a crude desk. Moreover, the dining halls were crowded with guests, meals lasting as much as three to four hours, sometimes with raucous entertainments. Privacy for reflection or study would have been unimaginable, gregariousness of the kind to which Paracelsus was so given, a matter of imposed necessity. Quarrels and inconveniences occurred in transit. The inquisitive Montaigne took note of the changing sovereignties and differing religious practices and doctrines. Fascinated by the latter, he engaged pastors and citizens in lengthy discussions of their religion. Like other visitors, he was favored by the local magistrates with a hospitality that accorded with his social rank and the political disposition toward his nation. Montaigne for his part preferred to avoid attracting notice. Had he not been a wealthy dignitary and former mayor of Bordeaux, but a "doctor of both medicines," without a fixed residence or steady source of income, self-promotion would have been at a premium.[102] Self-promotion, varying between approaches of eclectic harmonization and hostile assertions of fundamental originality, is a constant of Paracelsus's writing.

Among his very earliest medical-philosophical writings is the fragmented work that goes by the title of *Volumen medicinae Paramirum de Medica Industria*, and which in Sudhoff's volume one also bears the heading of "Fragments of the Book *Concerning the five Entia*" (*Brüchstücke des Buches Von den fünf Entien*). This fragmentary work appears to have been a rough draft. It attempts an unprecedented overview of five kinds of causes of disease and of five corresponding kinds of medicine. However, the work ends inconclusively, and in the subsequent writings the terms *ens* or *entia* retain only a minor significance, having been displaced by other terminologies. The inconclusive "Book of the five *Entia*" seems intent on pressing home the message to its readers that hegemonic claims in medicine are untenable, suggesting that the new medicine of the author is as valid as the other four kinds of medicine. If he accepts their validity, then the worthiness of his medicine should be above doubt. The tendency of his thought in this writing is irenic and inclusive. The opinion that this is his earliest medical writing gains plausibility from the fact that the author does not excoriate the medicine of his opponents or berate Galen or Avicenna as fools and knaves. Rather moderately, he avers that their theories have been misunderstood. The fact that he does not elaborate on the "three primary things" of his mature theory also sustains the judgment that this fragment on the *entia* or five substances of disease is among his earliest. It appears to be separated from the later writings by some abrupt turn in the development of his ideas.

Unfortunately, the interesting consequences of this priority have been camouflaged somewhat by a lavish praise for the *Volumen Paramirum*, which makes it rather difficult to see this fragment as an agonizing beginning rather than a work of serene genius. Far from serenity, the work tries to avoid confrontation by letting things be all ways at once. Disputes over causes and cures can be resolved, apparently, in a peaceful coexistence of diagnostic-therapeutic approaches. In this respect, the work on the five *entia* expresses a basic polarity in the thinking of Paracelsus: his will to harmonize all positions, a desire which, no sooner frustrated, swings to the diametrically opposite pole of his assertions of originality and furious assaults on detractors. For much the same reason, the work intimates the restlessness of his life and thought. We cannot be certain whether the tract was composed before, during, or after his sojourn in Salzburg, but it seems to convey an early hope that his originality can abide in harmony with other therapeutic approaches. This tendency of the *Volumen Paramirum* needs to be understood in the context of Paracelsus's perennially unsettled life.

One can imagine the author of the fragment on the five *entia* of disease, peregrinating across the margins of empire, through Hapsburg crownlands and church lands, imperial cities beholden only to the emperor, and Swiss cities beholden to none. He would have been confronted with a patchwork of territorial entities, as idiosyncratic in their urban constitutions, as piecemeal in their boundary lines, as diverse or uncertain in their ties of subordination, and probably as varied in their medical usages, as the five Paramiran "princes" of disease. In the definition of the author, the five *entia* are designated thus because each has the "power to rule the body" (*ens ist ein urprung oder ein ding, welchs gewalt hat den leib zu regiren*—I,1:172). The body lives under many different sovereign rulers, according to the author of *Volumen Paramirum*.

All the corporate entities faced common perils, one of which is discussed prominently in the *Volumen Paramirum*: the threat of plague. Not by chance, this is the first example, the touchstone case for explaining disease. Pestilence is a crown witness against the hegemony of humoral medicine. The *Volumen Paramirum* is quick to note against opposing arguments: "But you . . . err against us in stating that all pestilence arises from the humors. . ." (*aber ir halt euch also und irrent in dem gegen uns, das ir sezet, das alle pestilenz aus den humoribus entspring oder aus dem das im leib, da ir fast irrent*—I,1:172). Here, "pestilence" delivers the key argument against humoral medicine. Yet it is noteworthy that the author does not reason from the widespread occurrence of the plague to a single widespread cause of infection. His point is instead that one and the same disease can arise from five diverse causes; there are therefore "five pestilences" (*fünf pestilenz*), corresponding to the five pathogenic *entia* (I,1:174). Not only this: each of the five pestilences may stem from a single cause and origin, but then either remain internal, as fever, or become an open wound and pestilence (*wan febris und pestilenz haben ein ursprung, aber er bricht sich. ein teil gehet in die feule der inwendigen, als febres, und gehört dem leibarzt zu, der ander teil gehet in die pestilenz. . .*—I,1:166). The internal fever or pestilence is in the province of the physician, the external pestilence in that of the surgeon.

Paracelsus is known for introducing numerous variations in his diagnoses, analyses, and prescriptions. His theory of plague retains elements of constancy from the early fragmentary *Volumen Paramirum* to the plague tracts of the late 1520s. Moreover, in addition to this seminal prominence and relative constancy of his views on plague, it is also noteworthy that his views correspond to some previously expressed notions. Similar notions are found in the plague tracts that played such an innovative and prominent role in the public dialogue of medicine during the century and a half after the Black Death. The 141 *Pesttraktate* of German origin gathered by Sudhoff, roughly half of which were either composed in or translated into the vernacular, reflected the same notions found in those of other countries. Campbell's similar survey of *The Black Death and Men of Learning* offers an overview in support of her thesis that the cumulative impact of the plague altered medicine by upgrading the role of the surgeon, heightening the prestige of the medical professional, encouraging the practical orientations of anatomical dissection and the study of toxins in the body, and questioning the epidemiology of the ancients, Galen and Hippocrates, as well as by introducing the effective measure of quarantining the infected.[103]

Yet Paracelsus's book has its peculiarities. The discussion of the five substances of disease begins with a curious admixture of non-sequitur and tautology:

> You should know that all diseases are cured in five ways, and our medicine therefore begins with the cure and not with the causes, for the reason that the cure reveals to us the cause. To this [end] our argument is addressed that healing is fivefold. This is as much as to say that there is a fivefold medicine or a fivefold art or fivefold faculties or fivefold doctors. Among the five, each is a sufficient faculty to heal all diseases.

> *Du solt wissen, das alle krankheiten in fünferlei weg geheilet werden, und heben also an unser arznei bei der heilung und nit bei den ursachen, darumb das uns die heilung die ursach anzeigt. Auf das gêt unser argument, das fünferlei heilung sind.*

das ist als vil geret, als das fünferlei arznei sind oder fünferlei
künst oder fünferlei faculteten oder fünferlei arzet. under denen
fünfen ist ein iegliche ein gnugsame facultas der arznei, alle
krankheiten zu heilen. (I,1:165)

At first glance, this is not very satisfying. If the cure reveals the cause, why not begin, logically, with the cause? It seems that Paracelsus is in a hurry to arrive at his own kind of healing, and that the purpose of the broader context is actually to arrange an opening in the order of things. In later writings, the relationship will be reversed: the all-embracing theoretical context will require so much attention that he will lose sight of the specific tasks of healing diseases. Discussions of common ailments such as gout will implicate him as a medical theorist in discussions of the first and final things of all creation.

In this early essay, the spirit of inclusiveness encourages the pioneer to presume that there is room enough in medicine for every sort of theory and practice. Soon this expansiveness leads him into contradictions. Are we dealing with five *distinct* kinds of causes? In his haste to describe the five kinds of cures, he denies this: "thus not that we do not therefore demand for the five kinds of cure five causes of all diseases, but rather we describe five kinds of healing, of which each serves for all causes of diseases, as is set forth here" (*so merkt das wir nit drum forderen auf fünferlei heilung fünferlei ursach aller kranckheiten, sonder wir beschreiben fünferlei heilung, da ein ietliche deren dient auf alle ursachen der krankheiten wie dan hernach folget*—I,1:166) Against this, the reiteration of his characterization of the five cures immediately relapses, so that there turn out to be after all five causes: "five [in number] are the causes of all diseases' sources" (*fünf seind auch der ursachen aller krankheiten ursprung*—I,1:166). It seems then that, as far as healing is concerned, there are five distinct "sects"; but as far as the understanding of cause is concerned, there is only a single "sect" (*aber der heilung nach sind fünf secten, dem verstant nach auf wissen der ursachen nur ein secten*—I,1:167). The ambiguity is seminal: in the mature theoretical syntheses, Paracelsus still maintains that the true physician has to be knowledgeable in the four areas of philosophy, astrology, alchemy, and in what he calls the teaching of the "virtues." All of these presuppose a divine illumination and guidance, so that there are actually five sources of medical truth. In attempting to reconcile the diverse modes of explanation, the later writings likewise remain equivocal as to the precise causation of disease.

The five kinds of medicine are designated variously. In the main body of the *Volumen Paramirum*, the five medicines correspond to the five *entia* or five *substances* of disease. Paracelsus may have resorted to the term *ens, entia,* in an attempt to skirt the dilemma posed by the more logically unequivocal terms *ursache* ("cause") or *ursprung* ("source"). *Ens* has already been defined as a power from which the medicine associated with it derives its authority: *"ens* is a source or a thing which has power to rule the body" (*ens ist ein ursprung oder ein ding, welchs gewalt hat den leib zu regiren*— I,1:172). The five *entia* are *ens astrale, ens venale, ens naturale, ens spiritale,* and *ens deale. Ens astrorum* can only be the power of the stars—however, Paracelsus confines their influence to such a degree that here astrological medicine loses any pretension of hegemony. He accepts, albeit critically, the medieval and Renaissance precept that "the wise man rules over the stars" (*ein weiser man herschet uber das gestirn*—I,1:180). For Paracelsus, we recall, the stars are close. They appear to sustain the permanent being of the human creature, in the same way that, as he later says, air prevents the stars from crashing to the ground in the fragile cosmic egg (I,8:162).

In their visible aspect, the stars were the most permanent and orderly of all natural phenomena; hence, their stabilizing power is responsible for their influence on life:

> Now, life lives from the body [just as a fire burns from the wood that is its fuel]. Now, the body must have something so that it is not burned up by [the "fire" of] life, but rather retains its essence. That is the entity [ens] that I am going to tell you of; it comes from the firmament. You say, and it is true, that, if not for the air, all things would fall to the ground and everything that has life would be suffocated and die.

> *nun lebt das leben aus dem leib. nun muß der leib etwas haben das er vom leben nit verzeret werd, sonder im wesen bleib. das selbige ist das ding, darvon wir euch das ens erzelen; dises kumpt aus dem firmament. ir saget und ist also, so der luft nicht wer, so fielen alle ding gen boden und alles, das da leben hat, das selbig ersticket und stürb.* (I,1:182

The entity or medium that mediates between stars and earth, that holds things in place and transmits influences, is designated as the *Mysterium*. The *Mystery* is the most inclusive entity of all, and it is a vital medium: "the M(ystery) contains all creatures in heaven and on earth, and all elements live from it and in it" (*das dis M<ysterium> alle geschöpf enthalt in himel und erden, und alle elementen leben aus ihm und in ihm*—I,1:182–183). It is therefore a vitalistic substance. Presumably, just as the egg must contain a vital medium encompassing yolk and albumen to be and become what it has in it to be, so also, the cosmos must be filled with something more potent and more fundamental than its constituent elements and entities. Further explanation of the *Mysterium* is to be found in a work "on the first creation" (*wie aber das selbige euch zuverstehen ist, solt ir eingedenk sein de primo creato*—I,1:183). Paracelsus's early writings often refer to other planned or executed writings for further clarification.

Ens venale brings the author to the kind of medicine that interests him most pressingly: alchemistic medicine. *Ens venale* comprises the pathogenic substances of disease that surround the human being and that are ingested in food. The composition and use of poisons was an object of theoretical and (tragically for the guinea pigs) of practical research during the Middle Ages. However, it is on the foundation of his alchemy that Paracelsus now postulates that our environment and the food we ingest are replete with poison. The alchemist knows how to "separate the poison from the good" (*das gift das wir under dem guten einnehmen . . . vom guten scheiden*—I,1: 190). With this, Paracelsus seems to have achieved a salient breakthrough, both in recognizing the external causes of disease and in characterizing the process of digestion. Examined thoughtfully, the theory strikes us as less an anticipation of bacteriology and more a vestige of the great chain of being of an ancient metaphysics. There is a hierarchy in nature. Some things are more perfect (*volkomen*) than others. What is lower can be poisonous to what is higher. However, the lower must *yield* the higher: the grass the cow, the cow the milk, etc. The transformation of things is effected by an alchemy that operates by means of the "virtues" (*tugent*) or "forces" (*kraft*) in things (I,1:191–192). Paracelsus astutely recognizes that there has to be an alchemist within the body, effecting digestion and the tranformation of substances. He names this inner artist the *archaeus*. This recognition that digestion or metabolism rests on a process of chemical transformation may well be his most impressive insight attributable to deductions from empirical experience.

When it comes to the *ens naturale*, we might expect to find a discussion of Galenic medicine with its four humors. The author for the first time waxes polemical, deviating from the intended harmony of the five medicines. If the *ens astrale* comprised the macrocosm, *ens naturale* is the microcosm, the small counterpart of the firmament. The author acknowledges that he has accepted the term *microcosm* from certain rivals against whom he contends, but he avers that only he uses this term in its corrected sense (I,1:202). Clearly, he is adapting the term from opponents and, at the same time, incorporating it into his own arguments. Not only does the microcosmic condition presuppose a human firmament within us, it also presupposes that all things subsisting in the great world either are or can grow within the small human world: "Such growth is as much as the fruit of the earth . . . thus the growing nutriments of the body sustain its parts. Thus all things grow in the human being" (*solchs wachsen ist als vil als die frücht der erden . . . also halten die wachsenden nutrimenten des leibs die glider des leibs auf. also wachsen im menschen alle ding*—I,1:203). Within his scheme of the macrocosmic-microcosmic order, the elements and the humors can be accepted—albeit with a condescending air: "for they rule jointly in *ens naturale*. For some diseases originate from the seven [planets], some from the elements, some from the qualities, some from the humors, some from the complexions, as will follow here" (*dan die mitherschen in ente naturali. wan etliche krankheiten komen aus den siben, etliche aus den elementen, etliche aus den qualiteten, etliche aus den humoribus, etliche aus den complexen, wie dan hernach folgen wird*—I,1:210). Against the hegemonic assertions of the humors, Paracelsus responds with an alchemistic disquisition that contrasts the humors with the four tastes: "fiery, sweet, bitter, salty" (*feuri, süße, bitteri, selzi*—I,1:211). This is very odd, since it is not at all apparent why this should offer any sort of alternative. But the tendency is clearly away from the lifeless elements and toward the organic living qualities—toward meaning. In subordinating the four elemental humors to these four tastes, he vitalizes the *ens naturale* and integrates organic and chemical characteristics in its purview.

The *ens spiritale* requires a precarious definition, for the spirit intended by Paracelsus is neither angel nor devil nor the immortal human soul, but rather something "born from our thoughts without matter in the living body" (*dann der teufel ist kein geist. ein geist ist auch kein engel. das ist ein geist, das aus unsern gedanken geboren wird on materia im lebendigen leib, das nach unserm tot geboren wird das ist die sêl*—I,1:216). The *ens spiritale* is a spiritual entity or substance born out of the resolved will, in the same way that a resolved will gives birth to speech (*diser beschloßner wille und verhengter ist eine muter die da gebiert den geist*—I,1:219). The *ens spiritale*, which can effect sickness in the subject or in another who is an object of animosity, reflects the medieval and sixteenth-century notion of the power of imagination, a power that could imprint the form of an object contemplated or desired by the pregnant mother on the embryo of her unborn infant.[104] In this substance of illness, one can perhaps recognize an early intuition of the psychosomatic disorder of modern psychiatry. However, there is more to the *ens spiritale* than this. In his era of spiritual strife, Paracelsus recognized the activities of two realms, that of the bodies and that of the spirits. The spirits are at war in their invisible realm (I,1:218). *Ens spiritale* also gives an acknowledgment to a sorcery that operates by means of waxen images to cause illness in one's enemies (I,1:220–221). *Ens spiritale* is therefore akin to witchcraft as well. Since this *ens* is of the spirit, Paracelsus feels constrained to admonish sternly against confusing it with the power of faith: "to speak of faith or to connect it with faith is more foolish than wise" (*vom glauben zu reden oder einzureimen hierin ist mer nerrisch dan weisisch*—I,1:224). Subsequently, he is more willing to see imagination and faith as manifestations of the same power.

For the final medicine, that of *ens dei*, disease is treated as a punishment (*flagellum*, "scourge") from God. The first three *entia* pertain to the body; *ens spiritale* and *ens dei* both pertain to the spirit. Only *ens deale* falls within the purview of what is understood as Christian knowledge. In proceeding to discuss the *ens dei*, Paracelsus actually seems to disassociate himself somewhat from the valid truths found in the other medicines: "we write the other four books of practice not for the Christians but to the infidels . . ." (*wir schreiben die andern vier bücher der practic nit für die christen sonder zu den ungleubigen . . .* —I,1:225).

For the medical theorist, this conclusion presents a malaise — since his medicine aspires to be more than just faith healing. In the later works, the authority of God encompasses his entire medical theory. Here he may have arrived at his conclusion under some pressure from external theological challenges. There is a concluding tone of resentment toward them: "yet the theological writings should not trouble us . . ." (*wil uns nit betrüben noch die theologischen geschriften* . . .—I,1:234). He has reached an impasse in his thought. After initially begging the question of *ens* as cause, and after allowing for the possibility of several distinct realms of causation—all of them resulting in identical diseases—Paracelsus must either introduce a hierarchy of greater and lesser causes, or he must acknowledge that the human subject of medicine navigates through distinct causal realms separated by invisible boundaries. But instead of resolving the question, he concedes that *all* diseases must be recognized as instances of *ens dei*:

> therefore we employ in this tractate a Christian style . . . that we recognize that all our diseases are scourges and examples and a demonstration that God removes the same through our Christian faith, not through medicine in the heathen way, but rather in Christ.

> *darumb so sezen wir in disem tractat ein christlichen stylum . . . das wir erkennen, das all unsere krankheiten flagellen sind und exempel und anzeigung das uns got die selbigen hinnem durch unsern glauben christenlich, nit durch die arznei heidnisch son- der in Christo.* (I,1:228–229)

Paracelsus's later symbol of the *Labyrinth of Errant Physicians* seems ironically applicable to his own causal blind circuitry of five *entia*. The highest teaching of this early medical synthesis is that there is no true medicine of earthly origin.

In the *Volumen Paramirum*, the five *entia* and corresponding five schools of medicine correspond in a general way to variants of plague theory found in the older tracts. Recurrent ways of explaining plague epidemics had included the astronomical theory (epidemics result from catastrophic astral conjunctions); the widespread and enduring miasmic thesis (poisonous vapors released from the earth lead to mass infection); the theological theory (pestilence is a divine punishment); the spiritual-psychological theory (excited and malevolent passions such as fear and anger increase vulnerability); and, finally, variants of the Galenic theory that explained disease as humoral-elemental imbalance. The listing is not exhaustive, and in many cases theories were combined; but to say this is merely to acknowledge the tendency in the scheme of five *entia*.[105]   In the *Volumen Paramirum*, the above modes of explanation are matched by the *ens astrale* (the astral cause of plague), the *ens venale* (a more generalized parallel of the miasmic vapor which poisons the afflicted), the *ens deale* (for which Paracelsus also employs the term "scourge," *flagellum*), *ens spiritale* (the malevolence or anger that infects without material transfer or contact), and *ens naturale* (which Paracelsus expands beyond traditional humoral medicine). In both the early *Volumen Paramirum* and a later plague tractate composed for the city of Sterzing, the dual nature of plague as a disease that can either remain internal as fever or become external as bubonic plague calls respectively for the ministrations of the physician and surgeon (I,1:166; cf. I,8:376ff.).

It can therefore be said of Paracelsus's work on plague, as Campbell observed for plague in general, that it stimulated the combining of tasks of surgeons and physicians: "In this [matter], I would have it thus, that the surgical physician is the doctor and the plague surgeon, not the so-called surgeon" (*in dem wil ichs also haben, das der physicus chirurgicalis sei der arzt und chirurgicus pestis und nit der vermeint chirurgus*—I,8:376–377).   In the early *Volumen Paramirum* and the later Sterzing plague tract, the nature of the epidemic challenges humoral medicine, though the challenge does not lead to a clear deduction in either the earlier or the later work. In the latter, the author denies not only that plague is humoral but also that it is infectious in order to conclude with a "supernatural" reciprocality of astral and human influences (I,1:172; cf. I,8:375: *so ist auch pestis kein krankheit der superfluitet, ist auch nit humor, ist auch nit infectio, sondern intoxicatio . . .*). Moreover, the Sterzing tract bears striking witness to Paracelsus's credulous acceptance of legend as fact. His combined astronomical and alchemical explanations matter-of-factly include the action of the mythic basilisk, the legendary beast that could kill with its gaze: "The countenance of the basilisk kills, and likewise the countenance of Mars. . . . thus, too, there is a second poison through Mars in the pestilence. This has caused difficulty for those who have written about pestilence that they were foiled by the birth of the basilisk" (*das gesicht des basilisken tötet, also ist auch das gesicht martis . . . . also ist auch ein ander gift durch martem in der pestilenz. das ist mühe und arbeit bei denen, die sich in der pestilenz zu schreiben unterstanden haben, das inen die geburt basilisci gebrosten hat*—I,8:383–384). In the same passage, Paracelsus solemnly confirms the deadliness of the basilisk's glance: "For wherever the eyes of the basilisk turn, they look thither, and to whomever this glance is imparted, he receives the shot" (*dan da sich die augen hinrichten, da sehen sie hin, der disem blick zu teil wird der entpfacht den schuß*—I,8:384). The Sterzing tract expresses characteristic contempt for the gross stupidity of previous plague literature (I,8:371, 372). But the truth be told, some of the medieval tracts seem to have been more skeptical than he regarding this arch superstition of the pestiferous basilisk with its killing gaze.[106]

Here the important point is not to judge Paracelsus against earlier or later standards of enlightenment, but to recognize the strands of coherence in his profuse writings. The plague tracts reveal an underlying tendency of his work as a whole: the effort to forge out of diverse sources of authority one cohesive system of explanation. Alongside the killing gaze of the basilisk, the Sterzing tract undertakes to combine the two modes of explanation based on the stars and the inner life of the subject—combining the most external and objective of things with the most internal and subjective. Thus the outermost and the innermost of spheres are reciprocally in touch through the power of the "magical imagination" (*magica imaginatio*). Just as *ens spirituale* could bring about illness without material contact, Paracelsus observes that there is "an anger that overcomes its master [and] ruins his health" (*der zorn der seinen herrn uberwint, verderbet in seiner gesuntheit*—I,8:380). The force of this inner enmity "overcomes its enemies as it pleases without any swordstrokes" (*der uberwint seine feinde nach seinem lust on alle schwertschleg*—I,8:380). This same power can also pass into the astral influence which is a kind of medium between upper and lower, outer and inner:

> From the human being the effect goes into the influence, from which the impression goes to [the other] and the medium has been struck; thus plague remains in such an order. For all our poison, envy, hatred, deceit, anger, vice, and luxury return into the upper *magnalia*; in them lies [the power] to generate.

> *aus dem menschen gehet die wirkung in die influenz, aus derselbigen gehet die impression nach dem und das mittel getroffen ist;*

also bleibt pestis in solcher ordnung. dan alle unser gift, neid, haß, falsch, zorn, laster und uppikeit steigt zuruck in die oberen magnalia; in denen ligt es zu generiren. (I,1:380)

This spectral war, in which human viciousness literally escalates and exacts a spiraling toll, is rooted in the magical imagination and is at the root of epidemics:

So it is that *magica imaginatio* proceeds from us into [the heavens], and from [them] back upon us. And for this reason, *magicus intellectus* is the light from which every ground of the supernatural diseases is explained, outside of which intellect the medical men err in the description of plague.

darumb so gehet magica imaginatio von uns in in, von im wider auf uns. und also ist magicus intellectus das liecht, aus welchem erkleret wird aller grund der ubernatürlichen krankheiten, außerhalb welchem intellect die medici in beschreibung der pestis augenscheinlich irren. (I,1:381)

According to Pagel, Paracelsus adopted this theory from the Ficino he admired as the "best of Italian physicians."[107] The uncharacteristic use of the term *magicus intellectus* suggests the possibility of this influence. But the two distinct components of the theory, the role of the imagination on the one hand and of the stars on the other, were not foreign to the popular plague tracts either.[108] In combining them with the idea of plague as a supernatural disease, Paracelsus trod a precarious borderline between accepting plague as a divine punishment and elevating it into a supernatural operation: "It is well known to you what the firm imagination does, which is a beginning of all magical works" (*Euch ist genugsam wissend, was die strenge imagination tut, welche ein anfang ist aller magischen werken*—I,8:379).

Despite the apparent obscurantism, Paracelsus's theory of the accelerating inner and outer spiral of epidemic death rests on moral and religious premises: it condemns anger and fear and upholds human dignity, at least in a negative sense, by asserting that the human race is not tyrannized by the stars or elements; rather, the human will itself engenders the very catastrophe that would seem to defy all certain knowledge and self-determination. The imagina-

tion in this context is not faith, yet, like faith, it possesses a supernatural potency that can bridge the gap between inner and outer,
heavens and earth. The Tirolian beneficiaries of the plague tract,
however, did not appreciate its subtleties. They drove their would-be
benefactor out of town. Cities beset by an epidemic often at first
suppressed the scope of the danger in order to reduce panic and,
when worse came to worst, advised flight to the beleaguered city
dwellers. The advice offered by the plague tract was realistic
regarding human vulnerability, but it was hardly comforting:

> If we address the attack of plague, the truth is that we have no
> further knowledge, except that we might speak: watch out, take
> care, flee. For how little do we know of the [celestial plague] ray;
> it is born in the upper heavens, that we do know; . . . But we do
> not know where it will strike.
>
> *so wir sollen vom angreifen reden der pestis, so haben wir in der*
> *warheit kein ander wissen, das wir möchten sprechen, hüt du*
> *dich, du beware dich, fleuch du. dan als wenig wissens als wir*
> *vom stral haben, der wird in den oberen himeln geboren, das wis-*
> *sen wir; . . . wir wissen aber nicht, wohin er schießen wil.* (I,8:375)

After writing this for the citizens, Paracelsus was expelled from
Sterzing and soon afterward from Innsbruck.

But the Sterzing *Pestschrift* is not among the earlier works. It
is of the post-Basel period to which we digressed in order to gauge
the impact of the plague both in the beginnings and in the ongoing
development of Paracelsus's theories.

In summarizing the results of the analysis, we can see that the
Volumen Paramirum stands on a threshold. In the background, we
can perceive a rivalry of explanations in the tradition of the plague
tracts. In the foreground of works following the *Volumen*
Paramirum, we will discern the contours of an emerging pattern in
the thought of Paracelsus. We can arrange the features of this pattern into parallel columns. The causes commonly offered for plague
epidemics are seen to correspond roughly to the *entia* of Paracelsus.
To be sure, as to his later characterization of the disciplines that a
physician must command, discrepancies will emerge: the teaching of
the "virtues" is a later addition; and divine causation, though perennially present for Paracelsus, is afterwards no longer given as one
ens among four others:

Plague causes in popular tracts:	Five *entia* of Paracelsus:	Tributary medical arts of his later works:
humors (and elemental disturbances, such as earthquakes)	*ens naturale* microcosm	*philosophy*, concerned with the earth, nature
astronomical events: comets, conjunctions	*ens astrale* macrocosm	*astronomy*, the heavens
miasma, poisonous vapors in the air	*ens venale* omnipresent poison	*alchemy*, separates the poison from the good
imagination, black magic, anger, fear	*ens spiritale* [spirit as a distinct agent or medium]	*the "virtues"*
divine punishment	*ens deale*	*[divine authority]*

We should conclude our digression with a reminder that, although plague figures prominently in Paracelsus's writings, and although plague and its theories are well documented historically, for the sixteenth-century author, history and legend could blend into a single monolithic realm of shadows. Plague is not remembered as the Black Death that annihilated the populace of Europe in 1348. Of biblical fame, plague is "four thousand years" old according to Paracelsus (I,8:371). On the other hand, syphilis (*franzosen*) and gout (*podagra*) were revealing that in the autumnal times of the sixteenth century, the diseases were becoming different and more numerous than in the days of Galen. We shall see how Paracelsus is influenced by epidemic disease to theorize about new diseases and transformations of old ones. His thinking is in opposition to the underlying Aristotelian precept of a stable universe, and in stark contrast to the formulation of his supposed Ferraran professor Leoniceno, who reflected thus on the "French Disease":

When I reflect that men are endowed with the same nature, born under the same skies, brought up under the same stars, I am compelled to think that they have been always afflicted by the same diseases; neither can I comprehend how this disease has suddenly destroyed our age as none before. . . . For if the laws of nature are examined they have existed unchanged on countless occasions since the beginning of the world.[109]

Paracelsus is convinced that new entities are springing forth from the womb of creation. His theory of disease is of a piece with his understanding of time and creation.

Very generally, the notion of a universe of *entia* betokens the multiplicity of given sources of things; the world is made up of particular entities. Some entities are visible. Others are invisible. Some are temporal, others eternal. Some are animate, others inanimate. Change—birth, growth, death—is the dimension of the individuality of the entitites. Transformation embodies the emergence of what had been until then invisible. Therefore, what is novel is never altogether new. The new is rather a revelation of something theretofore concealed. Time is only the succession of things to be revealed, so that when all potential variety has at last been exhausted, the world must come to an end.

The individualist in Paracelsus knows that the differences among human beings is the mark of an eschatological progression which proceeds from Adam unto the end of world. This progression has been preordained by God through the nature of an *ens seminis* that contained all human forms, colors, and customs latent within it. This *ens* must unfold all its innate variants, until they are at last exhausted and the time of Judgment arrives:

> You speak further of the unlike forms of people, that from Adam on there has been such a long time with so many people without any one of them having been like another. . . . When the Final Day comes, all the colors and customs of people will be fulfilled; for it awaits the point in time when all colors, forms and figures, and customs of people are exhausted and none more can be born without having to look like another; then the hour of the course of the first world will have struck.

> *ir sagt auch mer von der ungleichen gestalt der menschen, das von Adam her ein solche lange zeit under sovil menschen nie keiner dem andern gleich ist gewesen . . . . so der jüngst tag kompt, so werden die farben und sitten der menschen alle erfüllt sein, dan er ist alein gesezt auf den punkten, so alle farben, form*

und gestalten und sitten der menschen für sind und keiner mer
mag geboren werden, er muß etwan eim gleich sehen. alsdan ist
die stunt aus des laufs der ersten welt. (I,1:181).

In the world of entities, the succession of time reveals the variety
encoded into a seminal entity—the seed of all things. The distinc-
tiveness of each entity in turn has both time (the potential variabil-
ity of things) and permanence (the imparted nature of the Maker of
all time) encoded into its particular being.

Assuredly, the bane of a world of particular entities lies in the
difficulty of subordinating particular to universal. The world of irreducible entities is the vista of peculiar objects in Dürer's painting of
Melancholia. Mysterious objects—a comet, a rainbow, a table of
numbers, an irregular figure, sundry symbols and puzzles without
clues—all surround a despairing angel. As an alchemist pondering
over substances and transformations, or as a physician searching for
the true ground of medicine, Paracelsus must have known this
melancholy irreducibility of the particular.

3 ■ Peasant War and Iconoclasm

We cannot ascertain with any real certainty when the *Volumen Paramirum* was written. Allusions in this and other works suggest that it might have roughly coincided with the Salzburg religious writings. The final section of the *Volumen* hints at a shift of orientation from "pagan" medicine to the *ens deale* of faith. In Salzburg, involvements of a rather mysterious kind confronted the speculative thinker with the conflicts and popular movements of the early Reformation. Though the precise nature and partisan adherence of his involvement is not clear, commentators of the adulatory school have dramatized his role in the events. The realities of his participation were probably more peripheral and ambivalent.

By the summer of 1524, Paracelsus was a settled personage in Salzburg. He had taken up residence near a bath and spa, a convenient location for a physician looking for new patients. Goldammer submits the plausible suggestion that Paracelsus chose Salzburg because it was under the rule of Cardinal Matthäus Lang.[110] An Augsburger by birth, Lang had come to Salzburg from Hohenheim's "second fatherland" of Carinthia, where he had been bishop of Gurk from 1505 until 1519. As the ecclesiastical and secular ruler of Salzburg, the cardinal was wealthy, powerful, and an influential figure in both the Empire and the Church. He was known as a friend of Humanists, hence a potential sponsor for new men. For his part, Hohenheim certainly knew how to stroke the heartstrings of Carinthian local patriotism. Lang might have seemed the ideal candidate for an inaugural and, one could hope, remuneratively obliging dedication of the kind that would grace every major treatise of Paracelsus.

If so, his hopes were tragically misplaced. This plan would go terribly awry, foiled by the events of the Peasants' War which gradually escalated in and around Salzburg, until in the heat of civil strife, people would be compelled to take sides, until even the aspiring young

77

man who had come to Salzburg with who knows what sort of ambitious plans would feel compelled to follow suit—probably against his original intention—by raising his voice to his harshest pronouncements denouncing the sacred symbols of established power and sanctity.

By 1524, the rising tides of reform and rebellion had begun to lap around this rock of ecclesiastical and imperial authority. Townspeople in Salzburg objected to Cardinal Lang's luxury and oppressive tax levies, the latest of which covered the expenses from his attendance of the coronation of Charles V. The towns and markets were to pay, while the upper estates were freed from obligation. Lang with his learned cohorts and armed mercenaries demonstrated their martial resolve by appearing in force in the central market of Salzburg. The burghers were forced to submit and swear an oath to desist from any action detrimental to their prince. These were the events of the so-called "Latin War" of 1523, when Lang and his learned councillors drew the rebellious populace up short. The bitterness was still in the air as the new physician set about launching his practice in the city.[111]

All the while, word of the new faith was being spread by emissaries, wandering folk preachers. Veterans and refugees of peasant uprisings were arriving in Salzburg from other parts to find employment and comradeship among the local miners. Around the beginning of the year 1525, a preacher from Tirol was tried and convicted of heresy in Lang's diocese. Before he could be incarcerated permanently, he was liberated by the common people. One of their number was arrested and beheaded without a trial on Lang's orders.

By now, the revolution was in progress in Salzburg: miners and townsmen armed themselves and were soon joined by peasants. Lang, his cohorts, and sixty-five loyal members of the nobility ensconsed themselves in the high fortress above the city. They spent the summer under a precarious siege, which was only lifted with extraterritorial assistance. A first relief force met with bloody defeat near Schladming. The popular forces occupying the city ruled with an iron fist.

Sometime during this uprising, Paracelsus fled. A later notarized inventory of the possessions he abandoned in Salzburg indicates that he precipitously departed the city, "in the past uprising" (*in der vergangen Aufruhr*).[112] It is possible, if far from certain, that he was interrogated before he entrusted his keys to the mother of his landlord and disappeared. In any case, he left too hastily to pack his clothing, but apparently not in such terror that he never expected to return and reclaim his possessions.

Two things should be remembered in evaluating his engagement in these events. First of all, the turmoil of the period was by rights both political or social *and* doctrinal. It is only our hindsight that separates these two aspects. The revolutionaries in Salzburg could not assail the prince-bishop without impugning both the secular and ecclesiastical systems of sanctification and power that coincided in his office and person. The twenty-four articles representing the popular demands gave absolute authority to their biblical-religious foundation, but went on to detail a comprehensive social and political program with a revolutionary character.[113]

At the same time, a second consideration should be kept in mind: the Reformation, like other great popular upheavals, was hardly a monolithic ice flow. It was an event enacted variously in the lives of its innumerable participants and groups. The popular, nonmagisterial "radical reformation" studied by George H. Williams followed eccentric and tangential courses within and alongside what might appear at a distance as the glacial flow of sixteenth-century history.

The evidence of the Salzburg writings indicates that the involvements of Hohenheim were as eccentric and peculiar as the remainder of his life. Judging by his allusions and diatribes, he entered the fray in 1524, in support of embattled doctrines, arguing in defense of the Virgin Mary and the saints. But the evidence suggests that his defense of established doctrines was far too idiosyncratic to meet with the approval of its intended beneficiaries. Representatives of the Church turned against him, and their apparent betrayal pushed him to his diametric opposite. He radically attacked their theology, with the result that he was forced to flee. His polemical writings indicate three phases in Salzburg. During the first, he argued in favor of established positions. During the second, he began to attract criticism, and, in response, articulated his doctrinal views more elaborately, thereby incurring even more critical objections. In the final phase of his involvement, he fulminated against all the symbols of Church authority and all the unjust practices of the secular or clerical rulers. This outburst may well have necessitated his flight to the safer territories of the Upper Rhine.

The first phase is that of the mariological works, including *De invocatione Beatae Mariae Virginis,* recently made available by Katharina Biegger, and of *De Virgine Sancta Theotoca,* which was published by Staritius in the seventeenth century.[114] A defense of the eternity of Mary is not what we expect from a man who is thought to have stood in the forefront of progress, and who was certainly one of the most independent minds of his time. But it must be remembered that such questions were hotly debated before, during, and after the Reformation. Official church theology was challenged, not only by the doctrines of magisterial reformers, but also by varieties of lay piety, some of which now appear more medievally Catholic than the concurrent doctrines of the Church. Scholars have shown that even some of the most radical popular reformers adhered to non-Lutheran or medieval doctrines in their creeds.[115] Paracelsus defended and exalted the divinity of the Virgin. Though critical of the cult of the saints, he maintained a lifelong belief in the existence of saintly persons who had the power to effect miracles.[116] From early childhood at the Swiss pilgrimage site of Einsiedeln, he had no doubt absorbed accounts of wonders and miraculous cures, even while witnessing all the grotesque fraud and venality that accompanied the veneration of Mary and the saints. His credulousness and criticism went hand in hand, in the same way that modern scientific minds are capable of maintaining an absolute faith in empiricism, while criticizing incompetent or fraudulent scientific work.

Politically, the polemics of 1524 reveal a stance that is both conciliatory and ambivalent. A concluding gesture of the *Liber de Sancta Trinitate* (September 1524) admonishes those to whom it is addressed that the Holy Spirit does not want the "senseless wars" (*unnütze krieg*) of those who "contend with such violence over heaven, each head according to its own opinion" (*so gewaltig umb den himmel streitt, ein ieglicher kopf nach seinem sinn*—II,3:265). Similar in tone and theme, *De Invocatione Beatae Mariae Virginis* concludes by admonishing its readers to desist from their false teachings concerning the humanity of the Virgin Mary: the false doctrines of their "four or six teachers" have been "fabricated only from the natural light, and not from the baptism of the Holy Spirit" (*allein aus dem natürlichen liecht gedicht, und nicht aus dem tauff des h. geists*).[117] But in the *Liber de Sancta Trinitate* of September 1524, the lay theologian is defending himself on two fronts: the tract begins by referring back to an earlier conversation or colloquium in which his interlocutors have accused him of a position counter to the Roman Church (*das alles, ir meldet, der römischen kirchen soll zuwider sein*—II,3:235–236). He denies having made statements to his interlocutors that were "heretical" in the understanding of the trinity (*wie ich gegen euch etwas ketzerisch soll geredt haben in meinem verstand der trinitet halben . . .*—II,3:235). It is clear from this that Hohenheim, even while contending against those who oppose the veneration of Mary, has embroiled himself in a dispute with the representatives of orthodoxy, and that he is addressing his "book" to the men of the Church in order to dispel the threat of anathema hanging over him.

Though the tract is intended to resolve this controversy by explaining his view of the trinity, it can only have made matters immeasurably worse. The commentary of Goldammer observes that the trinitarian doctrine articulated by Hohenheim in this context contradicts the theological mainstream of Christianity—with the conclusion that its author either fell prey to a misunderstanding or was influenced by traditions of some other kind. This might seem to imply that the tract was only a fluke or aberration. In fact, however, there is reason to suggest that this early writing on the trinity takes us as close as we can come to the seminal reasoning that led to the mature theories of Paracelsus.

Paracelsus's early interpretation of the trinity translates the inconceivable mystery of a God eternally three in one and one in three into his common sense world of natural entities:

In order that I instruct you how I understand the trinity, . . . God was in the beginning alone, without any beginning and not in three persons, alone *one* God, who was not called either God the Father, God the Son, [nor] God the Holy Spirit, or all three together. But rather God the Allmighty Creator and Destroyer of all was *one* God, *one* being, *one* divinity, *one* countenance, *one* person and no one with him. And [he] remained so long alone until it pleased him to wed and increase himself, and reveal himself.

Damit aber ich euch undterricht, wie ich die trinitet erkennen, . . . gott ist anfenglich allein gewesen; ohn allen anfang und nit in drei personen, allein ein *gott, der nit geheißen hat weder gott der vatter, gott der sun, gott der heilig geist oder all drei miteinander. sonder gott der allmechtig schöpfer und der zerbrecher aller ding ist gewest* ein *gott,* ein *wesen,* ein *gottheit,* ein *gesicht,* ein *person und niemandts bei ihme. und ist also lang allein blieben, bis ihm geliebt hat zu vermählen, sich zu mehren, sich zu erzeigen.* (II,3:238)

What is truly striking here is not so much the radical deviation from Christian doctrinal orthdoxy, nor the childishly absolute faith in certain biblical teachings, but rather the combination of doctrinal deviation with childlike faith: What is abstract and unimaginable in doctrine has been cast aside. What is picturable in images reflecting the world of natural entities is absolute. This remarkable combination lends sublime doctrine the quality of a folk fairy tale, as if he were recounting how a lonesome God once upon a time decided to couple, to multiply himself into three, and to reveal himself (*sich zu erzeigen*) through this increase. The sublime mystery of three in one is resolved genealogically: the three inherit the same power and force because the one has given rise to the three: "which has caused him to divide into three persons, into three kinds, into three beings, into three properties. Which all flows from one divinity in three streams . . ." (*das ihn geursacht hat, sich zu teilen in drei person, in drei art, in drei wesen, in drei eigenschaft. welches alles fleußt aus der gottheit an drei strümen . . .*—II,3:239). In addition to the three persons of the trinity, another person is called for in order to complete this scheme: "From the beginning of the number of the trinity God has first become double, that is, two persons in *one* person . . . (*Von anfang der zahl der trinitet ist erstlich gott selb ander geworden, das ist zwo personen in* einer *person* . . .—II,3:244). Evidently, Paracelsus does not intend to break the number of the trinity, any more than he deliberately sets out to undermine the Christian doctrine of one God in three eternal persons; in either case, he wants to avoid heterodoxy by means of further devices and considerations, though these could only have made his views all the more redolent of heresy to theologians. Far from any deliberate heresy, he intends to confirm the ineffable things of faith by projecting them into the realm of the palpable entities. Time in the *Volumen Paramirum*, we recall, was the succession of distinct entities, slated to end when the generation of distinct beings would be exhausted. The "time of the trinity" amounts to the division into three persons whose revelation is successive:

> Inasmuch now as time has a beginning in the number of the trinity, that is, that [the divine persons] have divided them-

selves, so that God has made out of himself a father, a son, and a holy spirit, with that the trinity begins and is understood, and before that [there was] only God.

Dieweil nun die zeit in der trinitet zahl ein anfang hat, das ist, daß sie sich haben zuteilt, also daß gott aus ihm selbst ein vatter, einen sun und einen heiligen gemacht hat, da ist nun die trinitet angangen und erkant worden, und vormals allein gott. (II,3:243).

But even before the division into three, there is a division of God which makes him mysteriously two in one:

From the beginning of the number of the trinity God has first become twofold (*selb ander*), that is, two persons in *one* person, and not one single person for himself, as God the Father is a single person with respect to the Son and the Holy Spirit, and they with respect to him, but rather two persons. And the two persons are *one* person and fulfill only *one* person in the trinity completely and make [that person] whole.

Von anfang der zahl der trinitet ist erstlich gott selb ander geworden, das ist zwo personen in einer person, und nit ein einige person für sich selb, wie gott der vatter ein einige person ist gegen dem sun und gegen dem heiligen geist, und sie widerumb gegen ihme, sonder zwo personen. und die zwo personen seindt ein person und erfüllen nur ein person in der trinitet volkomben und machen sie ganz. (II,3:244)

The intention here is clearly to establish a place in the divine family for a higher prototype of the Virgin Mary, a "goddess" (*ein göttin*) with whom the Father generates the divine Son in heaven prior to the birth of Jesus as God and man in this world:

Thus God made from himself, from his person, a woman. And although it is [the case] that from his person the Son comes and the Holy Spirit, they have not come into being from the person of the Father in the same manner as the heavenly queen [has come into being]. Rather, the Son is borne of two persons, namely from God and the goddess, the Holy Spirit from God the Father and from the Son, from two persons in *one* divinity. The queen, however, has been drawn out of his person, drawn in flesh and blood, and of an eternal blood and eternal flesh, an eternal woman, indestructible, immaculate, and unwed, for the reason that one person is in the trinity, be it her husband (*mann*) or her son, or the spirit of both.

Also hat gott von ihm selbst, von seiner person, ein weib gemacht. und wiewol das ist, daß aus seiner person der sun kombt und der heilig geist, so seindt dieselbigen in der gestalt wie die himblische künigin nit von der person des vatters worden. sonder der sun ist geporen von zweier personen, nemblich von gott und der göttin, der heilige geist von gott dem vatter und von gott dem sun, aus beiden personen in einer *gottheit. die künigin aber ist von gott aus seiner person gemacht, gezogen in blut und fleisch und eines ewigen bluts und eines ewigen fleisch, ein ewige frau, unzerbrechlich, unbefleckt und unvermähligt, aus ursach, daß ein person in der trinitet ist, es sei ir mann oder ir sun oder beeder geist.* (II,3:246)

This is an impossibly complex and contradictory notion, but its intention is clear: Mary and before her Eve have a prototype in a "celestial queen," an eternally pure being, both a person and not a person. She is necessary for generating the divine family, but not one of the three persons of the family. Yet she is also related to each as the necessary other that makes them distinct. One might compare her to the nullity that makes enumeration and succession possible: a null that has no power, but raises numbers to a higher power. However, it is not mathematical analogy that justifies the doctrine of the divine woman to Paracelsus. Nor is it a perceptible desire to elevate the status of women, a purpose Agrippa von Nettesheim pursued by extolling the virtues of human women. The rationale lies in the biblical core term of *image* and *likeness*:

For [the goddess] is of a heavenly nature and a heavenly kind and not of a human nature or a mortal kind. Therefore no fault is in her. And the same way as Eve was made of Adam, so too is the queen made of God himself. For the word was: "We will make a human being after our image and likeness." That is: as we see in form and manner, so too also the son of man [Jesus]. And just as we have made from us a queen and for ourselves a woman, so too, we make from Adam for him a woman who is mortal.

*dann sie ist eines himblischen wesens und einer himblischen art
und nit eines menschlichen wesens oder einer tödlichen art.
darumb kein befleckung in ir ist. und zugleicherweis wie Eva aus
Adam gemacht ist, also ist die künigin aus gott selb gemacht.
dann das wort war: "wir machen einen menschen nach unser
biltnus und gleichnus." das ist: wie wir sehen in formb und
gestalt, also auch des menschlichen sun. und wie wir von uns ein
künigin gemacht haben und uns selber ein weib, also machen wir
aus Adam ihm selbs ein weib, das tödlich ist.* (II,3:246)

The underlying reasoning from creation or generation as a making
of something in the image and likeness of the maker legitimates
Paracelsus's exaltation of Mary to a metaphysical plane. But in so
doing, this rationale also assimilates the human creature to the
divine Creator. A two-sided lever, the argument lowers the divine
into the conceptual space of the temporal at the same time that it
construes what is temporal as congruent with the eternal being of
the divinity. God is presumably like his own likenesses, only on the
higher plane of the perfect and eternal. Paracelsian theory con-
founds any interpreter intent to distinguish the enlightened from
the irrational by presenting an inextricable weave of the natural
and the supernatural. It is not empirical observation; it is the
undisciplined faith of folk piety and mariolatry that compels him to
superimpose nature upon the sublime mysteries of the deity.

In several respects, the early *Liber de Sancta Trinitate* of September
1524 reveals the foundations, the conceptual framework of the later
works. The *Liber de Sancta Trinitate* explains the "two lights," the
light of nature and the light of the spirit, in a manner anticipating,
yet surmounting, the contradictions found in the later uses of these
terms. The two lights designate the authority of the experience of
nature and of the experience of faith, respectively. In the tract of
1524, the two lights are distinct and knowledge of the trinity is
given to him who lives in the light of the spirit, not to him who lives
in the light of nature (II,3:249). Certainty in the Christian articles
of faith flows from the same source: "Such [things] flow from the
faith that must be in the human being. People have such a faith not
from themselves, nor from their flesh and blood, nor from their light
of nature, but from the light of the spirit" (*solches fleußt vom
glauben heraus, der da muß im menschen sein. solchen glauben
haben die menschen nit von ihn selbst oder aus irem blut und fleisch,*

noch aus irem liecht der natur, sonder aus dem liecht des geists—
II,3:258). In this early work, the pendulum of the two lights indeed
swings away from nature and toward the spirit; for the author notes
that what is known from the former—insofar as it does not conform
to the latter—may even constitute "a subtle seduction" (*nit aus dem
liecht der natur, welches oft ist ein subtile verfüerung*—II,3:259). The
context contains no reference to empirical observation; it has to do
with Christian articles of faith. This is why the author can immediately go on to confirm that *both* lights are from God, and the human
creature must live according to both, since the first proceeds from
God as creator and second from God as creator, redeemer, and spirit:

> There are two lights, human and spiritual and both come from
> God, namely the light of wisdom and the light of human life [;]
> and the light of faith and the spiritual life. By these two lights
> everyone should live.
>
> *Zwei liecht seindt, menschlich und geistlich und komben beide
> von gott, nemblich das liecht der weisheit und das liecht des
> menschlichen lebens und das liecht des glaubens und des
> geistlichen lebens. aus diesen zweien liechtern soll ein iedlicher
> leben.* (II,3:259–260)

Moreover, Paracelsus even suggests that the author of both lights is
the Holy Spirit. The spirit brings a knowledge of creation from the
Creator and a knowledge of redemption (and all attendant articles
of Christian faith) from the Creator *cum* Redeemer. This is the simple distinction behind all the apparent inconsistencies and contradictions: God reveals himself both through the creation and through
the person of Christ and his teachings. Either is a divine revelation,
though by different avenues and with different messages.

In pursuing the purpose of conciliation, the *Liber de Sancta
Trinitate* cites no less than eight times the "paramiran" writings
(*der paramirischen schriften*). He is sending these writings to his
interlocutors. He admonishes them to read them several times and
take them to heart, for their content is directly relevant or "of service to" (*dienstlich*) the matter at hand. The "paramiran writings"
(*die paramirischen schriften*—II,3:264), he assures, are relevant to
ongoing conflicts of faith that the author finds so reprehensible:

inasmuch as one battles over heaven, every mind in accordance with its own idea, and yet no one wants to understand the path on which he stands. Those are senseless wars, which truly do not proceed from the Holy Spirit.

dieweil man so gewaltig umb den himmel streitt, ein iedlicher kopf nach seinem sinn, und will doch keiner sein, der das verstehen will, den weg, zu dem er stellt. es seindt aber unnütze krieg, die für wahr aus dem heiligen geist nit komben. (II,3:265)

This is a poignant reminder that what we sometimes imagine in retrospect as the steady march of history beneath clear banners of progress or reaction was experienced by contemporaries as a melée of all against all: "useless wars" in which many are led by arbitrary fanaticism. But the conclusion of the *Liber de Sancta Trinitate* also indicates that Paracelsus himself was one of those who believed that his own view, if only it were accepted by all, would put an end to this senseless discord. His naive purpose of surmounting the "useless wars" of faith embodies both his poles, the irenic and the agressive, at once. The possibility that this also signals an overriding religious purpose of his authorship is suggested by the proclaimed decisive relevance of his "paramiran writings."

What, then, were these "paramiran writings" of his, to which Paracelsus alluded—urgently and no less than eight times—in his tract of September 1524? Did they include the *Volumen Paramirum*? Their designation suggests that they may be identical with or at least closely related to the later versions of the *Opus Paramirum* which are thought to have been composed only at the end of the decade. The odd mixture of Greek *para-* with Latin *mirum* suggests that the paramiran writings contain what goes beyond wonder, or a wonder of wonders. Paracelsus was not feeble in the invention of titles and names: it seems unlikely that he should have adopted the root *paramir-* for a work without any relation to the one alluded to here. Could the later *Opus Paramirum* have been written earlier and held back for a time, perhaps then taken up again and reworked? Goldammer suggests as one possibility that the *paramirische schriften* alluded to in 1524 are a separate body of *religious* writings, possibly including the work published in volume one of the Sudhoff division: *Das Buch von der Gebärung der empfindlichen Dinge in der*

Vernunft.[118] (To translate the title of this work requires interpretation; I suggest: *The Book on the Generation of Sensible Beings through the Power of Reason*.) This book is one of two; a second, similar work in Sudhoff's volume one bears the title, *Ein Büchlein 'De generatione hominis*.

Several things speak in favor of the possibilty that the *Book on the Generation of Sensible Beings* might have been written during the Salzburg controversies: it is a rough draft, poorly thought out and written in the heat of debate; more importantly, its first preface refers to the author's opponents as those who call themselves "earthly gods" (*die sich irdische götter nennen*—I,1:243). The work is written as a response to their challenge (*als auf ir schreiben antwort zu geben*—I,1:243). It is also apparent that the theme has been imposed upon the author; for in responding, he soon notices that the better reply would require addressing a rather different issue. Insofar as the question is the birth of a sensible human being, he writes that a man and a woman bring forth a child that is like its parents (*wan alein was do ist der empfintlikeit, das ist man und frau. aus einem solchen par wird volendet die geburt des kints, das gleich gestaltet und gleichförmig ist seinen eltern, von den es geboren ist*— I,1:245–246). In replying to opponents who have apparently cited Aristotle and Galen in support of what he calls their "earthly" opinions regarding generation and birth—perhaps in order to reject his apotheosis of Mary—Paracelsus is determined to demonstrate that humankind has something in it that transcends the immanent causes of life proffered by his Aristotelian opponents. Sparring and ambling toward the object of his argument, he mentions alternate species of sensible beings, the humanoid monsters whose existence was widely accepted in the sixteenth century. He soon comes to the point of human distinction: Christ, who could have chosen to become any other creature, chose to become human (I,1:248). He concludes his fourth preface by outlining the other species of sensible beings: the elemental spirits that are composed of and live within the elements of water, earth, fire, and air. The *Book on the Generation of Sensible Beings* will discuss these four species, doing so on the foundation of "philosophical experience" (I,1:251). The preface closes with an invocation to Christ and to the Virgin Mary, "who remained [a virgin] before his birth and afterward in eternity [and] thus remains immaculate in the holy trinity without end" (*welche eine*

bliben ist vor seiner geburt und darnach in ewikeit also unbefleckt
bleibet in der heiligen dreifaltikeit on end—I,1:251).

The treatise itself returns to the question of how humans are
generated. Though the train of the argument is extremely difficult
to follow, in its tendency it rejects a naturalistic view of generation,
the sort of view proposed by Aristotelians and by the anatomical
physicians, who write of "sperm" as if it were the key to conception:
"Why, then, do the blind physicians write so many chapters *de sper-*
mate, as if sperm were the seed, yet it is not the seed" (*warumb*
reden dan die blinden arzte von vil capiteln de spermate, als ob sper-
ma der same sei, und ist kein sam—I,1:255). Against an anatomical-
materialist analysis of human conception, Paracelsus marshals a
confusing concert of notions, seeming very much to suggest that conception depends on will, desire, speculation, and reason, in more
than the obvious manner. Oporinus reported that the master was
not particularly interested in women. The view of human reproduction expounded here might almost be that of a hermit monk:

> So that we inform you of the full ground, that God who created
> all things, placed only the human being in the light of nature, to
> be free and independent. Therefore he removed the seed from
> nature and did not imprint it in him on account of the eternal
> that is in him.

> *damit und wir euch den ganzen grunt erzelen so merken, das got*
> *der alle ding erschaffen hat, hat den menschen alein in das liecht*
> *der natur gesezt, frei und ledig zu sein. darumb hat er im den*
> *samen genomen aus der natur und im nit eingebildet von wegen*
> *des ewigen so in im ist.* (I,1:254)

The statement that God desires the purity of "the light of
nature" (*dan got wil vil mer das liecht der natur rein haben dan*
befleckt—I,1:257) in the context of a characterization of human conception suggests that there is a hidden agenda to make human
beings worthy of the Virgin by making them essentially virginal,
and to dignify the faculty of the medical philosopher with the nim-
bus of the *homo spiritualis*: "For in that which is pure dwells the
spirit and in the impure are the mute spirits" (*wan im reinen ist der*
geist und im befleckten die stummenden geister—I,1:257). Admirers

of Theophrastus have found a way to put a nice face on the message of the *Book of Generation* and the related fragment *De Generatione Hominis*, as if the garbled reasoning were intended to make a tidy ethical point about people not behaving like beasts. But the undeniable fact is that Paracelsus wants to show that the human reproductive *process* is inherently unlike that of animals, and this purpose embroils him in pronouncements that ought to be scandalous even for a sixteenth-century physician who claims here as elsewhere that his knowledge rests on "experience."

Our proper objective, however, is not to censure or praise Paracelsus, but to understand him on his own terms. The question to be asked here is: what are these disparate themes doing in one place, in these two fragmentary tracts outwardly devoted to human generation. What is the common denominator of such diverse topics as these: the existence of elemental creatures; Christ's choice of the human being as the vessel of incarnation; the denial that sperm is a necessary and efficient cause of conception; and the assertion that some sort of psychic faculty (reason, speculation, will, or imagination) instead acts decisively in conception?

I will suggest that the unifying context should be sought in medieval tradition. Scholars have debated whether and to what degree the Renaissance was anti-Aristotelian; and Kristeller has argued that it only became decidedly so in the time of Paracelsus and Telesio.[119] However, the coherence of Paracelsus's concerns has its roots in an older tradition of criticism which faulted Aristotle and the Aristotelians for limiting God's power. This medieval tradition rejected the Aristotle whose cardinal error was the presentation of nature as one, uncreated, and eternal, as if nature took precedence over God. Against this philosophy, a long tradition, beginning with the great papal condemnations of 1277, asserted the absolute power of a Creator who reserved the power and freedom to bring into being other worlds or alternate creations. Multiple worlds could testify to the omnipotent will of the Creator of nature. This encouraged a speculation that now appears akin to science fiction but which was at root rather a kind of "theology fiction" or "anti-science fiction." Edward Grant has written on the theological sources of the speculation on alternative worlds: "As a consequence [of the condemnation of Aristotle], it became respectable during the fourteenth century, as it had not been before 1277, to contemplate the possibility of simultaneously existing worlds beyond our own."[120] Oresme's speculation that every alternate world functions as does our own, and Ockham's precept that Christ could as well have chosen to be incarnated as an ass, instead of as the Son of Man, grew out of this initially anti-Aristotelian school of thought asserting the omnipotence and freedom of the divine will. When Nicholas of Cusa speculated in the fifteenth century that other planets were inhabited, his intention was to ascribe to the infinite Creator, whose being was characterized by an infinite actuality and by the coincidence of opposites, the actualization of every potential and conceivable predication. Cusanus's faith in the coherence of the universe led him to postulate that the alternate creations inhabiting the moon or Mars would have to reflect the elemental composition of those "planets": the moon people would have a watery nature, the Mars people a fiery nature, and so on. The Paracelsian spirits inhabiting the elements of water, fire, earth, and air, are alternate creations in this anti-Aristotelian tradition: their existence vouchsafes, at one and the same time, the infinite power of the Creator and the infinite mercy of the Redeemer. Paracelsus's elemental creatures are said to inhabit "a world" or "the fourth part of the world" (*dieweil wir spüren und erkennen das im wasser ein welt ist. . . . die geburt der vulcanischen völkern, so in dem vierten teil der welt wonen unter seim elementischen feuer*—I,1:250). Yet the salient issue is the Incarnation. It leads Paracelsus to submit the hypothesis that there surely must be something different about the human "sect": "inasmuch as Christ was of our sect and took on our form, who had the choice among all, or [the choice] to take any particular one, and [instead chose] to give himself into our [form] without any natural seed, we consider that the other sects are not perfect in form . . ." (*dieweil Christus unserer secten gewesen ist und unser form angenommen, der da die wal gehabt het under allen oder ein besondere zunemen, und sich in die unsere ergeben on natürlichen samen, achten wir das die andern secten nit volkomen in der form sind . . .*—I,1:248). "Without any natural seed"—this condition induces Paracelsus to speculate on the greatest possible distinction between the human reproductive process and that of any other living species.[121] Though the incarnation was a divine event, the human creature that, in its own humble way, attempts to emulate this incarnation—be it through vows of chastity or by leading, as does Paracelsus, the life of the spirit—must have something within its nature that predisposed Christ to become human and which therefore facilitates the human being in becoming christlike. This individual and theological point of departure induces the thinker-physician to denounce the errant medical men who analyze human conception in the anatomical and material terms, thereby ignoring what is distinctively human, namely, the *liquor vitae*, which in human reproduction supplants the animal function of the sperm: "For in the animal there is no *liquor vitae*, its seed is only its sperm" (*wan im tier ist kein liqour vitae, alein ist ir sam in irer sperma*— I,1:270). The material-anatomical approach pertains to that which is divisible; but the *liquor vitae* allows Paracelsus to conjecture about human generation in terms of the reproduction of the entire being, as if a "concealed human" or inner "microcosm" were to be liberated by the highest faculties of the human soul, in order to emerge and become visible through the processes of conception and birth:

> Thus in this way [the human being] has effected it and fulfilled his will in the speculation, so that the *liquor vitae* is ignited by speculation and becomes a seed of another human being. This is so in men and it is so in women. Otherwise, the *liquor vitae* remains only *liquor* and not a seed. But it becomes a seed, because it is distributed in the entire body. For the same reason, the entire nature, property, essence and kind of the members and of the spirits is in [the *liquor* or seed]. And as the body is in its form, so too is the *liquor vitae* [formed]. And the *liquor vitae* is nothing other than the hidden human being. And it is the visible [human being] that conceals him.

> *also so er nun das verhengt hat und sein willen erfüllet in der speculation, als da entzünt sich der liquor vitae von der speculation und wird zu einem samen eines anderen menschen. also ist dis im mannen und also auch in frauen. der liquor vitae wird und bleibt sonst ein liquor und kein sam. aber er wird zu einem samen, aus ursachen das er ligt in allem leibe ausgeteilet. desgleichen ist alle die natur, eigenschaft, wesen und art der glidern, der geisten in ime. und wie der cörper stehet in seiner formirung also stehet auch der liquor vitae. und der liquor vitae ist nichts anders dan ein verborgener mensch. dan der sichtig ist der, der in verbirgt.* (I,1:258)

Much is confusing and contradictory in this discourse, which sometimes accepts the agency of the sperm and sometimes denies it;

sometimes presents human and animal reproduction as being in the same category (compared to plant reproduction) and sometimes separates them implausibly; which elevates the role of reason and speculation in human reproduction, only to link their role to the power of imagination and desire. As he writes in the parallel fragment, *De Generatione Hominis*:

> God has given the human being the phantasy of lust and desire; he has given it so that it should become a material; this same material is the seed, of which will be reported here.
>
> *got hat dem menschen geben die phantasei des lusts und begirden, das selbig hat er geben, das es zu einer materi werd; dise materi ist der sam, davon wir hie meldung tun.* (I,1:293)

Given the point of departure and the objectives of this early medical-philosophical discourse, such difficulties were probably unavoidable. Nor are they alleviated when commentators fasten upon this or that reasonable statement in order to paint the whole undertaking in more favorable hues than it deserves.

What must be understood is the relationship of the early work to Paracelsus's developing theory as a whole. In denying the efficacy of sperm in humans, he intends to affirm that the more complex mixing of the total seed of a man and a woman gives rise to the successive individuation which he posited in *Volumen Paramirum*: "First of all, note that the man has a half of a seed and the woman a half; therefore the two make an entire seed" (*am ersten merken das der man ein halben samen hat und die frau ein halben; also die zwen machen ein ganzen samen*—I,1:261). "But the same mixture of the seeds of women and men yields so much tranformation that no human being can be exactly like any other" (*aber die vermischung der samen von frauen und mannen die selbig gibt so vil verenderung, das kein mensch dem andern mag gleich sein*—I,1:263). In roughly the same context, the author attempts to analyze human reproduction by distinguishing between "image" and "likeness"—an adaptation of the biblical usage that attempts to reflect the fact that human reproduction brings forth the new being that is both like and unlike its forebears. Referring in a subsequent section to the stages in which body, spirit, and soul are formed in the embryo, the author cites—as does the *Liber de Sancta Trinitate*—the forthcoming "piramiran" explanation of the matters under discussion: "you will find more on such births in *paramiris*, where the origin of the soul is treated" (*von solchen geberungen werden ir mer finden in paramiris, da tractirt wird vom herkomen der sêl*—I,1:271). With its polemical topicality and its tying of theological issues to an anthropological dogma that has medical implications, *Das Buch von der Gebärung der empfindlichen Dinge in der Vernunft*, indeed seems to pertain to a very early stage of Paracelsus's work.

The surviving tract that seems to conclude the Salzburg period bears one of his most trenchant and polemical titles, *De Septem Punctis Idolatriae Cristianae / Theophrastus Hohenheimensis Germanus*, *(On the Seven Points of Christian Idolatry . . .)*. Goldammer considers that the tract was written either late in 1524 or in 1525, in any case some months after a religious dispute participated in by Paracelsus, alluded to in his Mariological work *De virgine sancta theodoca* (II, 3: xxvii). The seven-pointed polemical work has something of the quality of a duel, since it is directed to two men, mentioned by name and nationality after the author's own name and nationality (*Germanus*) and the subtitle are given:

> *Theophrastus von Hohenheim etc. von der betrachtung und gottesdienst zu Valentio und Remigio Italis etc., der heiligen geschrift professoribus etc.*

"On contemplation and divine service, to Valentius and Remigius, Italians, professors of Holy Scripture . . ." It seems most likely that these two professors of Holy Scripture were the addressees of the previously discussed writings. Were they also among the retinue of Cardinal Lang—among the learned councillors who stood with him in his iron-fisted policy toward the people? Lang favored the company of intellectual Humanists; and their "professorships" *der heiligen geschrift* would have provided them the appropriate credentials for combatting the influence of the professor of Holy Scripture in Wittenberg, in what had become by now the antireformationist policy of the cardinal. The dispute with Valentius and Remigius may have induced Hohenheim's lasting claim to hold a doctorate of Holy Scripture.

The polemical tract against "the seven points of Christian idolatry" begins on an extraordinarily vivid personal note that renders abundantly clear where the author stands in the day-to-day struggle between new faith and old. The tract begins with a sweeping summary, both of the accusations against him and of the message of condemnation which he has preached to the people:

> Your daily cavilling and inciting against me on account of the truth which I have spoken, occasionally and several times, in taverns, drinking places, and inns, against the senseless attendance of church, luxurious ceremonies, fruitless praying and fasting, alms giving, making of sacrifices, tithing . . . confessing, taking of the sacraments, and all other priestly commandments and [priestly self-] support; moreover [your having alleged] against me, this was in drunkeness, because it happened in taverns, and taverns prove to be unseemly places for truth, and because of which [you] called me a mountebank preacher (*winkelprediger*) . . .

> *Euer täglich widerpellen und scharpfreden wider mich von wegen der warheit, so ich etwan und etlich mal in tabernen, krügen und wirtshäusern geredt hab wider das unnütz kirchengehn, üppige feier, vergebens petten und fasten, almusen geben, opfern, zechenten . . . peichten, sacrament nemben und all andere dergleichen priesterliche gebott und aufenthaltung, auch mir dasselbig in ein trunkenheit gezogen, darumb, daß in tabernen geschehen ist, und die tabernen für untüchtige örter zu der warheit zu sein anzeigen, und uf das mich ein winkelprediger genant . . .* (II,3:3–4)

This paints a lively picture of a folk preacher of a kind common to the period. That he has been accused—he freely admits: with cause—of having preached in taverns, need not detract from the popular image, nor from the presumed piety and sincerity of the author. The message of the Reformation was transmitted in no small measure by popular preachers and inns were important meeting places. But his rejoinder to the accusations that follows immediately throws his stance in peculiar relief:

> Why do you do this to me now at this time, inasmuch as you were silent and well pleased when I spoke in the taverns, [saying that] people should make sacrifices to you and follow you,

and not say anything against you? If that was proper in the taverns and a service for you, then accept now the truth that is spoken in the taverns. For in the taverns, I was faithful in you, but now I am faithful in Christ and no longer in you.

warumb tuet ir mirs ietzt in der zeit, dieweil ir mir geschwigen habt und euch wol gefallen hat, da ich redt in den spelunken, man sollt euch opfer geben und folgen, euch auch nit einreden? ist das billich in der spelunken gewesen und ist euch ein dienst gewest, so lassent euch auch ietzt die warheit in den tabernen gefallen. dann in der spelunken war ich glaubig in euch, aber ietzt bin ich glaubig in Christo und nimmer in euch. (II,3:4)

Here is a frank admission that during the earlier religious and political turmoils, Paracelsus actively spoke out to defend the institution and office of the Church and its representatives. As the *Liber de Sancta Trinitate* reveals, those who were to benefit from his support (had he hoped to advance through them to contact with Lang?) had scorned his words. As we have seen, the book on the trinity can only have elicited an even sterner reaction. If he avoided heresy charges, this was presumably because Salzburg was already tottering on the brink of a revolutionary uprising. Instead of bringing formal charges against him, those whom he considered his former friends and allies must have ridiculed him, as the charge of his drunkenness indicates, or as a reference made elsewhere to his stuttering suggests.[122] (Even before the fiasco of Basel, Theophrastus may have found himself ridiculed as *Cacophrastus*). With the rage of a betrayed ally, he mentions an accusation of sedition against him: "You complain long and much that I have completely alienated the peasants from you, so that they no longer make sacrifices and think little of you and indeed nothing at all" (*Ihr klaget sehr und fast, ich hab euch die pauern widerspennig gemacht, daß sie nimmer opferen und wenig uf euch halten und schier gar nichts*—II,3:5).

His polemical reply is massive and sharp. With a sweeping gesture, he obliterates the patristic tradition of his opponents: "I reject your holy fathers, for they wrote according to the body, and not [according to] the soul" (*ich widerrede eurn heiligen vätern, dann sie haben dem leib geschriben und nit der seel*—II,3:6). Just as summarily, he asserts the highest and most immediate authority: "What I have spoken is from the Holy Spirit. It is therefore the gospel" (*was ich geredt hab, das ist aus dem heiligen geist. also es ist das euangelium*—II,3:6). In a conscious parody of the seven sacraments or seven deadly sins, the polemic then proceeds against what he denounces as the seven articles of Christian idolatry: 1. Senseless church services and rituals which are a waste of time, a service to the devil, a sin against Christ and the Holy Trinity (II,3:10). Because of such idolatry, the official church is nothing other than a "church of walls" (*maurkirchen*—II,3:15). The true church is the spiritual community of all the just and faithful. 2. He is against prayers spoken in the churches of stone. Instead of singing the liturgy, the faithful should do good works for their fellows: "Therefore, whoever is in the faith is full of love for all those who are hungry . . ." (*also welcher im glauben ist, derselbig ist aller liebe vol gegen allen denen, die hungerig seindt . . .*—II,3:20). 3. Against costly and worldly religious holidays which have even been perverted into a "path to heaven" (*ir habt aus dem feiren ein weg gen himmel gemacht*—II,2:28). 4. Against fasting, since it involves idolatry and implies that this is the way to combat the devil. 5. Against the institution of almsgiving—as opposed to giving alms out of love for the poor—and especially against alms for cloisters (II,3:37). 6. Against pilgrimages, including those made to his birthplace of Einsiedeln (II,3:42); and against the religious orders, scholars, legal spokesmen, and the like—all of whom serve in the army of Lucifer (II,3:48). 7. Finally, he polemicizes against everything within or outside the church or convent that can be construed as an object of veneration: bells, altars, pulpits, cloister, pictures, ornamentation. All these things are fashioned by the devil. All such things contrast with true faith. The true faith proceeds from within outward and not in the manner of a tumult from outside inward (II,2:51). The seventh point is therefore a recapitulation of all the others. The entire polemic builds toward and climaxes in its condemnation of the archidolatry of religious images: "For in all images is idolatry" (*dann in allen bildern ist abgötterei*—II,3:55). The point is softened somewhat by his concession that "pictures are the books of the laiety" (*wiewol die bilder der laien pücher seindt*—II,3:55). This may refer to the *biblia pauperorum*, the medieval picture Bible produced for the illiterate. The concession could allow Paracelsus to distance himself from the iconoclasm that emptied churches of artwork and destroyed it as idolatrous. However, the basic message of Paracelsus's sevenfold fulmination against Christian idolatry lies not so much in any measures or tactics; it lies in the radical rejection of every practice and symbol embodying ecclesiastic authority. *The Seven Points* makes a clean sweep of every visible, humanly crafted, or overtly performed manifestation of the sacred. All such things are instruments of manipulation and exploitation. This radical rejection opens the door for Paracelsus's move to transfer the notion of the true image of God from all fashioned symbols and images to nature itself, from all the things created by human hands to those created by God.

The Seven Points and the *Book of Justice* (*Liber de Justitia*) are the highwater marks of Paracelsus's affinity with the radical reformation that followed Luther in basing all justification on inner faith, but surpassed him in the radicalism of its rejection of all outer ceremonies and tokens of sanctity: "If the ground of justice is properly regarded and understood, everyone should know, that it is to be sought inwardly and not outwardly" (*So der grund der gerechtigkeit betracht und gehalten soll werden, soll ein ieglicher wissen, daß derselbig inwendig soll gesucht werden und nit auswendig*—II,2:153). "In faith is justice, and whoever follows faith, also follows justice" (*Im glauben stet die gerechtigkeit, und welcher nachfolgt dem glauben, der folget nach der gerechtigkeit*—II,2:153). Proceeding from, but not confining himself to, the Lutheran contrast of law and grace, Paracelsus criticizes the harsh laws and punishments that were meted out so prodigiously in the aftermath of the Peasant Wars: "That is no justice, that a murderer is broken on the wheel on account of his murder. . . . That is justice, however, that the same murderer is broken [by the power of] faith, from which flows his penitence and contrition, in faith and not in body" (*das ist kein gerechtigkeit, so man ein mörder von wegen des mords radprecht. . . . das ist aber die gerechtigkeit, daß derselbig mörder in den glauben gebrecht werde, aus wellichem ihm fleußt die reu und buß, im glauben und nit im leib*—II,2:155). Along with this rejection of a law that he sees as embodied in the unjust ordinances both of the world and of the Church, Paracelsus recognizes the basis of a radical egalitarianism in faith and gospel:

> Therefore no commandment shall stand nor exist among people that is to serve [to bring] blessedness, nothing but the teaching of the Evangelists, in which it is shown: Believe only that the Holy Spirit baptises you. Then, every human being is his own prince, his own king and master, to command himself.

darumb soll kein gebott stehn noch sein undter den menschen,
was zu der seligkeit dienen soll, nichts denn allein die leher der
euangelisten, darin angezeigt wird: glaub nur, daß dich der
heilig geist tauf. alsdann ist ein ieglicher mensch sein fürst, sein
könig und sein herr, selbst zu gebieten. (II,2:159)

In embracing tenets of a radical reformation, Paracelsus finds a
foundation for his egalitarian sentiments; and this confirms his
sense of sovereignty in matters of the spirit. The affinity with the
Reformation does not lead Paracelsus into a close allegiance with
the theology of Luther. His idiosyncratic character and ideas and
his tendency toward moral generalization and frontal opposition
prevent such involvement. However, one can agree with Hartmut
Rudolph's tentative acceptance of the authenticity of a letter
addressed by Hohenheim as of the end of March 1525, to Luther,
Bugenhagen, and Melanchthon. Not only do the phrasing and date
and address of the letter fit both into the situation of the Wittenberg
reformers and into that of Paracelsus during or soon after the
Salzburg period;[123] equally characteristic is the appeal to an influential and high-placed figure for recognition of one of his writings,
in this case an exegesis of the first five chapters of the Gospel of St.
Matthew. Many of Paracelsus's writings adapt the terminology of
faith and works, of outer and inner, spirit and flesh, to purposes of
medical discourse.

But the approach represented by the letter to Luther and by his
most radical Salzburg tracts are only steps toward the future path
of his thought, not its final destination. The frustrated search for
support and recognition has led the young Theophrastus to a radical rejection of the old faith and its manifestations, has led him to
sympathize with and seek refuge in certain tenets of the new faith
in its most iconoclastic and Spiritualistic form. The future course of
his speculation will recapitulate his dual impulses of agression and
irenicism, combining them in an attempted resolution of the two
principles of authority, of the outer, already shattered for him by his
iconoclasm, and of the inner, not yet clearly interpreted by him as to
its locus as spirit in nature. Paracelsus has yet to merge the outer
and the inner into a theory recognizing the inner truth of the spirit
hidden beneath the outer visible entities of nature.

4 ■ The Liberation of the Divine Image

Paracelsus resumed his wandering. Was he fleeing after having led or participated in the armed uprising that nearly toppled Lang? The change from an advocate of the embattled ecclesiastical order to a leader of the fight for freedom would not have been without parallel in the year 1525. This was the banner year of Müntzer's glory and fall, the year in which a young secretary to the Bishop of Brixen named Michael Gaismayer stood guard before the gates of the episcopal palace to prevent the insurgent peasants from sacking it, only to march off the next day as their elected leader in a well-conducted military campaign to transform Tirol into a Protestant republic with a Swiss-style autonomy.

However, it seems more likely that Paracelsus passed through the impassioned stages of his doctrinal evolution in the shadow of the revolutionary events unfolding in Salzburg. The Salzburg insurrection was set in motion and encouraged by the flood that spread from Wittenberg. The insurgents embraced Lutheran tenets and cited the Bible in order to transform the oppressive regime of the episcopal state. The grievances of the burghers, miners, and peasants of Salzburg were relatively down-to-earth, as were those of the Tirolians under the leadership of Gaismayer. More like Müntzer than Gaismayer, Paracelsus was driven by eccentric speculations and inspirations, by doctrinal issues and disputes (though, unlike Müntzer, the medical reformer did not court martyrdom for his doctrines—a distinction that should not be overlooked in evaluating Paracelsus's affinities with the radical reformation). One can readily imagine the populace of Salzburg aroused by sharp controversies; inns and marketplaces filled with crowds, improptu debates, preachers on streetcorners, rabble rousers, visionaries and prophets. But when the insurrection was in full swing, its leaders and active participants might have had little patience for discussions of the secrets of the trinity or hypotheses on the generation of living things through the power of reason and imagination. Paracelsus's reverence for the

101

Virgin Mary would have distanced him from many among the activists. He may have respectfully written to Luther, Melanchthon, and Bugenhagen during this period; however, he remained somewhere between the boundaries that were being staked out to demark the confessions of the future. After 1525, these lines began to rigidify and become more dogmatic, while Paracelsus's doctrinal independence remained both idiosyncratic—and surprisingly flexible.

After Salzburg, he was drawn westward, across boundaries of invisible realms that were in flux, to Ingolstadt, the university town of Dr. Eck, who was Luther's most agile doctrinal opponent in Germany. In Ingolstadt, Paracelsus is said to have enacted one of his miraculous cures.[124] Then on along the Danube into Swabia where he is said to have cured an abbess at Rottweil,[125] and then westward, after various other sojourns, to the Upper Rhine. On November 30, 1526, he purchased the rights of citizenship in Strasbourg. A document from the city records reports a puzzling affiliation with the guild of grain merchants, millers, and starch makers. According to Sudhoff, the surgeons belonged to this guild in Strasbourg.[126] Paracelsus had obviously been in the city long enough to make the right connections. Important surgeons, Hieronymus Brunschwig and Hanns von Gersdorf, had resided here, as did the self-promoting medical author and anatomist Vendelinus Hock, whom the students in Basel would characterize as his victorious rival at a public dissection.[127] In joining the guild and purchasing citizenship, our man clearly reckoned with a permanent stay.

The choice of Strasbourg is significant: not a university city, not a Catholic city, but also not one of extreme Lutheran sentiments or violent conditions. This was a large, prosperous city, conservative by some standards, yet rather open and even flexible in times of stress. In Strasbourg, the Humanists wrote of the Eucharist in classical verse forms. Sebastian Brant had published the first international bestseller in German, *The Ship of Fools*. Printing presses flourished.[128] In the early 1520s, the city rapidly and peacefully accepted and began implementing the reform. Well before this turn of events, voices were heard in and from Strasbourg calling for reforms of the clergy and the schools. As the Reformation developed in Strasbourg, the city embraced religious leaders, such as Capito and Bucer, who were not natives. Even dissenters persecuted elsewhere found a relatively tolerant society here.[129] Leaving Salzburg and other less than pacific regions behind him, Paracelsus should have had sound reasons for choosing Strasbourg. Here were abundant patients in a large wealthy merchant center. The city was open to outsiders, with active intellectual circles broad enough to accommodate every impulse from mariology to Spiritualism, with excellent publishing opportunities and a diminished likelihood of getting beheaded or burned at the stake. In 1526, the defeat of the peasants in widely scattered uprisings and the increasing persecution of the Anabaptists by every confession was already giving rise to a migrant population of displaced and disaffected souls, radicals and visionaries, who were, like the Salzburg refugee, in search of a safe haven and a sympathizing community. A man who alternated between radical iconoclasm and an idiosyncratic conflation of theology with other sources of knowledge would have encountered kindred spirits and fellow sufferers, as well as some well-placed potential benefactors in Strasbourg. In a sense, this was also home country for Paracelsus. For the Alemannic Southwest included Swabia, where the Hohenheim family had its origins, and Switzerland, where he had been born, as well as Alsatia with its urbane metropolises of Strasbourg and Colmar. But here too, troubles were germinating. By 1525, the rift between Luther's Wittenberg and Zwingli's Zurich, implicating other cities of the Upper Rhine region, had become irreparable. A protracted controversy between Luther and the reformers of Strasbourg and Basel would only be resolved after many years of uncertainty and contention.

However, before Paracelsus could get settled in Strasbourg, he received the impressive offer from Basel to take up the dual position of professor of medicine and official city physician. Scholars are on the whole in agreement about the reasons for this offer. Paracelsus's fame had been spreading on the Upper Rhine. He had won the favor of the Humanistic and reform-minded burgher circles in the city, that is, the influential publisher Johannes Froben, whom he treated with much short-term success, Erasmus, with whom the physician corresponded briefly but amicably, as well as the Amerbach brothers, young patrician Humanists, and the reformer Oecolampadius. Froben and Erasmus were sufferers who eagerly accorded recognition to a new medicine that promised to alleviate their maladies. However, there was also a political side to the offer. The city council would have had an interest in bringing him to Basel as a city physician and perhaps as part of an initiative against a stubborn university that clung to the old faith. Already in February 1524, a similar event had nearly taken place when François Lambert, the liberal-minded Franciscan and friend of Agrippa von Nettesheim, had attempted to hold a public disputation under the auspices of the city council with published theses that had struck an Erasmian note, only to have the event boycotted by the Church and the Catholic university.[130] A later sixteenth-century source mentions Oecolampadius, the struggling reformer of Basel, as the driving force behind the appointment of Paracelsus. As an embattled theology professor who lectured in German, as Paracelsus intended to do, Oecolampadius would have had sound reason to support the appointment of such a resolute and kindred voice of innovation and protest: truly a potential *Lutherus medicorum,* so it must have seemed. Before coming to Basel, Paracelsus already enjoyed contacts with the Strasbourg reforming circle of Hedio.[131]

It was under these circumstances that Paracelsus came to Basel, to a situation that demanded finesse and circumspection, neither of which he possessed. He might either have shown the university all the deferences demanded by such an institution in an attempt to curry the favor of the academic establishment, or he might have made up his mind to brook every insult and ride the general wave of reform over the heads of contemptuous colleagues to an inevitable victory. Unfortunately, he did neither the one nor the other. Paracelsus got off to a brave start with the announcement of his program of lectures early in the year 1527. His decision to lecture in German, to openly oppose the ancient authorities in medicine, to proclaim a new standard of "reason and experience," *ratio ac experientia,* and to symbolically fling down the gauntlet by burning the old *summa* of medicine on June 24 rang in his professorship with the fanfare of a dramatic reform of medicine in the spirit of the times. Resistance came in the form of taunts from students, no doubt encouraged by hostile colleagues, in favor of Galen and against the new terminologies introduced by the outsider. Instead of ignoring these taunts, Paracelsus repeatedly demanded that the council act against the offenders and became increasingly incensed when nothing was done. He was sensitively wounded when his adversaries posted a Latin verse diatribe in the form of "Galen's reply," *Manes Galeni adversus Theophrastum, sed potius Cacophrastum.* This was the source of the long-remembered "theft" of his good name and perhaps a motive for the invention of his even more exalted pseudonym. *Cacophrastus* may have alluded to his stuttering;

the poem ridiculed the invention of unheard of terminologies, such as *Yliadum* or *Archäus*, and his alchemistic ("spagyric") dreams.[132] By the end of the year, his fortunes had turned sour. Froben, his patient and patron, died. A conflict with another prominent patient over payment of a fee induced the lecturer and official physician to make rash statements. There was a recurrence of the rage, born of his sense of betrayed trust, that had preceded his flight from Salzburg. As in that city, Paracelsus again reverted from worldly ambition to a world-defying fury, thereby putting an end to his academic prospects forever.

Between the works dated 1524 and 1525 in Salzburg and the works written in the first few years after his flight from Basel, Paracelsus found himself thrust by circumstances into a hothouseatmosphere which elicited the great body of his medical work that would give him the fame or ill-repute of a reforming physician in the eyes of contemporaries and posterity. During this relatively brief and, for a scientist, hyperactively extroverted interval, he produced a prodigious variety of pronouncements on specific diseases and a mass of alchemical receipts and procedures. What I want to show here is that the applied work on specific diseases and alchemical procedures is contextualized by his theories—as evidenced by the jibes in *Manes Galeni*. Furthermore, his theory was structured not, or at least not predominantly, by inductive conclusions from practical research—this would have been almost inconceivable given the unstable circumstances under which he was compelled to work—but rather by the transferral of his religious speculations to nature and medicine. There is no evidence in his lectures that he acknowledged this transferral at the lectern; but it is suggested in certain pronouncements originating during this period. After Salzburg, where religious pronouncements had led to danger and flight, reticence must have seemed advisable, all the more so given the multilateral fronts in the religious conflict that was heating up to its local eruption at the time of his arrival in Basel. Perhaps Paracelsus would have fared better (he could not have fared much worse), if he had openly based his authority as a physician and professor on theological precepts, as he did in his later writings. The situation in Basel was in any case volatile, with the reforming parties divided even among themselves. Paracelsus both rebelled against and accommodated himself to what was expected of a professor of medicine. In the end, he was defeated as much by his temper as by the vested power of his conservative academic opponents. Caught up in the throes of reform, the city closed the university soon after his debacle.

According to Sudhoff, Paracelsus's work called *Archidoxis* is a product of the period of wandering between Salzburg and Basel. It would indeed seem to be an early work inasmuch as the triad of Sulphur, Mercury, Salt, nearly ubiquitous in the mature writings, is not mentioned—despite the fact that the main body of the book of *Archidoxis* is devoted to an alchemistic material that would appear to be the most probable empirical source of the triad.[133]

In introducing *Archidoxis* with a *prologus de microcosmo*, the author suggests a much broader context and purpose for the work. The rhetoric is entirely that of a reformation just now breaking free of the centuries-old bondage to false ideas and false books. "If we should and must consider our wretchedness and abandonment, dear sons . . ." (*So wir unser elend und verlassenheit sollen betrachten und müssen, lieben filii*—I,3:93). The work solemnly begins by invoking the sense of spiritual forlornness which must have been invoked by reforming preachers. But *Archidoxis* does so in order to dramatize the degradation of medicine and knowledge. The prologue has the confessional tone of a voice rising up *ex profundis*: the author had not been able to lift himself up while in bondage to the old medicine (*das wir nit zu grünen noch zu ufrichten komen mochten, also lang und wir der arznei, wie die alten beschriben hatten, nachfolger waren, sonder mit vil armut und jamer gefangen und bittern ketten gebunden . . .*—I,3:93). He postulates, then, a line every bit as sharp and decisive as that proclaimed by the preachers of the new faith. On the one side stands his new medicine, on the other the dishonest doctors who have arrived at great wealth in the path of the old (*und vil der doctorn seind, die durch die alten zu großem reichtumb kumen und seind, aber mit wenig lobs, sondern mit vil liegens erlanget haben*—I,3:93). As the author has cast off the chains of the old false medicine, his reformed medicine will activate the "mysteries of nature," in "such forces" as are liberated by cleansing substances of their impediments—just as a prisoner is liberated from his bonds to become spiritually free (*so ist also mysterium naturae in solchen kreften, so sie entlediget wird von seinen impedimenten, wie do ist der gefangen man, der entledigt wird von seinen banden, dem all sein gemüt frei ist*—I,3:93). The multifaceted casting off of chains—the false teaching, the material impediment, and of course the physical ailment—has an emblematic forcefulness. The things themselves bear "this sort of flaw" (*ein solcher prest*). "As [this flaw] is removed, there occurs the art of separation, which, compared with the art of aromatics [the use of smoke or incense sold by the apothecaries], is like a light in darkness" (*so der hinweg kompt, ist gleich die kunst diser separation, gegen der kunst aromatariorum, wie ein liecht in einer finsternus*—I,3:93–94). Not only is the characterization of the new medicine saturated with religious metaphors, it in fact *is* religion, *is* knowledge of the divine mysteries:

> We want then to approach with a good spirit the mysteries of nature [and] by experience separate [off] the corporeal impediments, and consider, first of all, what is most useful and noble for the human being, to know but the mysteries of nature, from which is to be regarded what God is, what the human being is, what the exercise of both is, celestial in the deity, earthly in the perishable. From which then arises, what theology is, what justice is, what (rhetoric) is, how alone the life of man is constituted by the mysteries of nature, to know and to pursue them, through which God and the eternal good may be recognized and attained.

> *wollen wir mit gutem gemüt anfallen die mysteriae naturae <und> durch die experienz scheiden von den impedientibus corporibus und am ersten bedenken, was dem menschen am nüzlichsten und am edelsten ist, alein zu wissen die mysteria naturae, daraus betrachtet wird, was got ist, was der mensch, was ir beider übung seind, himlischen in der gotheit, irdischen in der zerbrechlikeit. daraus dan entspringt, was theologia ist, was ius ist, was (rhetorica) ist, wie alein die mysteria der natur das leben des menschen ist, zuwissen und denen nachzufolgen, dadurch got und das ewige gut mag erkennet werden und erlanget.* (I,3:94)

The language is turgid, the sense enigmatic. Yet this leaves no doubt whatsoever that the medical-alchemical art of separation is as much theological as natural. And notwithstanding the repeated references to the mysteries of nature and human life, the mode of paralleling the earthly with the eternal and of proceeding from nature to God is at least as old as the theology of Hugh of Saint Victor, or the visionary mysticism of Hildegard of Bingen. What is new with Paracelsus is that nature is not merely the visible symbol of the invisible things of God. Nature is increasingly understood as a revelation from God about the perishable realm, a revelation of the divine forces that effect healing. The mind travels from the perishable to the eternal in order to return to the perishable. This approach is recommended against the false pride and greed of the "theologians" and against the opinionated law and order of the jurists; it is offered against them in order that they should not ruin the common good (I,3:94–95). It seems, then, that the opponents here are still those against whom he had railed in Salzburg, not yet those against whom he will polemicize in and after Basel. Although the treatise moves on to a detailed discussion of the alchemical separation of elements, the sense of moment conveyed by his invocation of profound crisis intimates a reconfiguration of all life in accordance with the divine image.

It is necessary, the author begins afresh, to comprehend the microcosm in order to recognize how it can receive and merge with medicine and be governed by it. Three things must be understood: how the five senses react to the mysteries of nature; what it is that stimulates and animates the body to its motion; and how it is that all the power within the body distributes and transforms itself in the individual parts and limbs of the body, and yet "remains by origin a single nature" (*und ist doch anfenglich ein einige natur*— I,3:96). Considering the materials in the book of *Archidoxis*, it is evident that the author has to bridge the gap between crude experience of alchemical forces on the one hand and his view of the animate, human, and divine meaning of medicine and alchemy on the other. With respect to these animate aspects of life, he is aiming at a threefold division. This implies that there is a twofold body, spirit and matter. Regarding salvation, he draws a twofold division: "that there are two bodies, eternal and corporeal, enclosed in *one, ut patet de generatione humana*, but medicine works to purify and cleanse the house in which the *corpus spirituale* may sufficiently spend its essence. . ." (*das zwen corpus seind, aeternum und corporale, in einem verschlossen, ut patet de generatione humana aber die arznei wirket in dem, das sie das haus erleuteret und reiniget, dorin dan der corpus spirituale mag gnugsam verbringen sein wesen* . . .—I,3:97). The mortal gap between the animate and the lifelessly material facing medical alchemy has to be bridged along with that between the eternal

and the corporeal confronting theology. It is because these two difficulties coincide that the medical-theoretical problem can aquire its
eschatological significance, encompassing the very scheme of creation. Throughout his work, the necessity of closing the gap dictates
a variety of solutions. Here, the transforming passage from the
material body to the animate one is effected by the power of the will
as imagination: "*intentio vel imaginatio* ignites *virtutem vegetativam*, as a fire [ignites] wood . . ." ("*intentio vel imaginatio zündet an
virtutem vegetativam, wie ein feur ein holz . . .*"—I,3:98). This igni-
tion is therefore like the action of the "mysteries of nature" in bodies: "For *mysterium naturae* in bodies is like a fire in wood that is
wet and would like to burn but can't because of the moisture" (*dan
mysterium naturae in den corporibus ist gleich wie ein feur in eim
holz, das naß ist, und gerne brinnen wolt, das vor nessi nit mag*—
I,3:93). Paracelsus's *Liber de Longa Vita*, attributed by Sudhoff to
the immediate pre-Basel period, similarly presents fire as an image
of life fueled by *humor vitae* and burning with *spiritus vitae*: "Thus,
if we see life as a fire that thus burns and also lives, then what life
and fire is is now modelled for us materially, visibly and sensibly" (*so
wir also das leben sehen wie ein feur, das do brent und auch lebt, so
ist uns da iezt materialisch fürgebilt, sichtlich und empfintlich, was
das leben und das feur sei*—I,3:229). Was it an intuition of this kind
that gave rise to the theory of the three principles which are eluci-
dated as three aspects of the combustion process?

Similar to his reflections in the prologue to *Archidoxis*, the fragmentary tract called *De viribus membrorum* or *De Spiritu vitae* dis-
cusses the distribution of powers in the parts or limbs of the body.
In its oneness, this vital power transmits and is united with a cosmic power: "From all the stars and influences of the entire heavens
as far as the firmament extends lies the force of the *spiritus vitae*
and is like an invisible celestial vapor and is united with [the heav-
ens] as cold and warmth in order to make a temperature" (*Aus allem
gestirn und influenz des ganzen himels, so weit das firmament
begreift, ligt die kraft des spiritus vitae und ist gleich einem vapori
coelesti invisibili und unirt sich mit dem als kelte und werme so sie
ein temperatur machen*—I,3:17). The theory of the *spiritus vitae* had
the advantage of sustaining the notion that nature as a whole and
in particular contained healing powers which were the same powers
that enliven the body. The *spiritus vitae* offered a new etiology of
disease as blockage. Where the *spiritus* cannot penetrate, disease

arises (*Nun auf das merket, wo der spiritus vitae nicht hin mag, da gebirt sich eine krankheit* . . . —I,3:16). The fragment on the *Spiritus vitae*, like *Archidoxis*, is mainly filled with alchemical analysis or procedure. When the author turns from the divine and cosmic prologues of these writings to the main discussion, there is a stark contrast, a quick descent from lofty generalization to practical detail and instruction. This conveys the real dilemma that faced Paracelsus in any attempt to legitimize his alchemical medicine: the gap between the inanimate and the animate could only be bridged by reducing animate to inanimate or by elevating inanimate to animate.

Since Paracelsus can only choose the latter option, he is driven in his argumentation to embrace every sort of miraculous report or claim suggesting the ascendancy of spirit over matter. Thus, in one of many characteristic asides, he reports that cows can spend an entire summer in the Alps without drinking and that there are some people who go for years without eating, "inasmuch as it is attributed to God on account of the piety of the person, which we do not want to judge upon (*wiewol solchs got zugelegt wird, von der frombkeit wegen der person, das wir nicht urteilen wollen*—I,3:99). This is reminiscent of controversial sixteenth-century miracles of pious souls who were said to live on nothing but the sacramental host. However, Paracelsus cannot be pinned down to a specific doctrine on such matters. A bit later, we find him associating those who venerate the healing powers of saints with evil magic. Significantly, Paracelsus brings to nature and medicine the terminologies of contemporaneous religious debate, the contrasts of faith and works, of the outer and the inner, of flesh and spirit. This usage is very much more in evidence than is any counterposing of Hermetic and Neoplatonic ideas against the authority of church tradition and the Bible (although, as Rudolph has recently shown, there is some evidence of a Platonistic terminology in his statements).[134] During this decisive period of his career, Paracelsus does not choose the side of Renaissance philosophy against a Reformation fideism. Quite to the contrary, he attempts to extend faith to the domain of nature and medicine. This was also the period in which theologians who had no interest in nature philosophy were being compelled *nolens volens* to make pronouncements about substance in response to the sharpening of the controversy between Luther and his critics over the doctrine of Christ's substantial presence in the Eucharist, a question to which Paracelsus addressed many theological tracts. Given the contemporaneous controversies over the sacraments coinciding with Paracelsus's Basel professorship, it is quite understandable that the fundamental philosophical problem of the relation of matter to spirit, the interactions of the two, and the transformations of one into another, should have appeared to be what it in fact is in his work taken as a whole: a problem at once naturalistic and theological.

The solution to the complex difficulty of bridging the gaps between matter and spirit, between earth and heavens, the created and the eternal, visible and invisible, begins to announce itself in metaphors and figures of speech which crystallize to a central term of Paracelsian theory: the term or family of terms for *image* (*bilt, biltnus, einbildung, form, gestalt, figur*, and more). *Image* is the root of a magically engendering imagination and the biblical measure of the likeness of divine and human natures. In created matter, process reflects the power of the Creator Spirit. Impression is the mode of influences of heavens upon earth. Just as imagination can "ignite" arcane virtues and impregnate with life, just as fire "models" (*für-bilt*—I,3:229) the image of the process of life, the alchemist's fire conveys the image of being *qua* process: the three symbolic aspects of combustion. Image as *bilt* is something made that also takes after or bears the mark of its maker. With this in mind, it is possible to arrive at a clearer understanding of the unifying thread that runs through every ramification of Paracelsian theory. Already in his *Book of the Holy Trinity*, one finds the paradoxical argument that we know less about God than the wild animals know about us (II,3:241). Yet the biblical dictum that the human being has been created in the image of God is also an absolute certainty (II,3:240). As late as the *Astronomia Magna* of 1537–1538, one still finds these same two assertions paradoxically side by side:

Inasmuch as it is so, that neither I nor anyone else, can or may know of the image of God, as it is, except for what we understand and may abstract from Christ and Scripture. For it has been left to us that we should learn to understand and recognize the invisible in it, for it is invisible. But it is no less the case that God is the person. Inasmuch as the person is, there is also an image, for a person cannot be without image, and image is a form and figure. Thus, as the human being is formed [*gebildet*], thus also is God formed [*gebildet*], after whom the human being has been formed.

*wiewol das ist, das ich, noch keiner, kan noch mag wissen von der
biltnus gotes, wie sie ist, alein was wir von Christo und von der
geschrift verstehen und ausnemen mögen. dan sie ist darumb
uns verlassen, das wir sollen das unsichtbar in ir lernen verstehen und erkennen, dan sie ist unsichtbar. aber nit minder ist es,
got ist die person. dieweil nun die person ist, so ist auch ein biltnus, wan ein person mag on ein biltnus nicht sein und biltnus ist
ein form und figur. also wie der mensch gebildet ist, also ist auch
got gebildet, dem der mensch nach gebildet ist.* (I,12:289)

Absolute skepticism about the nature of God, and at the same time
absolute certainty of the biblical dictum of likeness, constitute the
ambiguous core of Paracelsus's theories. Scripture, which, taken as
meaning, is invisible, has been given to us so that we may recognize
what is invisible: the spirit beneath the letter. The creation of
nature is this same rendering of the invisible visible:

> But thus now God has made the world not to be invisible but
> rather visible; that is, he has created that which beforehand was
> nothing, and from that which was nothing heaven and earth
> have been created, and thus his word, which had been invisible,
> [is] made visible, inasmuch as his word has become that which
> we touch and see.

> *so nun aber got die welt beschafen hat, nicht unsichtbar zu sein,
> sonder sichtbar, das ist, er hat sie beschaffen, die vorhin nichts
> gewesen ist, und aus dem das nichts gewesen ist himel und erden
> beschaffen, und also sein wort, das unsichtbar gewesen ist, sicht-
> bar gemacht, als das sein wort ist worden, das wir greifen und
> sehen.* (I,12:291)

The creation through the Word, the divine Son, the visible person of
the trinity, is a motif common both to medieval cosmology and to a
long tradition of so-called Logos mysticism, spectacularly represented in the ninth century by Erigena, the philosopher and mystic of
nature and Logos. Implicit from the beginning of the Paracelsian
writings, this conclusion closes the triangle of his premises: the person of Christ, the Scriptures, and the nature that has been created
as the divine Word made visible—all render the invisible things of
God visible; and although the human being is the only creature with

an eternal soul, in some sense all must reflect all as word, image, and sign. The human creature is also heaven and earth, visible and invisible, and a threefold being of *body*, sidereal *spirit* (or sidereal body), and *soul* or the eternal spirit and breath of life (*spiraculum vitae*). All things have an inner spirit. As signs, they are also word-like. Hence, nature, too, is corporeal, spiritual, and verbal.

Those who prefer to see Paracelsus as a Renaissance thinker contend that his signatures are of popular-superstitious origin, and that the vital spirits in all things derive from Renaissance Gnosticism, Hermetism, popular pantheism, or other nonbiblical influences. This search for determinants other than the biblical passages emphasized by him embodies the procedure of a quest for errors. To Paracelsus's believing mind, the very convergence of sources could only have testified to the truth of his bible-based conception. The fact that magic and imagination work their will by means of *images* could only have confirmed the divine ontology of the image, though in a debased form. That the stars operate on earthy life by means of *impressions* could only have confirmed the centrality of image, even if the stars are not divine. All transformations act by imposing a new image. The arcane forces that effect change are a "new birth" (I,9:88). The diseases are microcosmic pictures of macrocosmic events. To say that the one is *analogous* to the other puts rather too prim a face on things, as if we were to suggest that he did not really intend to equate an earthquake with the trembling of the body, but was only, as we say, *drawing an analogy*. Very much to the contrary: the great world is the "father" of the small world, of the human being. This is why Paracelsus can write that in order to understand the patient, one must know his father (1,8:98–99). The quasi-paternal relation of maker to made is the ground of the individual images of disease: flatulence as the image of wind turbulence, trembling as the image of an earthquake. More will be said below about the particulars of such diagnoses and about the corollaries of this central notion of the image, which extends a universal pattern to the discussion of religion, nature, and the Paracelsian medical subdisciplines.

Before turning to the further applications of the concept, we should consider the mental advantages and disadvantages of the notion of image taken in itself. One advantage was that *image* could be intuitively connected with entities in a way that such nonentities as insubstantial form or number could not. No matter how vaguely, the notion of process as image-creation invokes the perceptible appearances of things. Likeness and image represent themselves as terms of common experience; they intuitively equate objects from different realms of experience. The disadvantages are equally evident: likeness between fundamentally unlike things is a matter of subjective intuition. Paracelsus maintains the likeness of material and immaterial things by positing *invisible* entities. This is the rationale for the "spirit-materiality" (*Geistleiblichkeit*) in his thinking that has fascinated many of his admirers.

A crystallization of his thinking can be traced through the fragments thought to have been composed in the mid- to late 1520s—works that attempt to systematize the knowledge of alchemy and medicine and to relate them reciprocally to one another as in the *Archidoxis. Das Buch de Mineralibus* is such a work. In it, the author sets out to correct previous theories of ore: where they failed was in not having grasped *ultima materia*. For whoever does not grasp the ultimate matter *ipso facto* cannot grasp *prima materia*. Since the naturalism of Paracelsus is unquestioningly eschatological, metal ore has to be understood with reference to its first and final states. This is so, he stresses, for the same reason that a theologian must know his end and that an astronomer must know the starlight (I,3:31). The progression of inanimate things is as much the subject matter of the naturalist as the origin, history, and end of the world is the subject of the theologian. Paracelsus's knowledge of *ultima mineralium materia* confers on him an authority surpassing that of his predecessors (I,3:31). This must include the Aristotle who considered nature and matter to be uncreated and saw species as immutable. The terms *materia prima et ultima* are employed in an alchemistic context, distancing his usage from the Aristotelian view of an uncreated nature, even while echoing the Latin jargon of Scholastic science.

The *Book of Minerals* compares the minerals to fruits that ripen in the earth. All things were created alike in process, though the human being is the unique image of the Creator:

> For all things that God created he executed in the corporeality of like process. But differently [was] the human being created, differently the tree, differently the stone, and the human being [was] made so much more, in that he is created after [God's] image, for in [man], too, is the eternal, which is not in the other created things.

dan alle ding, die got beschafen hat, die hat er in der corporalitet gleicher proceß ausgefürt. aber anders den menschen gemacht, anders den baum, anders den stein, und den menschen sovil mer gemacht, darumb, das er nach seiner biltnus gemacht ist, das auch in im ist das ewig, das dan in den andern creatis nicht ist. (I,3:39)

We notice here that, although man is created in the image of God by virtue of the eternal, *all* things are made "in the corporeality of like process(es)." This is a complex thought that has several implications: The three primary things are in all of nature as a process which is at the same time imparted by God and homologous with the trinity. Therefore, the chemistry of nature is the same as, or at least contiguous with, the chemistry of animate life. The process of digestion in the human being is the same as the work of the alchemist in transforming substances. But Christian doctrine stands against the materialistic or pantheistic tendency in this, so that Paracelsus must also assert a special sense in which the human being is made after the image of God: namely, as body, soul, and spirit. Wilhelm Kämmerer has documented the two tendencies of Paracelsus toward the dualism of body and soul and toward the trichotomy, including spirit.[135] With this inclusion, the body can also be spiritualized through the arcane forces and virtues, and the soul spiritualized in the creative imagination which corresponds to the creative power of the *spiritus creator* that hovered above the dark waters in the creation according to the Book of Genesis. As Regin Prenter has observed, Luther was similarly taken with the real connection between spiritual rebirth and the creation of the cosmos:

> The groaning of the Spirit toward God is a real raising from death, a new creation. When the gospel says that no one can enter the kingdom of God without the new birth of water and the Spirit it simply means that the old man must be destroyed totally. *The old man must become as the earth which was waste and void before the first creation so that God the Holy Spirit can create the new man out of nothing.*[136] [Italics added]

As Prenter observes, Luther frequently linked the intercession of the spirit in the pain and conflict of the soul with the creative activity of the spirit in Genesis 1:1. Prenter observes that for Luther this was not idle allegorizing. Similarly for Paracelsus, the homology of creation and salvation is extended even further, beyond soteriology, to the power of medical healing.

Without abandoning the Christian doctrinal distinction between human and nonhuman, Paracelsus therefore established a framework in which all things could have their being in process. As process, the outlines of the divine image became discernible in inanimate nature as well. All the transformations of nature presuppose a single divine pattern. Within all things, and most especially in the element of water, which has primacy because of its pride of place in the biblical account of creation, all sorts of fruit are latently present:

> and the same *prima materia* is nothing other than sulphur, salt, and mercury, which are the soul of the element, its spirit and its proper substance. And the three things here mentioned have in them all metals, all salts, all gems, etc.

> *und das die selbig prima materia alein ist sulphur, sal und mercurius, die aber nun sein die sêl des elements und sein geist und das recht wesen. und die drei ding, wie genent seind, die selbigen haben in inen all metallen, alle salia, alle gemmen etc.* (I,3:41)

The divine pattern which is tantamount to "nature," together with the predestination borne within the seeds of all things, assures that chaos and conflict will yield to order and fruition:

> As if one had, thoroughly mixed up in a sack, all the seeds in the world together. And if one were to sow it in a garden, nature would be there and give to each seed its own fruit to the end that each would come into its own being and perfection, without harming the other.

> *als wan einer het in einem sack durch einander aller der samen, so nun auf der welt seind, bei einander. und so ers nun in garten seet, so ist die natur do und gibt einem ietlichen samen sein eigene frucht zum end, also das ein ietlicher semen in sein wesen kombt und perfection, dem andern on schaden.* (I,3:41)

In order to account for the variety of things, Paracelsus must postulate a variety within the *prima materia*:

Now as you have heard, the *prima materia* is together in the mother, as if in a sack, namely composed of three parts. Now, however, as many as are the kinds of fruit, even that many are the kinds of sulphur, salt, and also mercury. A different sulphur is in gold, a different one in silver, a different one in iron, a different one in lead, tin, and so on.

Nun wie ir gehört habt, das die prima materia bei ein ander sei in der muter, als in einem sack, nemlich von dreien stucken zusamengesezt. nun aber so vilerlei frucht, so vilerlei seind auch der sulphur, sal und sovil auch mercurii. ein ander sulphur im golt, ein ander im silber, ein ander im eisen, ein ander im blei, zinn etc. (I,3:42)

Yet the universality of the pattern proves that all in nature arises from one source, and that nature divides genus, as the alchemists say, by a process of separation:

that nature then has comprised everything in one fist, and then hands out each genus, so that in it is the best and strongest [nature]. Thus nature divides into a special kind the metals, and each genus in particular. . . .

das also die natur solchs alles zusamen hat in ein faust gefaßt, und aus der gibts heraus ein ietlichs genus, das in ir ist bei dem besten und sterkisten. scheidet also in ein besondere art die metallen, und ein ietlich genus besonder. . . . (I,3:43)

Alternative to this order imposed by *natura naturans* is the chaos and conflict of the things that struggle to be born: all elements are in all other elements. The strongest imposes its properties on the others. In human conception and birth, the seed that is strongest, be it male or female, imposes itself as the gender. Paracelsus offers glimpses of the disorder of a nature viewed without reference to the pattern and purpose of creation. It was a view that undoubtedly bespoke the heartfelt intuition of those who lived through this period of conflict. Calvin for one knew how to summon all the horrors of a nature depraved and rife with enmity. Paracelsus reacted to a nature perceived as in conflict and confusion by discerning a divine pattern within flux itself.

Attempts have been made to keep Paracelsus's natural theory as free as possible of theology by characterizing the discovery of the three principles as a result of practical alchemical study or epidemiology. It is true that at times the light of nature is portrayed as independent of the light of revealed religion. In the work on metals, not God but "nature" fashions created things. Nevertheless, any attempt to conclude from this that Paracelsus asserted the independence of nature against divine intervention would rest on a very tenuous foundation indeed. In the tract *De Genealogia Christi*, which is dated by Goldammer around 1530, in any case prior to the year 1532 (II,2:XXXII), Paracelsus writes:

> and that in this manner in three things all things have been created . . . namely, in salt, in sulphur, and in the liquid. In these three things all things stand, whether they are sensate or insensate. . . . for in the same manner as God has spoken: "we create the human being after our image." So, too, you understand that in the same manner that the human being is created, so too, all creatures are created in the number of the Trinity, that is, in the number three.

> *und daß in den weg in drei ding seindt alle ding beschaffen . . . nemblich in das salz, in den schwebel und in den liquor. in den dreien stehn all ding, es sei empfendlichs oder unempfendlichs. . . . dann zugleicherweise wie gott gesprochen hat: 'wir schaffen den menschen nach unser bildnus.' also verston ir auch . . . daß dergleichen alle creaturn geschaffen seindt in die zal der trinitet, das ist in der zal drei.* (II,3:63)

It would be farfetched to suppose that Paracelsus had possessed all the theological premises needed to arrive at the conclusion that the triadic form of creation is a trinitarian one, but had forgotten his premises just as he began developing the theory by means of practical medical or alchemical research, only to reintroduce his forgotten theology after the fact. It is far more likely that he contemplatively superimposed the triad on his observations, but deemphasized its theology during his professorship in Basel. The doctrine of the three principles began to acquire its ascendancy in and soon after Basel, when Theophrastus was struggling to rebuild his devastated fortunes and reputation.

One recognizes this in the collation included in volume one of division one under the title of the *Eleven Treatises on the Origin, Causes, Signs, and Cure of Specific Diseases* (*Elf Traktat von Ursprung, Ursachen, Zeichen und Kur einzelner Krankheiten*). As we have seen, the dating of this work in or around 1520—the misconception originating in the date stated but later rescinded by Sudhoff—has encouraged the untenable thesis that Paracelsus began writing by working out the main ideas of his philosophy of medicine, and only later episodically came into contact with the religious controversies of the time. A more careful reading of the *Eleven Treatises* would have shown not only the later date of origin and the roots of the work in Paracelsus's struggle to gain acceptance in Basel, but also the fundamental rootedness of the medical theory and practice in a biblical creation theory.

Though not seminal, the work is arguably pivotal: in it, the theorist overcomes the vision of a world of entities governed by five distinct yet overlapping "monarchies." He deemphasizes, but does not by any means rescind, the notion of a universal spirit entity such as the *spiritus vitae* or the *limbus*, understood as the causal basis of disease and health. Where the *Volumen Paramirum* knew five causal realms whose interpenetration was not explained, the *Eleven Treatises* moves toward a mode of explanation guided by the implicit concept of a correspondence and harmony of the great and small worlds. At the authoritative center of the new theory as it appears here is the theological elaboration of the "image." Implicitly grouped around this center, the works soon to follow after 1530 will recognize the corollary authorities of philosophy, alchemy, and astrology. The new theory that emerges after Basel will be in tendency opposed both to Galenic medicine and to physiological anatomy.

Disease in the *Eleven Treatises* is analyzed with reference to the correspondences of macrocosm and microcosm. This means that the symptoms of an illness are comparable to meteorological or geological events: colic or gas is the microcosmic equivalent of macrocosmic storms of the four winds; stroke equivalent to a lightning bolt; hydropsy is nothing but a microcosmic inundation. To understand the former, one must discern the latter: hence the physician must be a philosopher, astronomer, and alchemist. The connection is in every case based on similarities of appearance: microcosm is the image of macrocosm. The author is compelled to pose and answer the question why it is the case that the human being has the equivalent of the great world, with its heavens, within:

It stems from the fact that he also has within him his own separate heavens, like the external [heavens], and a like constellation; therefore, he does not sense time from the external [heavens], but from the internal [one]. The planet in the heavens rules neither me nor you, the one within me does. The astronomer who judges the nativities from the external planets is in error, for they effect nothing in the human being: the inner heavens with its planets does it; the external [only] demonstrates and is an indicator of the inner; for the human being is like this rustic example. The sow is in anatomy like the human being, thus, too, is the human being like the heavens.

doher kompt es, das er in im sein eigen sundern himel auch hat, wie der eußer, und ein gleiche constellation; drumb so empfint er der zeit, nit <von> den eußern, von den inner aber. der planet im himel regirt mich noch dich nit, der in mir aber. der astronomus der aus dem eußern planeten judicirt die nativiteten, der irrt, dan sie tunt nichts im menschen: der inner himel mit seinen planteten der tuts, der eußer demonstrirt und ist ein zeiger des innern; dan der mensch ist also auch, wie dis beurisch exempel. die sau ist in der anatomei wie der mensch, also ist der mensch auch wie der himel. (I,1:78)

Paracelsus's seemingly progressive—if by no means consistent—rejection of the influence of astrology here entails a rejection of causality itself in favor of the imprecise postulate of the microcosm as the image of the macrocosm. The outer stars remain as indicators of the inner human ones (*der eußer demonstrirt und ist ein zeiger des innern*). The real import of this shift is the relegation of authority from stars or observational astrologers, to God, nature, and the divinely inspired theorist. The "works" of God are image-signs conveying their meaning directly, without need of the intricate calculations of the mathematicians: "Thus the works give the sign of what it is [*sic*], as a painted picture gives its sign that it is a picture . . ." (*Also geben die werk das zeichen selbes was es ist, wie ein gemalts bilt gibt sein zeichen, das ein gemelt ist . . .—*I,1:79). "For the sign is the work itself" (*drumb ist das zeichen das werk selbs—*I,1:70). What does it mean, we must ask, when Paracelsus denies that the external star or heavens "rules" the human being, yet asserts that stars and heavens demonstrate or indicate the inner human heaven? It can only mean that macrocosm and micrcosm both mirror their maker. Paracelsus expresses this in a key passage:

> Therefore the signs that in themselves show what it is teach the physician what he too should be. For the one who made the great world made man last from the limbus and in that way both worlds are made. The one who put the winds and seas, sun, moon, etc. in the heavens, he put it in the human being as well, and said that you are, etc. Thus did the Creator who made the world prove his goodness. For what is the entire world but a sign that it is of God and has been made by God? Just as a carved image is a sign of its mason or carver, so too, with all other things, God has made these works and [they are] signs that they are his production. Now the great world is visible, the small world not, except in the figure of the divine image, the other is hidden in us. For so too, Christ was visible in person, as the great world is visible before our eyes.

> *also die zeichen, die sich selbs anzeigen was es ist, lernen den arzt, was er auch sein sol. dan der die groß welt hat gemacht, der hat am lezten aus dem limbo den menschen gemacht und also sind beid welt gemacht worden. der die wint und die mêr, sunn, mon etc. geben hat in himel, der hats auch geben in menschen und gesagt, das bist du etc. also hat der schöpfer, der die welt gemacht hat, bewert sein güte. dan was ist die ganz welt als ein zeichen das sie gottes ist und das sie got gemacht hat? als ein geschnizlet bilt ein zeichen ist seines steinmezers und schnizlers, also auch mit allen andern dingen hat got die werk gemacht und sind zeichen, das sie gottes arbeit sind. nun ist die groß welt sichtig, die klein nit, als alein in der figur göttlicher biltnus, das ander ist verborgen in uns. dan also auch ist Christus in der person sichtig gesein, wie die groß welt sichtig ist vor unsern augen.*
> (I,1:79–80)

To make the heavens the overriding cause of human life might have been a sacrilege. Therefore, the link with astronomy is asserted by making the two worlds into real signs or images as God's work. The devout physician recognizes the correspondence and meaning of things and restores the harmony of worlds. The intention of the passage only becomes unclear at the end: the great world is the visible world; its structure is concealed within the microcosm—except "in the figure of divine image." The passage goes on to explain with an analogy: "For thus too Christ was visible in the person, as the great world is visible before our eyes. But now, however, in turn, he is invisible in another form, that likewise is not that which it is" (*dan also auch ist Christus in der person sichtig gesein, wie die groß welt sichtig ist vor unsern augen. nun aber widerumb ist er unsichtig in einer andern form, die auch das nit ist, das es ist*—I,1:80). Just as creation was a divine revelation, Christ on earth was God become visible. But now Christ is invisible in another form—just as the great world is invisible within the human being—a form "which is not what it is." This form is the Eucharist, which is and is not the bread and wine in containing the invisible Christ concealed beneath it. The argument takes flight from the phenomenal realm. Etiology is grounded in the Bible. The correspondence of external nature and human anatomy is backed up by the miracle of divine presence in the host. Knowing that Christ is invisibly present beneath the material makes it possible to accept that the cosmos is invisibly present in the human organism.

Compared with the anatomical studies that were in progress in Paracelsus's time, this sort of thinking is unscientific and crude. Yet even the recognition of its worst faults should not induce us to overlook one impressive aspect of the Paracelsian theory of corresponding images: in asserting unlike likenesses, Paracelsus is compelled to discover a third term of comparison, namely that of the process. An analysis of nature that primarily recognizes things and likenesses of forms encounters a protean riddle in the transformation of entities. If one thing can be transformed into another, it must have been invisibly present in the one. Paracelsus explains the mysteries of transformation by postulating agents of change—the arcane forces, quintessences, virtues, and *magnalia* of nature; he charts process by recognizing in it an image of a divine process. The inner and the outer, the human and the meteorological, are alike in the processes one sees writ large in the heavens and pursues in detail in the alchemical laboratory.

This is evident in the etiology of the malady of stroke: "But now you should know that stroke, called in Latin *gutta*, is in every property and essence like the celestial flash (*stral*), also with [respect to] its birth, and also in its effect and wondrous work" (*Nun sollen ir aber wissen, das der schlag, auf latein gutta, gleich sei in aller eigenschaft und wesen dem himlischen stral auch mit der geberung, auch mit der wirkung und wunderwerk*—I,1:83). The pathology of a stroke is thus like the generation of a lightning flash in every important respect. By virtue of the comparison, either event receives an aura of the wondrous. Since the chemistry of the great world makes visible what is concealed in the small world, the key lies in explaining meteorology. The thunder that comes with lightning arises from three things: "There are three things that make the thunder, sulphur and salt and the fire of the firmament" (*Drei ding sind, die den fulgur machen, der sulphur und das salz und das feur des firmaments*—I,1:90). Another version of this tract combines analogy with causal analysis to spell out in greater detail the process by which sulphur, salt, and fire merge to make thunder: as the alchemist gathers up the materials for a *bombarda*, including saltpeter found in niter and fire as sulphur, the heavens use the same materials to the same end. The explosion of gunpowder appears like lightning (I,1:94).[137]   Since both have the joltingly destructive effect of a stroke, the likeness of effect implies a likeness of cause. Beyond this uncharacteristically lucid causal analogy, the three principle things now cited increasingly in explanations of every sort of natural event are an image and signature of the divine Maker. Just as God is a craftsman, the heavens too are a master craftsman. The metaphor is a privileged one: it enhances and at the same time humbles human artifice. A human craftsman is dependent on the quality of his materials; but the heavens are a "master" who crafts living images from rotten or dead things (*der himel aber, der ir meister ist, der nimpt faul ding und macht legendig bilder doraus, do sunst <die> von menschen nur holz seind und metallen und farben, dise aber leben*—I,1:115).

With even more striking insight, the same kind of comparison is used to account for the transforming activity of the stomach: "Every sculptor has his tools and in his brain the image which he wants to carve and make; that is, he has the art within him. The stomach likewise" (*Ein ietlicher bilthauer der hat sein werkzeug, und bei im in seim hirn das selbig bilt, das er dan hauen und machen wil; das ist, er hat die kunst in im. also ist auch dem magen*—I,1:127). This is surely the triumph of Paracelsus's application of alchemy to medicine: "For it [the stomach], the matter is the same as for a spagyric [i.e., the alchemistic artist of separation and combination] who renders all things subtle and separates them, purifies in many ways, now this, then that way, for as long as it takes to find what he desires" (*im ist auch gleich einem spagirischen, der die ding alle subtil auftreibt und scheid, reinigt und in vil weg, iezt in dem weg, darnach in ein andern weg, so lang bis gefunden wird das jenig, das er begert*—I,1:127). The stomach is an alchemist, or a miner who searches for ore, sometimes finding it, sometimes ruining it in the search (I,1:128). In discussing digestion, Paracelsus harks back to the insight of the *Volumen Paramirum*. Everywhere there is poison: "For there is no food that does not contain within it poison. . . . Therefore, the stomach is such that it must separate things afterward and make them excrement and expel them . . ." (*dan kein speis ist nit, sie hab in ir gift. . . . drumb ist nun der magen also, das er die ding hindan scheidet und zu kot machet und austreibet . . .*—I,1:123). However, the stomach can go too far and begin to digest this excrement—a cause of diarrhoea.

In his Basel university lectures, Paracelsus advanced many arguments of this kind, citing the three primary things and the transforming activity of the digestive organs (cf. I,4:200, 268, 270, 550, 563). His subsequently elaborated concept of the "tartaric diseases" is anticipated in his speculation on the interaction of the three primary things in a reflection that characterizes the *tartarus* as a variant of salt, a solid or coagulated residue from the process of digestion (*nun hierauf folget auch die krankheit: aus dem liquore eine, das ist mercurio, aus dem brennenden, das ist aus dem sulphure, aus der eschen, das ist der tartarus, den ich hie anfenglich under den dreien büchern sez*—I,5:133). With respect to the process of digestion and tranformation, the stomach, liver, and kidneys are "all three fires, which separate these three from the others" (*magen, lebern, nieren, welche alle drei feuer sind, die do scheiden dise drei von ein andern*—I,5:134). The same context in which internal organs and digestive processes are both construed triadically contains another of the references to the long-promised "paramiran works" (*den ich melt in paramiris*—I,5:134).

In the *Eleven Treatises*, the three primary things surmount the static character of elemental nature and humoral medicine. After citing the three principles to relativize the importance of the seemingly inert elements by multiplying four elements times three principles in order to project twelve substances (I,1:13), Paracelsus cites the three in order to go beyond their number in discussing *caulis romana*, an herb that is significant regarding the process of digestion:

There is in each thing all species of the three first, under which all genuses are included, but so subtly in quantity that it is impossible to weigh or see them. As an example, *caulis romana* is among all herbs the noblest to eat. But now what is *caulis romana* in its nature? It is a thing composed of all species of minerals, of fruits, of *tereniabin* and of degrees.

Das ist in eim ietlichen ding, alle species der dreien ersten, under denen alle genera begriffen werden, aber so subtil in seiner quantitet, das unmüglich ist zu wegen oder zu sehen. als ein exempel, caulis romana ist under allen kreutern das edelste zu essen. nun aber, was ist caulis romana in seiner natur? es ist ein zusamen gesezt ding von allen speciebus der mineralium, der früchten, der tereniabin und der graden. (I,1:129)

One cannot help but notice the logical contradiction in this: If everything contains through the first three all species and all genuses, yet in such a fine amount that they cannot be weighed or seen, how does Paracelsus know this to be the case? And if all things are in all, what makes the *caulis romana* special? He feels that he knows such things, undoubtedly, because he is the spagyric artist who works until he obtains the desired substance; he feels that he knows, because, even when encountering failure, he fervently believes in the God of whom he says in his treatise on metals (*Das Buch de Mineralibus*): "it is he alone, all in all, he is *rerum prima materia*, he is *rerum ultima materia*, he is who is all" (*er ists alein, alles in allem, er ist rerum prima materia, er ist rerum ultima materia, er ist der alles ist*—I,3:34). This was the complex experience—of outer and inner, of real and imagined things—that enabled Paracelsus to claim the authority of *magia* for his medicine while disputing aspersions of *zauberei* (sorcery). It is the experience intimated by Oporinus's memoir of his master in Basel, obsessively bent to his alchemical fire and absorbed in processes of transformation. In the *Book on Metals*, the rare and ecstatic passage cited above goes beyond the light of nature to affirm a sort of pantheism, or more precisely, panentheism. The heavens likewise make the earth into what it is by virtue of their *impressions*: "the earth is nothing without the impression of the heavens" (*die erden ist nichts on des himels impression*—I,1:4). Undoubtedly, Paracelsus was reflecting here in part on the action of the so-called celestials—the sunlight that bleaches cloth and all the other seasonal effects wrought by the shell of the world—however, the term *impression* makes these actions appear again as a mode of image-forming. We recall that in the *Volumen Paramirum*, gender in the process of conception was an impressing of the "image," of seed or matrix, whichever is strongest (I,1:263). Sorcerer's magic employed crafted images: a perversion of sacred generation. But then the profane only has its power as an inversion, a debased image, of the sacred.

As the logic of entities *qua* images is gradually altered into a theory of universal homologous process, Paracelsus viewed the three primary things as aspects of a process exemplified by transforming fire. Applying the three things to the discussion of specific diseases such as "St. Anthony's fire" (*brant*), the Basel lectures universalize the significance of the three in order to account for life in the organic being or the unity of the inorganic object: *quod homo consistit ex tribus, id est mercurio, sale, sulphure. . . . nam nulla res est quae consistere possit sine his tribus; ubi alterutrum deficit, perit res* (I,4:270). Sulfur is defined as that which burns; salt as the fixed or the alkali; and mercury as smoke or liquid (I,9:83). It seems paradoxical that the conjunction of these three should constitute the unity of things and not their separation. If the three are separated, the corpus ceases to be an entity; the animate body becomes lifeless. During the Basel period, there are further attempts to account for such diverse diseases as ulcers and leprosy by speculating on the three primary things (I,5:493, 502).

When the three are separated, unity or life is at an end. This is a striking vision of things, reminiscent of Heraclitus: to subsist is to be caught up in a perpetual process of change, like the world that reaches its end when at last two beings are born exactly alike. It is rather as if the crudely realistic Paracelsian universe of the entities had been smashed to pieces by an earthquake and the fragments set to flame. In Paracelsus's conception, all things have their substantial being in a firelike process. How else could one interpret this dynamic unity if not as an image of the triune God? The signature of God is impressed on the inner being of entities as the pattern of the inseparable three things, these irreducible essences which sustain the divine order in the world of irreducible entities.

Is this the deity of orthodox Christianity? Or is it the heretical divine family of the *Liber de Sancta Trinitate* of 1524? The Salzburg trinitarian theology had postulated the semiperson of the "goddess" and presented the three persons of the trinity as an evolving family. This aspect of an evolution is projected onto the philosophy of the three primary things. The becoming of the divine family projects its mirror image in the process that constitutes the unity and life of entities. The rationalization of the Virgin Mary as the passive goddess-mother who both is and is not the same as the trinitarian father corresponds in the Paracelsian philosophy to the elements which are not dropped but only subordinated to the three primary things. The elements are redefined as *matres* or *mütter,* "mothers." A more sublime aspect of the female principle in creation is the *labor sophiae,* defined as "the other paradise of this world, in which no disease grows, no disease remains, no poisonous creature dwells or enters . . ." (*das ander paradeis diser welt, in dem kein krankheit wechst, kein krankheit bleibt, kein vergiftiges tier wonet noch einge-het . . .*—I,3:238). "[The long life] lies solely *in labore sophiae,* in which the *operationes elementorum* occur in the fullness of their powers . . ." (*das selbig ist alein in labore sophiae in dem da geschehen die operationes elementorum mit volkomener wirkung ganz mit kreften . . .*—I,3:23). The elements can only approach the divine female principle Sophia in this heightened labor in which their powers achieve the fullest activation. In the evolving projection of the Salzburg trinity, the heavens or macrocosm correspond to the trinitarian father. The domain of alchemy, instructed in its art by the heavens, corresponds to the trinitarian son, since the alchemist exercises the Christlike office of redeeming and transforming substances. The virtues in all things, as well as the *spiritus vitae* as a whole, correspond to the third trinitarian person.

As we have seen, the heresy and the science of Paracelsus emerges, ironically enough, as a hypertrophied medieval religious tradition. In the twelfth century, Hugh of St. Victor had helped to found this tradition when he wrote that, just as human beings speak and mean with voices, God means or signifies with things (*Voces ex humana, res ex divina institutione significant. Sicut enim homo per voces alteri, sic Deus per creaturam voluntatem suam indicat*).[138] The reading of things and creatures in nature as divine "voices" or "meanings" was integrated into the fourfold meaning of Scripture: Jerusalem was the geographical city in the *historical* sense; the Church in the *allegorical* sense; the soul of the believer in the moral or *tropological* sense; and the heavenly City of God in the *anagogic* or mystical sense.[139] Any object in nature referred to by any word in

Scripture could be interpreted as a divine signifier. With the tendency of popular piety to embroider such religious teachings, the spiritual senses could be readily interpreted to sanction the divine signatures. For Paracelsus, these were primarily images impressed on things, signifying their healing virtues, their concealed divine powers. If it can be said that Luther radically simplified the fourfold meaning by concentrating on the literal or historical foundation of the fourfold sense, Paracelsus can be said to have inherited the ruins of the spiritual meanings, when these were dislocated by his radical iconoclasm and reapplied to his nature, shored up by a now all the more literal historical sense. The meanings purged from ceremonies and churches were reallocated to nature. For, as he put it: "the entire world is a church" (*die ganz welt ist ein kirch*).[140]

Elsewhere, I wrote that, "Paracelsus and Agrippa were men who would know all things; Luther was the man who would know the one necessary thing."[141] One can contrast Paracelsus's many interests with the Luther whose mental life was centered on the Bible, but in the final analysis *a theological pattern* grounds the thought of Paracelsus as much as that of Luther. Understanding all things requires the contemplation of nature as a creation that bears the stamp of its Creator. The despised ancients erred in regarding nature as uncreated and eternal. For Paracelsus, the image of God, the signature of the Creator, is stamped onto all created things. *Bilt* is the unifying term of his thought and the unspoken but everpresent religious principle of his rejection of Aristotle and Galen.

5 ■ The Voyage of Medicine

The Basel period elicited a body of smaller works directed to the particulars of disease and organized into disquisitions, small tracts, or chapters suitable for university lectures. After Basel, the outcast gradually returns to the grand summary or synthesis, to the declaration issuing from the illuminated summit of all knowledge. The diseases addressed in the years after Basel are epidemic rather than individual. Paracelsus writes on syphilis and plague, matters of existential concern to the community as a whole. Around this time, he also turns his attention to hospitals and to surgery. As we have seen, it would be premature to conclude that Paracelsus abandoned claims to the divine source or context of his *theorica* in Basel, but neither did he stress it. Appealing to the authority of *experientia ac ratio* and attending mainly to specific diseases, he momentarily set aside the grand theorizing so characteristic of the *Volumen Paramirum*, *Archodoxis*, or of the later *Paragranum* and *Paramirum*.

As we have seen, the fanfare of the *Intimatio* that heralded the beginning of Paracelsus's abortive activities in Basel can only have made his proposed reform of medicine appear parallel to the ecclesiastic reform which in 1527–1528 was still undecided in that city. It must be remembered that when Paracelsus arrived to assume his position, Basel was divided among those with loyalties to the old faith, to Luther, to the moderate and reform-minded Humanism of Erasmus, to the Humanistically schooled thoroughness of Zwingli, to the iconoclasm of urban enthusiasts, and to the separatism of the Anabaptists within the city or in the rebellious countryside outside Basel. Even if Paracelsus had been eager to compromise, it would have been difficult to decide with whom. His erstwhile supporters were themselves divided by the issues of Reformation, the Humanists Erasmus and Bonifacius Amerbach on one side and Oecolampadius on the other. Exiled from Basel, life could again become simpler—if much grimmer and more hopeless. Campaigns could again be conducted with universal theoretical manifestos, as apodictic as a catechism or an ultimatum.

Two letters written by the ex-professor *cum* city physician from the safe haven of the Alsatian city of Colmar to Bonifacius Amerbach exude a becalmed state of mind and an eagerness to return. The tone belies how gravely the exile underestimated the damage inflicted on his interests. As to the cause of his calamities, there is not the least doubt in his mind. The city of Basel has reneged on its promises and cast contumely and contempt on his person and reputation. He concedes that he may have been too open in his response to the magistrates. Yet what he said to them rested on truth; moreover, the whole affair only proves that the truth attracts hatred (I,6:36–37). The pattern is that of the Salzburg period: after seeking, and for a time even enjoying, recognition from established elements in Basel, after appealing to the magistrates to intervene against his academic detractors, Paracelsus explodes with sweeping condemnations of the wickedness and stupidity of his tormentors, no doubt thereby alienating old friends and potential allies. When the damage has been done and can no longer be undone, he reacts like a man recovering from a delirium, attempting to woo back individual supporters and restore the high-minded reforming aura heralding the start of his activities in Basel.

As in Salzburg, it is not the self-possessed development of the scholar, thinker, and spiritual pilgrim, it is the extreme situation that sways and guides the direction of his work. After his first fruitless efforts to return, he searches for other opportunities. In Colmar, his welcome wears thin. In Nuremberg, he finds a city nearly as intellectually thriving as Basel, but equally luckless for a wandering physician. After Nuremberg, he seeks solace more often than not in lesser places such as Beratzhausen, Sterzing, and Sankt Gallen. Without changing the thrust of his ideas, the situation imposes its revised agenda. Instead of the practical reforms attempted in Basel, Paracelsus again accentuates his central theoretical constructs and surrounds them with an aura evoking the pristine correctness and persecution of the Lutheran Reformation.

A reforming work on phlebotomy that may have been composed as his plight in Basel was drawing to a close imitates the trope of a restoration of pristine truth corrupted by venal sophistry: "For if one truly searches for the origin of medicine, the first physicians were quite simple [and were] not surrounded by any cunning or

deceit" (*dan so dem ursprung der arznei wahrhaftig wird nachge-
grünt, so seind die ersten arzt gar einfeltig leut gewesen und mit
keiner listikeit oder betrug umbfangen*—I,4:393–394). The author
does not indicate who these simple physicians were, but it might not
have been necessary. Readers would have thought of the true apostolic simplicity, uncorrupted by Roman falsehood, as evoked by
Protestant reformers; or they might have thought of a prelapsarian
Adam who learned his arts directly from nature or God. Paracelsus
increasingly sought to surround his personal plight with the background of a cosmic-eschatological conflict in the works that follow.
The first and last things of creation are increasingly evoked in his
work.

The preface to the *Three Books of Surgery* (*Drei Bücher der
Wundarznei, Bertheonei*), a work assigned by Sudhoff to the post-
Basel period, reacts, rather naively, to the preceding debacle by
attesting that what is most necessary for the doctor, the end of his
work, is the health of the patient and the honorarium of the healer,
as if these two things were comparable (I,6:41). The wrath occa-
sioned by the loss of an honorarium is transferred to the entire tradition of his opponents and even to their entire races.
Commentators who lend an almost absolute credence to every tirade
against apothecaries and academic traditionalists have sometimes
omitted to comment on his indistinguishable judgments that the
Greeks were always liars (*die alzeit verlogen leut seind gewesen*—
I,6:50), as were the baptized and unbaptized Jews in medicine
(I,6:45; cf. 171). Paracelsus's sense of his mission is marked especially at this juncture by eschatological nationalism, a loud prophetic megalomania which lashes out with varying emphases against
everything foreign, Jewish, Humanistic, and against those who pur-
portedly misapply his discoveries and insights. But the "last ones"
have not yet been awakened. A new truth therefore has yet to be
born in Germany (I,6:55). He was echoing a nationalism that was
coming to life during the period of the early Reformation. Of course,
his sense of mission sat well with the *Zeitgeist* before and under
National Socialism, when a torrent of literary and journalistic publications celebrated the German and European significance of
Paracelsus; and even the famous surgeon Ferdinand Sauerbruch
lectured on him in occupied Prague.[142]   In post-war Germany,
Paracelsus and Sauerbruch became icons of a revived Hindenbur-
gian style of authoritarianism: the uncorruptible steadfast leader

who rants at all incompetence and commands with a firm hand in order to spare lives, the surgeon symbolizing the notion that the knife can be wielded benevolently.[143]

After 1945, the image was also refurbished in universal and irenic tones. Unfortunately, this meant that the underpinnings of the Paracelsian bigotry were ignored—his desperate struggle to legitimize his theories by placing them in an eschatological context. His is an eschatology that contains two opposing but correlated impulses. The one impulse stresses that the theorist must consider every entity with respect to what is first and last and must therefore recognize the natural multiplicity of organic forms which have been generated in the image of the triune deity, the one God who is all in all. The other impulse polarizes into the dualistic conflict between truth and falsehood, a conflict in which the opinions Paracelsus rejects as outmoded appear in lurid tones: as lies and deceptions born out of the mendacity and greed of foreigners—of Greeks, Jews, Arabs, of arrogant professors in Montpellier and Paris, and of course of all who accept their kind of machinations. The first eschatological impulse recognizes the one in all, affirming a divinely sanctioned individuality in the pattern of creation. The second impulse is patterned on a Day of Judgment that calls down divine wrath on his enemies, among whom are the deceitful Jews in medicine, toward whom Paracelsus's rage becomes more prominent after Basel. His antisemitic strain attracted the admiration of German nationalists and ideologues of Nazi medicine in the Third Reich.[144] Unlike Luther scholarship, which chose to acknowledge the antisemitism of the reformer, Paracelsus research has remained silent about this side of his mentality. In his political views, the dualistic aspect weighs more heavily than its alternate, more than the pluralism that tended to prevail in the Spiritualism of Sebastian Franck and Jacob Boehme. This is said, not to impugn the motives of those such as Goldammer who have argued elements of tolerance and universalism in Paracelsus.[145] Indeed, the implications of the eschatological motives which Goldammer himself has so effectively demonstrated in the thought of Paracelsus[146] may only become fully apparent when and if one recognizes that the exhortations of Christian love are matched by equally fervent effusions of hatred.

The background of ultimate conflict tinges the discussions of syphilis in the two massive volumes directed to the "French disease" in 1529: *On the French Disease, Three Books. Para* (*Von der französischen*

Krankheit, drei Bücher. Para., November 23, 1529), and *On the Origin and Provenance of the French Disease, with Prescriptions for its Cure, Eight Books* (*Von Ursprung und Herkommen der Franzosen samt der Recepten Heilung, acht Bücher.*, 1529). By taking up an epidemic illness that threatened whole communities, Paracelsus hoped to gain recognition in Nuremberg for his theories of medicine. The three-book treatise and the eight-book work that follows it discuss not only the "French disease" but nearly the entire range of Paracelsus's medicine and philosophy, placing them within the context of a historical and catastrophic conflict between truth and falsehood. Cryptically, the first work bears the designation *Para* in its title, heralding a return to the *paramiran* revelations promised in Salzburg. The three-book work is dedicated to Lazarus Spengler, a leading city official who was influential in and beyond Nuremberg. The urban administration that he served was one of the most effective in the Empire, his extended city-state one of the wealthiest and most powerful, a city until recently adorned by such luminaries as Willibald Pirkheimer and Albrecht Dürer.[147]

However, Paracelsus might also have known or ascertained that, though Nuremberg was a place of competing doctrines, the city was in the throes of expelling its dissenters. Hans Denck and the so-called "godless painters," doctrinally unorthodox apprentices of Dürer, had already been banished; and the prolific Sebastian Franck, a Spiritualist and Humanist who was still in the city when Paracelsus arrived, would soon be forced into exile.

In a work published soon afterward in Strasbourg, Franck recollected his encounter with the legendary physician:

> Dr. Theophrastus von Hohenheim, a physician and astronomer. Anno 1529 this same doctor came to Nuremberg. A remarkably wondrous man who ridicules almost all doctors and authors of medicine. He is supposed to have burned Avicenna publicly at the university in Basel, and is quite alone against all medical men with his formulas of medical judgments; and carries on disputes with many. Whose practices are opposed to all, as if he were a second Lucian.
>
> *D. Theophrastus von Hohenheim, ein Physikus und Astronomus. Anno MDxxix ist gemelter Doctor gen Nürnberg kummen. Ein seltzam wunderlich Mann, der fast alle Doctores und Scribenten*

in Medicinis verlacht. Den Avicennam soll er verprent haben zu Basel in offenlicher Universität, und allein schier wider alle Medicos ist, mit seinen Recepten Judiciis Medicine und vil Widersinns mit vilen helt. Des Practiken schier wider all ist, gleichsam ein ander Lucianus. (*Chronika, Zeitbuch und Geschichtsbibel.* Strasbourg, 1531, Blatt 253)[148]

This recollection conveys a sense of wonder, but not necessarily a sense of unequivocal admiration; and certainly it offers a far more plausible explanation for the failure of Paracelsus to gain a foothold in the city than speculations about the intrigue of Prof. Stromer in Leipzig, the author of the opinion against the publication of his books which was received by the city council after Paracelsus had departed. Around this same time, the city solicited an opinion from Luther sanctioning measures against heretics and dissenters. As we shall see, it cannot be denied that the works on the "French disease" contained ideas that would have been at least suspect to the authorities during this period of doctrinal retrenchment. The fact that Paracelsus dedicated his three-book work on syphilis to Spengler is more likely to have aroused the caution of this Lutheran patrician, a man not likely to have been easily flattered or wooed by the unsolicited attentions of a wondrous stranger who disputed with the established physicians, some of whom would have been longtime friends or acquaintances of the administrator. To be shut out by the exclusive ranks of a proud city may be an ugly experience, but it is not quite the stuff of a martyr's legend.

The treatise in three books dedicated to Spengler begins, faithful to the resolve expressed in his prior work on surgery, with a sweeping and detailed refutation of all medical error: the first book attacks twenty kinds of medical "impostures" that have been applied with ill effect in the treatment of syphilis. The "impostures" include, the author writes, those that have abused his medicine (I,7:72). This perhaps reflected the spread of the pseudo-Paracelsian medicine, which was soon to give rise to many pseudepigraphic writings circulating under his name. However, it may also suggest that Paracelsus was attempting to counteract his ambiguous reputation by denouncing his purported imitators. In any case, the author makes a gesture of sweeping aside all the imposturing sects that are obstructing the institution of his true medical reform. The impostures typically include the humoralists, who profess that there are only four kinds of syphilis when there are actually a hundred kinds (I,7:74); as well as many impostures of treatment, such as annointing, smoking, washing, bathing, cutting, burning, and even the misuse of alchemical remedies. Considering the catalog of dire remedies, one might venture to surmise that Paracelsus's frequent counsel to allow nature to heal itself was by default the most sensible and compassionate recourse. He recognized that harsh cures and impositions of abstinence attacked the patient along with the disease: "From this it follows that the body loses its powers, which it cannot regain" (*daraus folgt das dem leib abgehet an seinen kreften, das er nimermer erlangen mag*—I,7:155).

Albeit with limited fanfare, his reform of medicine is here reflected in the three primary things: they are contained in the explication of the formula for an *essentia mercurialis* offered by Paracelsus (I,7:110–111) as a cure for syphilis. Its adoption, he admonishes, would require "a new teaching and school" (*ein neue ler und schul*). As is increasingly the case after the flight from Basel, Paracelsus's survey of the ranks of the medical false brethren includes the translators of medical terms from Hebrew, Greek, Chaldean, and Arabic writings, and not least of all the vicious Jewish medical cabal guilty of "lies and deceit" (*lügen und betrug*—I,7:98).

In this tract dedicated to a guardian of Lutheran orthodoxy in Nuremberg, Paracelsus also implicates certain adherents of the old faith, which still had its adherents in the converted lands. He targets the common medieval belief that individual saints are in charge of specific diseases. Paracelsus is not satisfied to discredit this as superstition: he alleges that the efficacious cures associated with the saints were actually effected through sorcery for which hagiolatrous veneration only provided a cover:

I must reveal their art in some measure. You know that there are many forms of sorcery; should they occur in the name of sorcery, no one would allow it; it would hold no respect, but rather would be repulsive to the world. Now, one has to cover it up and ascribe it to the saints, then it has a venue.

Ich muß ir kunst etlichs teils eröfnen. ir wissent, das zauberei mancherlei ist, solt sie beschehen under dem namen einer zauberei, niemants gestattets, het auch nit sonderlich ansehen, sunder were ein scheuen vor der welt. nun muß mans plenden und den heiligen dasselbig zulegen, so hat es ein furgang. (I,7:95)

If one is to attribute Paracelsus's attacks on Jews to a common prejudice of his age, his calculated attack on the healing cult of the saints defies such an interpretation. As bigoted as those he slanders, Paracelsus does not deny the results attributed to the saints, but instead associates this competing "medicine" with sorcery, a recrimination that could lead to torture and death. In a period of *angst* and repression, Paracelsus apparently sought to dissociate himself from the disreputable vagrants, monks, and old wives (*lantstreicher, münich, alte weiber*—I,7:140), from the sort of "empirics" condemned by academic medicine. He attempted to evade denunciation by calumnifying others, not only Jews and all foreigners, but even Catholic-recidivist faith healers with whom he had much in common. There is a side of Paracelsus that is inadvertently rendered all the uglier by the contrasting beatific portrayals of certain scholarly admirers. However, this contrast of the saintly healer with the passionate hater should not lead us into the opposite onesided error of overlooking his unselfish motives, his adherence to ideas and ideals. In the writings of the post-Basel period, Paracelsus descends to his lowest point. The nadir is also a turning point and a return to the beginnings of his theoretical outlook. The early, often recited promise of the "paramiran writings" is at last fulfilled.

More generally, the treatise on syphilis surrounds disease and medicine with an alarmist air of natural and historical catastrophe, a common vision in this time haunted by nightmares of cosmic disaster and divine punishment. Because syphilis is a new epidemic disease, all the old cures and theories are outmoded in every respect: "From this, it arises that, for as long as the French [syphilitic] species endures, all the old books, writings, and prescriptions will never again prove effective for us as they did for those of old . . . " (*aus dem entspringt das alle die alte bücher, schriften und recepten, dieweil die französisch art lebt, nimermer mögen ir wirkung bei uns wie bei den alten erzeigen . . .*—I,7:139). All the diseases are being transformed by a "new birth" of disease: "several diseases will be transformed into other diseases; therefore a different theory and practice must be [instituted] which cannot happen without great knowledge of the stars" (*etliche krankheiten werden verwandlet werden in andere krankheiten; darumb ander theoric und practic sein*

*müssen, welche on grosse erfarenheit der astronomei nit bescheen
mögen*—I,7:144). From the standpoint of epidemiology, the view
that diseases can be transformed is undoubtedly of considerable
interest; however, in attending to it, one should not overlook the
extent to which this view is conditioned by a catastrophic sense of
epoch, a sense that ignores what he might have known about the
history of plague. He dates the advent of epidemic syphilis around
the year 1480 (I,7:189). It can hardly be said that prior to that time
the treatment or prevention of any form of plague was more effective than in 1529. To Paracelsus, the incurability of pestilence is due
to the changed nature of the heavens (I,7:144). The newness of
syphilis results from a sexual licentiousness and an astral-constel-
lation of Venus that "transmutes" "old diseases" into the new disease
(*also wissent den ursprung der franzosen, das sie aus den alten ver-
legnen krankheiten, die, in maßen wie angezeigt ist, sich durch den
luxum und durch die constellation veneris in der vermischung
frauen und mans transmutirt und in das geschlecht der franzosen
verkert wird*—I,7:194). In part because of the misguided medical
practices, medicine faces a new epoch of disease. Indeed, medicine
is like a ship navigating the perilous and unknown seas of time:

> For the end of new diseases has not yet been born. . . . Medicine
> is directed into the world like a ship on the sea, which has no
> permanent place, but rather is guided by the helmsman by that
> which he encounters, not by the wind of yesterday, but of today.
> . . . Now, be informed as well that some diseases arise from
> faulty medicine and can never be healed.
>
> *dan der neuen krankheiten end seind noch nit geborn. . . . die
> arznei ist gericht in die welt gleich einem schiff auf dem mer, das
> kein bleibende stat hat, sonder durch den schiffmann gefurt nach
> dem und im begegnet, nit nach dem gestrigen wind sonder nach
> dem heutigen. . . . Nun wissent auch, das etlich krankheit
> entspringen aus unpillicher arznei, die nimer zu heilen seind.*
> (I,7:148, 149)

This vision of the transmutability of diseases and of the voyage of
medicine is a striking one when one considers that we are now beset
by new epidemics, and that we know that bacterial strains mutate
to become resistant to overused antibiotics. However, a real fire

doesn't necessarily make every alarm siren prophetic. Here it should not escape notice that the lesson for Paracelsus's helmsman of the ship of medicine is to become an astrologer.

The influence of the stars occupies the author in writings devoted to prognostications and astral phenomena around 1530. These short writings can best be understood as shadows ominously cast by the conflicts and anxieties of his time. There are lurid premonitions of two great insurgent sects and of two great rebel leaders who will invade (I,7:460ff.). Wars, epidemics, economic calamities, and religious rivalries are foreseen (I,7:462–463). A confederation led by Germany will extend from Lübeck into Italy. It is not an empire, but an apocalyptic "confederation," as was Switzerland. The Swiss areas where the Rhine originates will experience strife and can expect a strong dose of astral poison (I,7:472–473). In auguring with the cryptic-prophetic figures of Johann Lichtenberger, Paracelsus voiced his characteristically uncosmopolitan opinions of the peoples of Europe in this tract.

Astrology reflects Paracelsus's fears and animosities, but of equal importance for the articulation of his thinking during the post-Basel period is the renewed correlation of his medical theories with a theology that expresses his generosity and hope. In exile and despair, this correlation—always implicit—became more overt than in his university lectures and medical handbooks designed for practical use. The eight-book treatise on syphilis reaches an impasse of despair in acknowledging that, just as some men are not healed or redeemed by Christ, some patients cannot be healed by the best of physicians. An irrational ground of health rooted in desire, imagination, and faith is not open to treatment for the good: "For the human being is subject to the imagination; and the imagination, though invisible and intangible, nonetheless works corporeally in a substance and through the substance, as if it were substance" (*der mensch ist der imagination underworfen, und die imagination wiewol unsichtig, ungreiflich, noch so wirkt sie corporaliter in ein substanz und durch die substanz, als sei sie die substanz*—I,7:329). He goes on to cite a widespread view (found in Montaigne and others of the sixteenth century) that the imagination and desire of a pregnant mother can physically alter the body of the child.[149] His understanding of the imagination as a power acting on and becoming substance goes beyond this folk superstition. According to Hebrews 11:1, "faith is the substance of . . . things unseen." Although not cited verbatim, *fides est non apparentium* is the guiding subtext. Regarded in the larger context, the notion that substances and powers materialize in a human or divine imagination, imbued with faith and longing, is linked to Paracelsus's declaration in his *Hospital Book* (*Spital-Buch*, 1529) that, "The highest ground of medicine is love" (*der höchste grund der arznei ist die liebe*— I,7:369)—a work that has as its guiding subtext the Pauline hymn of love in 1 Corinthians 13. The Pauline text tells of the emptiness of spiritual gifts without love; the author of the *Hospital Book* recites the vanity of titles, offices, fame, and honor without the combined love and healing art. According to the author, these are a gift from the God who taught Adam language. The pristine language of Adam was thought to express the invisible essences of things. Just as God imparted language to Adam, he enabled the physician to fathom the invisible things in nature and creature:

> Thus, medicine should be grounded in and learned by the doctor as miraculously as language [is founded] in Adam. For just as we cannot see in an herb what (power) is within it, so we cannot see in a human being what his nature wants. . . . The knowledge of concealed things in nature has its teacher outside of nature, from which in consequence experience grows.

> *also sol bei dem arzet die arznei gegründet und gelernet sein, so wunderbarlich wie die sprach in Adam. dan als wenig wir mögent in eim kraut sehen, was darinen ist, als wenig mögent wir auch in einem menschen sehen, was sein natur begert. . . . verborgen ding in der natur zu wissen, nimpt außerhalb der natur seinen lermeister, aus welchen nachfolgent die erfarenheit wechst.* (I,7:370)

The *Hospital Book* contains an exhortation to the rich to aid the poor (I,7:378): there are repeated references to the "psalmist"—an apparent allusion to his long commentary on the psalms, a work already in advanced progress in July 1530. The associations and allusions point toward the focalization of his themes in passages that appear to labor toward the rebirth and revitalization which becomes evident in the great works of the so-called "*Para*-period" (Sudhoff) around 1530. In the context of the eight-book tract on syphilis, faith and imagination are linked; and although only the former is religious, both convey a supernatural power:

For imagination can cause sickness, fear can cause sickness; and so too, joy can cause health; and just as imagination can be good or evil, so, too, it can make healthy or sick. From this it follows that imagination is more than nature and rules it, [that it] takes away the inborn quality and transports the human being, so that the heavens no longer know him, nor the nature of the earth; for he has departed from them all through the imagination.

dan kan imaginatio krankheit machen, kan erschrecken krankheit machen, so kan freude gesundheit machen; und so imaginatio gut und bös sein mag, so mags als wol gesund machen als krank. daraus dan folget, das imagination mer dan die natur ist und regirt sie, nimpt die angeborne eigenschaft hinweg und entsezt den menschen, das in der himel nicht kennet, noch die natur der erden; dan er ist durch imaginirung denen allen entwichen. (I,7:329–330)

Even if there are idolatrous saints or false prophets who seem to effect miracles, the real power effecting these things stems from God and brings about its results through "faith and imagination," "through hope and love" in God:

For there is no one who regards him as a god, who calls himself a prophet or a saint. For all people know that such things [miracles] proceed from God and not from the human being; whether by a true or a false prophet, faith and imagination proceeds [singular!] through hope and love to God.

dan niemant ist da, der den für ein got halt, der sich schon ein propheten oder heiligen nennet. dan alle menschen wissen, das aus got und nicht dem menschen solches get; es sei durch ein rechten oder falschen propheten, so get der glaub und die imagination durch hofnung und liebe in got. (I,7:332)

This is why there are miracles, prophets, and saints among the heathens, too: a problem that still disturbs the author who had once puzzled in the *Volumen Paramirum* over the incongruity of a non-Christian medicine that might be effective. Imagination and faith are overlapping circles of force. In Hebrews, the context of faith as the substance of things longed for but unseen refers to the creation of the visible universe from that which had been invisible. ("By faith we understand that the universe was formed at God's command, so that what is seen was not made out of what was visible.") For Paracelsus, the entire art and skill of the physician lies in discerning the invisible from the visible, the inner from the outer. Commenting on Psalm 110 (111), the author harked back to the iconoclasm of his early work against Christian idolatry. Not shadows nor dreams nor chattering nor singing nor ceremonies can testify to faith in God, but rather the tangible covenant (*bund*) of the Lord's Supper (*das testament des nachtmals Christi*—II,5.2:145). Even the heathens can recognize the things of nature as creations of God. However, the Christian recognizes the Eucharist as an institution or work of God's hands:

> Now it is a work of his hands, for the reason that he created it at the Last Supper. For he has created it who created heaven and earth, as a reminder by the same God that he gave us the day with the sun, fruit with the summer, and so on.

> *nun ist es ein werk seiner hend, dann ursach also hat ers geschaffen uf dem nachtmal. der hats geschaffen, der himel und erden schuf, bei derselbigen gottes gedechtnus zu haben, daß er uns mit der sunnen den tag geben hat, mit dem sumer die frucht und dergleichen.* (II,5.2:147)

The heathens who recognize the visible things of nature as divine works live by the "letter"; the Christians, who are taught by the Holy Spirit to recognize the invisible things of God, live by the invisible spirits—the "virtues" which they recognize within the letters of the world. Paracelsus refers to the visibility of the fruits or grains of the earth not only in this psalm commentary:

> just as little as the grain in the field is a shadow, even so little may we carry out the remembrance of Christ in the Eucharist without the body, blood, and flesh of Christ. For only the body of each thing is the remembrance of God.

> *als wenig das korn im felt ein schatten ist, also wenig mugen wir im nachtmal Christi die gedechtnus volbringen ohn den leip, blut und fleisch Christi. dann allein der leip eins ieglichen dings ist die gedechtnus gottes.* (II,5.2:146)

Elsewhere, too, he evokes the miracle of fruition. He refers to the natural wonder in the eight-book treatise on syphilis, where the growth of grain is described as an alchemistic work:

> Let the gold be the seed, sow the growing power. Let the athanor be the earth, and thus you will raise the gold into fruit. . . . Therefore, what increases there, here in the *corpus* increases in the virtues. In this stands the preparation of medicine. Thus, the effect of the Creator goes forward, as was designed from the beginning.

> *laßt das golt den samen sein, seie du die wachsent kraft. laß den athanor sein die erden, und also wirst du das gold aufbringen in die frucht. . . . also auch was dort am corpus zunimpt, das nimpt hie zu in tugenden. in disem stehet die bereitung der arznei. also gehet des schöpfers wirkung für, als von anbegin fürgenomen ist.* (I,7:265–266)

As we have seen, Paracelsus was like Luther in attaching signal significance to the notion of rebirth and to the doctrine of Christ's real presence in the Eucharist. The universe of the entities, the visible and invisible, the material and spiritual entities, provided Paracelsus a single framework to encompass both the transformations in perishable nature and those in the realm of salvation. This is evident in Paracelsus's work on the Eucharist, *Das Mahl des Herrn* (*The Lord's Supper*), a work composed sometime between 1523 and 1534 (the dates of the reign of Pope Clement VII, to whom the work is dedicated).[150] There are two creatures within the human being: a mortal one created from Adam and an eternal one created from Christ. However, both creatures are substance, for, the tract asserts, without material substance there would be nothing. Without body nothing happens, he concludes, thereby, in tendency, leaning toward the Lutheran position on the Eucharist.[151] To Paracelsus, this means that we have two bodies: the one is from the Father (who is invisible, but whose works have been made visible in creation), the other from the Son (who was made visible in Christ, but whose works are invisible). And both bodies must be fed: the former requires the nourishment that is transformed into flesh and blood by the *archeus*, the alchemist in the stomach; the latter feeds on the bread and wine which are transformed into the invisible spiritual body (ch. 1-5).

Though it appears that the breaking of bread can occur in faith without physically taking the Eucharist, the believer is in any event reborn out of Christ: "Thus, he gives birth to us anew and yet does not break our old form and image" (*Also gebiert er uns neu und zerbricht uns doch die alte Form und das Bildnis nicht*—ch. 12). It is evident that the visible and invisible creatures are united in one as images of God so that a bodily resurrection is assured. Independently, commentators studying Luther and Paracelsus have observed that their eucharistic doctrines are implicated with their respective doctrines of the resurrection. With reference to Paracelsus, Hemleben wrote of the primacy of the doctrine of resurrection in the theology of the Eucharist: "It is clear that Theophrastus was preoccupied, before all theology of the Lord's Supper, with his understanding of the resurrection, [i.e., with] the resurrected body . . ." (*Deutlich ist, daß es dem Theophrast vor aller Abendmahlstheologie um ein Verständnis der Auferstehung, des Auferstehungsleibes geht . . .*).[152] Sommerlath made the similar observation with respect to Luther that, "In the Lord's Supper it comes about, as it came about upon the death of Christ. . . . The body is thus drawn into immortality. . . . Luther could not give express scriptural citations for this view" (*Es geht im Abendmahl, wie es beim Sterben Christi zuging. . . . So wird der Leib hineingezogen in die Unsterblichkeit. . . . Auf ausdrückliche Schriftstellen konnte sich Luther bei dieser Meinung nicht berufen*).[153] Neither Luther nor Paracelsus could offer strict scriptural proofs for the transforming power of the Eucharist. However, the prologue of the Gospel of John, with its evocation of the creation through the eternal Word, was cited by both in favor of their respective interpretations (the Word in John 1:1 and the body of Christ are interpreted by Luther,[154] as well as by Paracelsus,[155] as the same thing). This implies that the visible-material realm interacts with the invisible-spiritual one; and it implies that the corporeality of things is wordlike, so that entities can be seen as bearers of divine meaning. In pursuit of nature and medicine, Paracelsus carried his reading of nature further than did the theologian Luther; and yet his medical-philosophical ideas never relinquished their intended adherence to biblical authority, so that even after he had fallen into disfavor with Protestant critics such as Erastus and Hunnius, attempts understandably continued to be made to synthesize Paracelsian and Lutheran doctrines.

The syntheses and affinities of Paracelsism and Lutheranism must remain as unfathomable and elusive as a fleeting conjunction in the kaleidoscopic metamorphoses of Christian doctrine—unless the relationship of their respective doctrines is approached in a way that is mindful of the differences of their perceived world from our own: the world of Paracelsus and Luther was smaller, bounded on every side by the power of Creator and Redeemer, but also more complex, in enfolding the invisible and visible realms within one another and envisaging an omnipresent struggle among the elements or between the powers of Satan and God. A clearer sense of their crisis-racked experience of being-in-the-world might reveal more about the faith commanded by their doctrines than can apologetic explications presenting their opinions as more coherent and more compatible with modern experience than they really are.

Despite the wretchedness of his failures and homelessness, the ideology of Paracelsus's medicine was being reconfirmed for him in every discipline. In philosophy, the physician sees beyond the outer surface of the body or element to recognize the powers or virtues hidden within; and he operates with them, like God bringing forth the visible creation to reveal invisible intentions. In alchemy, the work of separation is comparable to the Creator's separation of light from darkness (I,7:271), or the Redeemer's resurrection and conferral of rebirth. The imagination of the patient must be informed by faith. The office of the physician fulfills the commandment of love. The theorist of nature sees through the outer surfaces of entities to their life-sustaining virtues, just as the exegete of Scripture looks beyond the outer letter to the essential spirit of truth. Medical and natural theory reflect the clearer light of theology. Theology thus illuminates Paracelsus's pilgrimage through the valley of despair after Basel and Nuremberg.

6 ∎ The World as Mirror

In the year of the Augsburg Diet, 1530, the turbulent and tragic decade of reforms and reversals drew to a close with Germany tottering in an uneasy balance between religious war and the various provisional accords that staved off war without offering any real hope of permanent stability. The prospects included at one extreme the enforcement of the Edict of Worms in a general persecution of all "heretics" and at the other the universal recasting of authority in pursuit of some new and unheard-of order.

In 1530, the world is as adrift in change as Paracelsus is unmoored in neverending peregrinations. In the Spring of 1530, he is granted a brief respite south of Nuremberg at Beratzhausen in the Upper Palatinate, where he is welcomed or tolerated by a Protestant baronial house known for its defiant independence[156]; and this important station, about which unfortunately too little is known, gives him an opportunity to survey his life and work.

Looking back, the pilgrim without a destination nurses his festering anger toward Basel. He recognizes a forlorn condition of wretchedness. It had begun in Esslingen before his season in Nuremberg; and it had been confirmed in that city. With livid contempt, he now recollects the apothecaries and physicians, the wives of wealthy medical men, their eyes as poisonous as snakes (I,8:42).

One can of course ask, with justifiable skepticism, whether these colleagues were truly as wicked as Paracelsus saw them as being, and to what degree his opinion of them projected his own opportunism and ambition. But one should also bear in mind that others reacted similarly to the disappointments of the era. When the expectations awakened by the new religious initiatives went unfulfilled, other voices of protest, similar *cris de coeur*, were raised against the false letter of the new creed and for its true spirit. For Sebastian Franck and the other disappointed radical reformers of this period, faith contracted into dichotomies that were, if less vitriolic, no less manichean than those expressed in Hohenheim's enmity. Passions rose and fell together in this troubled world that had gone into labor to be reborn.

It is not by chance that the Paracelsian terms of moral opprobium, *luxury* and *poison*, are employed by him in analyzing syphilis. Given the nature of the disease, the precarious state of the common weal, and the catastrophic outlook of the outcast, it is not surprising that he should have written in his pivotal work of this period that syphilis "is the greatest disease of the entire world, than which no worse has been found, which spares no one . . ." (*die größte krankheit der ganzen welt ist, da kein ergere nie erfunden, die niemants schonet . . .*—I,8:62). What is surprising, however, is that amid his furious diatribes filled with anxiety and frustration, the characteristic formulations of the *Para*-period came into being in the drafts of *Opus Paragranum*, his seminal treatise on the four pillars of medicine. *Paragranum* presents the "seed," *granum*, of the *Opus Paramirum* that followed immediately afterward. Long heralded by Paracelsus, the debut of the "paramiran" works looks back to the project he had announced in Salzburg, where the "paramiran writings" promised to clarify theological questions; as well as to Basel, where the similarly announced work *in paramiris* was cited in a lecture in a context having to do with the digestive process and its residues (I,5:134). The paramiran writings were intended to provide the keystone of the Paracelsian corpus as a whole. And they do.

If there is an ecstasy of rage, a state that seizes and lifts the mind above itself, crystallizing thoughts that are inchoate yet central to the meanderings of reflection, the *Opus Paragranum* of 1530 was written in an ecstatic rage of this kind. "Reader" (he begins his terse apology, difficult to translate in every word, yet unequivocal in its import): I have meant to bring forth my books, and have not been hindered by any idleness or by my peregrinations, but only by the scorn and derision that I have encountered in Basel and elsewhere. In Basel, I was ridiculed as *Cacophrastus* by those who would steal my good name. They claimed that I had stolen my work. Yet nothing of the kind has ever been written. My writing shows six hundred new formulas (*inventiones*) of which none has ever been heard of or allowed by any ancient or modern philosopher or *medicus*. What is more, my library does not comprise six sheets of paper; and my secretaries can testify that what I write proceeds from my mouth and that in ten years no book has been read by me (*das solches vom*

mund get und in zehen jaren kein buch gelesen offenlich ist—I,8:33).
He goes on to deny the obvious inference that he is a magician: those
who say so are in fact "inventing from the magical in order to wound
me" (*aus dem magischen erdenken, mich zu verlezen*—I,8:33). They
do this, he says, in order to steal his medicine and his good name.
One could add, his identity. Furiously, he reflects upon the "pride"
(*hochmut*) and "winged phantasies of my opponents" (*die fliegenden
fantaseien meiner widersecher*—I,8:35).

Now it is his intention to write about syphilis, though his detractors deride him for not being able to write about any other disease.
He will do so because it befalls rich and poor, and all lands from
Hungary to Spain. They accuse him of malpractice, as he them.
(*Wie gern sprechen ir, du verderbst auch!*—I,8:35) He replies that
they themselves utilize wood, quicksilver, burning, and cutting more
than nature can bear; so that their wood (guiac) is destroying all
patients. And who should drive out the surfeit of quicksilver from
their "bones, brains, or bellies" (I,8:36)? Reading this, one wonders
whether the malpractice alleged against Paracelsus in Nuremberg
might have resulted from the quicksilver treatment of syphilis—an
antidote to which he was theoretically committed, and which was
the major alternative to the guiac that he rejected—but one that had
the bad effects that he described elsewhere graphically as, "a great
winter, from which your body and spirit trembles; thus in mercury
there is a concealed winter, coldness, and snow" (*zu vergleichen
einem großen winter, aus welchem dir zitert dein leib und gemüt; also
ist im mercurio ein verporgner winter, kelten und schnee*—I,7:157).
To have so vividly captured the macrocosmic image of mercury poi-
soning, its uncontrollable shivering and the grey or pallid "snow" of
death, he must have at least witnessed it in person, whether in his
own patients or those of his competitors. "But tell me, what have I
ruined or killed, tell you wretches!" (*sagt mir aber, was hab ich
verderbt oder getöt, sagt ir lauren!*—I,8:36).

He recalls the slur against him that he is a medical Luther, an
association that actually should not have worn so badly in Lutheran
Nuremberg or Beratzhausen. The ulterior motive in calling him this
is to see Luther burned as a heretic, and him too. During the
months of suspense after the Edict of Worms was reinstated against
Protestants in 1529, this countercharge, tantamount to a charge of
cowardice and betrayal, might have touched to the quick those who
were now challenged in their new faith. But to the *Lutherus medicorum*, these aspersions are denigrating for another reason:

Do you think I am only Luther? Insofar as I am gifted beyond that which is required of a Christian, namely, with more of an office than an apostle (that is, with medicine, philosophy, astronomy, alchemy) and you think that I am only Luther? . . . Why do you do this [i.e., cast these aspersions]? Because you hope that Luther will be burned and Theophrastus shall be burned also.

meint ir, ich sei allein Lutherus? dieweil ich uber das so eim christen zustat, sonderlich mit mererm ampt dan ein apostel begabt (das ist mit der arznei, philosophei, astronomei, alchimei) und sol nur Lutherus sein? . . . warumb tunt irs? darumb, ir verhoffent, Luther werd verbrennt und Theophrastus sol auch verbrennt werden. (I,8:43–44)

One might regard this as nothing more than an overweening boast; however, the exact references to medicine, philosophy, astronomy, alchemy do not allow us to do so. Nor do his repeated assurances that he has been made a doctor by God, that his medicine is from God.

The "four pillars" change slightly in the draft prefaces to the *Opus Paragranum*. After this initial reference to a distinct quadrivium (medicine—which should be the sum of all—included as if on an equal plane), he reduces the number to the last three as the pillars on which medicine stands (I,8:49). This is what one might expect: aside from the three primary things, Paracelsus has a habitual impulse to find three things in any analysis. The next draft preface, only slightly calmer than the first, repeats many of his fulminations about Basel, Nuremberg, "Cacophrastus," and the divine calling of medicine; it was written from the same mood and intention. But the second preface knows a quadrivium, a different one, yet one deliberately offered and long maintained: philosophy, astronomy, alchemy—and "the virtues" (*der tugenden*, I,8:54; or *virtutibus*, I,8:68). Sometimes the fourth "pillar" is referred to in the singular, but at least as often in the plural. This makes it doubly incongruent: not a science like the others, and not a singular object. Considered closely, the others are a strange ensemble as well. One would think that philosophy might have subsumed them all. And why isn't anatomy, that is, his own distinctive version of it, included? *Opus Paragranum* has much to say about it, yet it is not included as one of the pillars of medicine. As the pillars are explained by the author, each of the four seems to overlap with the others and to yield further subdistinctions—of invisible and visible, outer and inner, above and below—distinctions that undermine conceptual integrity and obscure definitions.

These confusions can only be obviated when one recalls that, beginning with his earliest Salzburg writings, Paracelsus's mind has been guided by the notion of the created entity as the image of its Creator, and of creation as a crafting of likenesses. The medicine that comes from God is an image of the divine being; it is in fact a reflection of the heretical *quaternary* of the deity: divine father, goddess, son, and spirit, as presented in the *Liber de Sancta Trinitate* of 1524. The first-mentioned three pillars were not sufficient to serve as an image of the deity, because the first, philosophy, corresponds to the passive role of the "goddess," as do the "elements," which are also called *matres* or *mütter*, "mothers." Like the goddess, philosophy is a reflection, no more independent of the thing it reflects than the non-making aspect of the Maker-God. As the *Book of the Trinity* puts it: she is not "powerful" (*gewaltig*); however, she stands in God's place and renders the father "revealed and complete" (*erfült sie gott des vatters statt und macht ihn als einen vatter offenbar und volkomben*—II,3:246). She reveals the father in knowledge, in the mirroring of the mind which is and is not what it reflects. The *Opus Paramirum* makes no mention of the goddess—perhaps because it would have been an inopportune time to do so—but philosophy and nature now stand in an equivalent relation of identity and difference:

So now if the physician is to grow out of nature, what is nature other than philosophy, what is philosophy other than the invisible nature? One who recognizes sun and moon and knows with closed eyes how sun and moon are, has the sun and moon in him as they stand in the heavens and firmament. Now that is philosophy: that it stands in the human being as [it stands] outside impalpably, like someone who sees himself in a mirror.

So nun aus der natur der arzt wachsen sol, was ist die natur anders dan die philosophei, was ist die philosophei anders dan die unsichtige natur? einer der die sonn und mon erkent und weiß mit zugetanen augen, wie die sonne oder der mon ist, der hat sonn und mon in ihme, wie sie im himel und firmament stehen. das ist nun die philosophei, das sie im menschen wie außerhalben ungreiflich stande, wie einer der sich selbs im spiegel sicht. (I,8:71)

In the universe of the entities, consciousness is and is not its intuited object; an intuiting subject is and is not the object of consciousness. The other represents the one and reveals it, just as the goddess with no power of her own is and is not the same as the omnipotent divine Creator. Nature as an object of reflection is the mother of the reflection in the mind—is mind.

> And when the outer is no longer there, the inner is no longer in the steel [mirror] either; for the outer is a mother of the inner. Thus, the human being is an image in a mirror, put into it through the four elements, and with the passing of the elements follows the passing of the human being.

> *und wan das eußer nimer da ist, so ist das inner auch nit mer im stahel; dan das eußer ist ein mutter des innern. also ist der mensch ein bildnus in eim spiegel, gesezt hinein durch die vier element und nach der zergehung der elementen folget die zergehung des menschen.* (I,8:72)

If any thought expressed by Paracelsus can be appropriately taken out of its context to reveal new and equally suggestive meanings, it is this notion of reciprocality. Outer and inner, nature and soul, are there for one another. With nature, the soul vanishes, a sobering thought in view of the current destruction of species. But for Paracelsus, the context and intentions are mystical: the female divine principle in nature is the elements in a passive state and *sophia* in an active one. The *labor sophiae* effects a transcendent activation of the elements (also known as *matres*—material as the womb of things), yielding a "second paradise" in which there is no disease (I,3:238). In the sphere of knowledge, "philosophy" is a mirror image: "Thus philosophy is nothing else but the entire knowledge and recognition of the thing, which gives the reflection in the mirror" (*so ist die philosophei nichts anders, allein das ganz wissen und erkantnus des dings, das den glanz im spiegel gibt*—I,8:72). What follows then is a knotted utterance that seems to indicate that the utter nullity and dependence of the figure in the mirror constitutes knowledge of it. We might say that by being nothing but what it reflects, the reflection is "a dead image" (*ein tote bildnus*), hence a true one, a dead certainty, so to speak. As material (as elements or "mothers"), the creature is transient. However, a kind of divine philosophy appears as an elevating true mirror image of things, and *sophia* as a perfected magnification of debased matter. The debased mothers and the transcendent *sophia* occupy their places within the scheme of ideas as projections from the divine female principle in the scheme of creation and reflection.

Just as *philosophy* corresponds to the elements as "mothers" and to the "goddess," *astronomy* corresponds to the Father in the trinity, *alchemy* to the Son, and the *virtues* to Spirit. Philosophy and astronomy overlap in a way that makes sense only because they are the image of a transcendent unity:

> Now that the human being in his composition shall be considered by every physician, so know now in the second ground of astronomy, which is the upper part of philosophy, through which the human being can be entirely understood, how their bodies are to be understood and recognized through the upper sphere as in the lower one of the microcosm, as one firmament, one star, one nature and one being, which is subdivided in figure and form.
>
> Now astronomy is here the second ground and comprises two parts of the human being, his air and his fire, just as philosophy has comprised two parts, earth and water. Now as was said in [respect to] philosophy, I also want astronomy to be explained in particular, thus that in the human being are the heavens. . . .

> *So nun der mensch in seiner zusamensezung sol ganz fürgenomen werden durch einen ieglichen arzt, so wisset iezt in dem andern grund der astronomei, das dan der ober teil der philosophei ist, durch den der mensch ganz erkent wird, wie ir corpora sollen verstanden und erkannt werden durch die obern sphaer also in der undern microcosmi, wie ein firmament, ein gestirn, ein natur und ein wesen da sei under geteilter gestalt und form.*
>
> *Nun ist die astronomei hie der ander grund und begreift zwei teil des menschen, sein luft und sein feuer, zugleicherweis wie die philosophei begriffen hat auch zwen teil, die erden und das wasser. nun wie gesagt ist in der philosophei, wil ich auch, das hie in sonderheit gehalten werd in der astronomei, also das im menschen der himel sei. . . . (I,8:91)*

Astronomy is not usually identified by Paracelsus as a part of philosophy, and not usually identified with two elements; but it is often identified with the heavens that exist both above and within. Moreover, the heavens that are known through astronomy are frequently, as here, referred to as a "father" of the human being: "Therefore, it is furthermore my intention to add that the human being has his father in the heavens and also in the air, and is a child that is made and born from the air and the firmament" (*Also ist weiter mein fürnemen fürzufaren, das der mensch sein vatter habe im himel und auch im luft, und ist ein kind, das aus dem luft und aus dem firmament gemacht ist und geborn*—I,8:92). This does not mean simply that God the father of the human being is in heaven. The heavens are the father of the human being: "Thus inasmuch as the human being is made like the stars and the stars before him and he from them, thus there must be paternal work in the son as in the human being" (*Also dieweil der mensch gleich ist gemacht dem gestirn und das gestirn vor ime und er aus ime, so müssen vetterlich arbeit im son ligen wie im menschen*—I,8:98). The relationship is hierarchical and at the same time cognitive: "For the son follows after his father and not beside or with him" (*dan der son get nach seim vatter und nicht neben im oder mit ime*—I,8:98). The notion of a celestial paternal lineage transfers anatomy from observation to mystical intuition: "Shouldn't it be [obligatory] for the physician to consider how the human being inherits and possesses his father's anatomy? And no one can take that from him, and the son cannot be recognized without the father . . ." (*sol es dan dem arzt nicht sein zu betrachten, so ein mensch seins vaters anatomei ererbt und besizt? und das mag im niemants nemen und der son mag on den vater nicht erkent werden, sonder durch den vater. . .*—I,8:98). What this means is that the functioning of the human organism, as well as disease, is "inherited" from the heavens: "Now the heavens are also sick. . . . [For] the human being inherits this; for his [human] heaven follows after the father . . ." (*Nun ist der himel auch krank. . . . der mensch erbt das; dan sein himel folget dem vatter hernach . . .*—I,8:105). Paracelsus goes on to add a stipulation that makes it possible for the human being not to become ill from the heavens; but the stipulation does not obviate the paternal image relationship, nor does it render the whole notion any more empirical or any less mystical.

The final draft of *Paragranum* explains alchemy as the third pillar of medicine in a manner suggesting the completion of a flawed creation through the Redeemer:

Now further, to the third ground on which medicine stands, [it] is alchemy. If the physician is not skilled and experienced in it in the highest and greatest [degree], everything is in vain as far as his art is concerned. For nature is so subtle and keen in its things, that it cannot be used without great skill; for it brings nothing to light that is perfect on its own; rather the human being must complete it. This completion is called alchemy.

Nun weiter zu dem dritten grund, darauf die arznei stehet, ist die alchimei. wo hierin der arzt nicht bei dem höchsten und größten geflissen und erfaren ist, so ist es alles umbsonst, was sein kunst ist. dan die natur ist so subtil und so scharpf in iren dingen, das sie on große kunst nicht wil gebrauchet werden; dan sie gibt nichts an tag, das auf sein stat vollendet sei, sonder der mensch muß es vollenden. dise vollendung heißet alchimia. (I,8:181)

Just as nature acting through the stars and the season of summer brings fruit to ripeness, and just as the stomach transforms things into flesh and blood, so also medicine through alchemy serves to transform and to perfect, doing so in accordance with the hidden *arcana*, the forces or virtues in nature:

Thus is alchemy the external stomach, which prepares for the stars what belongs to them. It is not as they say, that alchemy makes gold, makes silver; here the project is: make *arcana* and direct them against the diseases; that is the end, that is the ground. . . . Thus nature and the human being are to be joined and brought together in health and in diseases.

da ist nun alchimia der eußer magen, der da bereit dem gestirn das sein. nicht als die sagen, alchimia mache gold, mache silber; hie ist das fürnemen mach arcana und richte dieselbigen gegen den krankheiten; da muß er hinaus, ist also der grund. . . . also wöllen die natur und der mensch zusamen in gesuntheit und in krankheiten verfügt werden und zusamen vergleicht und gebracht. (I,8:185)

The refinement of the health-giving arcane virtues is a "second birth": "Inasmuch as by one process all *arcana* are born in fire, and fire is its earth and this earth [has] the sun with it, and earth and firmament [are] *one* thing in this second birthgiving" (*wiewol durch ein proceß alle arcana werden im feur geboren, und das feur ist sein erden und dise erden ist die sonn damit, und ist erden und firmament e i n ding in diser andern geberung*—I,8:187). What has already been associated with philosophy and astronomy—mother and father, earth and heavens—is implicated in this process of a "second birth" by fire. A life-giving death, this process is the same as that by which the seed that rots in the earth grows and rises out of the ground: "And as the seed that becomes rotten in the earth before it grows and thereafter goes into its fruit . . ." *(und wie das korn, das faul wird in der erden, vor dem und es wachst, und darnach in seine frücht gehet . . ."*—I,8:187). Like Christ at the Judgment, the alchemist separates good and evil:

> Who would contradict that in all good things a poison lies hidden and exists; everyone has to confess that this is so. And since this is so, my question is this: mustn't one separate the poison from the good and take the good but not the bad? Indeed, one must.

> *Welcher ist der, der da widerrede, das nit in allen guten dingen auch gift ligt und sei; dis muß ein ietlicher bekennen. so nun das also ist, so ist mein frag, muß man nit das gift vom guten scheiden und das gute nemen und das böse nit? ja, man muß.* (I,8:197)

The notion that poison infects all things appears as the medical or alchemical equivalent of Luther's sense of the omnipresence of evil. This affinity with the Lutheran worldview is underscored by the fact that Paracelsus does not offer any evidence to prove the presence of poison in all things, but instead appeals to the reader to confess as much: "everyone has to confess that this is so" *(dis muß ein ietlicher bekennen).*

Moreover, just as philosophy revealed by way of reflection, and astronomy by giving rise to its son, alchemy too has the task of revealing what would otherwise lie concealed in nature:

> Thus [what] is contained in alchemy, to be acknowledged here [as a part of] medicine, is the cause of the great concealed virtue that lies in the things of nature, which are not revealed to anyone, unless alchemy makes them manifest and brings them forth.

So nun so vil ligt in der alchimei, dieselbige hie in der arzneit so
wol zu erkennen, ist die ursach der großen verborgenen tugent, so
in den dingen ligt der natur, die niemand offenbar sind, allein es
mache sie dan die alchimei offenbar und brings herfür. (I,8:191)

The virtues concealed in nature are revealed by the alchemist, just
as the Holy Spirit is made manifest after and through the Son. In
nature, the virtues are many and varied: "Now you see that a thing
does not have only one virtue, but rather many virtues. As you see
in flowers that they don't have only one color. . . . Thus, too, are to be
understood the manifold virtues that lie in the things" (*nun sehet ir,*
das ein ding nit allein ein tugent hat sonder vil tugent. als ir sehet in
den blumen, die nit allein ein farben haben. . . . also ist auch von
mancherlei tugenden zu verstehen, so in den dingen ligent—I,8:192).
Each of the four pillars of medicine has its double, macrocosmic and
microcosmic, aspect. The fourth is both the moral virtue in the
physician and the objective virtues within nature: "the fourth pillar
is virtue and it should remain with the physician until death; and
[it] concludes and maintains the other three pillars" (*die vierte seul*
sei die tugend und bleibe beim arzet bis in der tot, die da beschließ
und erhalt die anderen drei seulen—I,8:56). What he says of astronomy and philosophy can be said of all four pillars: "they are not, however, separate arts or separate knowledges, that is, sciences; for one
is in all" (*es seind aber nit geschiden künst oder geschidene wissen,*
das ist scientiae; dan eins ist in allen—I,8:147). "everything is one"
(*ist alles e i n s*—I,8:146). This is not pantheism or materialism: the
one that is in all things is the divine image which is both creation
and birth, a likeness that relates all to one as offspring or artifacts
are related to their sire or maker. This is why the humors that correspond to the elements—defined since Aristotle as divisible and
seen as part of a nature that is eternal and uncreated—are not the
avenue to knowledge or healing for Paracelsus. The informing
divine image constitutes things as indivisible in a life process that
has a beginning and an end, a creation and a destruction that follows the general restoration of all things in the *Annus Platonis.*
This is why Paracelsus can declare that, "medicine is the end of all
things" (*die arznei ist das end der dingen allen*—I,8:147). Many
alchemists would have taken Aristotle to task for denying the muta-
bility of species; but for Paracelsus, Aristotle is especially odious
because he is perceived as alien to a nature that is the true teacher

of the physician (I,8:69-70). Obviously, Paracelsus underestimated Aristotle and overestimated himself. But we should not lose sight of the point of disagreement: nature clearly demonstrates that the entities are subject to transformation; and in the view of Paracelsus only alchemy and not medieval Aristotelian science recognizes this great truth.

The instructive wonder is that all things hang together in the chaos-infused shell of the cosmos:

> You see the air: that it is a corpus of the firmament, for it stands in it. Now, it is no corpus at all and yet is that which carries the stars, and no one can touch it. Thus is the nature and mystery of these things, that the chaos (air) lifts and supports the stars, sun, and moon. We do not see this chair, nor this support.
>
> *Den luft sehet ir, das er ist ein corpus des firmaments, dan er stet in im. nun ist er kein corpus und ist doch der, der das gestirn tregt, und niemants greift in. also ist die natur und mysterium derselbigen, das der chaos hebt und tregt das gestirn, sonn und mon. wir sehent disen stul nit, noch disen trager.* (I,8:162)

What follows is the usual comparison of the cosmos to an egg. In this case, the stars are the yolk and the element of air or chaos is the albumen that holds them in place. Even when it is twisted out of shape, the guiding idea of likeness governs the thinking of Paracelsus. The stars shine through and impart "impressions" to the human creature, as sunshine passes through an open window (I,8:163). In order to receive the astral force, there has to be a medium in the human creature that carries it and attracts it: this medium is the "great divine order," the order comparable to that of the cosmic one, but within the human being (I,8:163–164). The heavenly bodies have their counterparts within, for

> all planets have within the human being their likeness and signature and their children, and the heaven is their father. For the human being is made after the heavens and earth, for he is made out of them, as the child must be like his parents. . . .
>
> *alle planeten haben im menschen ir gleich ansehung und signatur und ire kinder, und der himel ist ir vater. dan der mensch ist nach himel und erden gemacht, dan er ist aus inen gemacht.*

so er nun aus inen gemacht ist, so muß er seinen eltern gleich sein. . . . (I,8:164)

Here, three ideas are connected in showing the relation of what is above to what is below: the ideas of the "signature," of the likeness, and of the offspring. The first pertains to the realm of the sign, the second to that of the picture, and the third to that of paternity. In order to comprehend Paracelsus's understanding of causality, it is necessary to take into account how interbred and tainted with one another are his notions of meaning, making, and spawning. A cause does not cast across a void in order to conjure up an effect, different in kind and indifferent in value or meaning. For Paracelsus, effect is utterance, imprint, child. Causes engender their effects in a continuous transformation of the whole, in the egg of the world. As an armchair philosopher in a more secure century, Hume could question the attribution of causal determination to events that repeatedly occur in sequence. Paracelsus, whose recognition of causes was a matter of life and death for the patient and of honor or disgrace for the physician, was driven by the agonizing uncertainty of causal relationships both to reify and personify causality, to assimilate it thereby to doctrinal patterns and mental habits of faith.

The *Opus Paramirum* of 1531 recalls the *Volumen Paramirum*, the early work on the five *entia* of disease. In order to gain an overview of Paracelsian theory in its evolution, the reader would do well to consider the parallels of plague etiology and the five "substances" of disease as delineated at the end of chapter two; the heretical divine quaternary in chapter three; the parallel of the divine persons with the three principles of sulphur, salt, and mercury at the end of chapter four; and the importance of the eucharistic substance or body of Christ, as discussed at the end of chapter five. In the next chapter, it will be demonstrated that these parallels constitute what Paracelsus himself regarded as his *theorica*, a "theory" that also incorporated a semiotic dimension in the doctrine of the signatures. We cannot refer to the parallels among his terms as a system. There are too many inconsistencies, too few coherent definitions. Yet in order to interpret Paracelsian theory, it is surely necessary to observe that motives are recurrent. Intuitive similarities or likenesses anchor the authority of his speculations concerning the objects in nature, the terms of knowledge, and the qualities of life; concerning the role of the *elements or humors*, the *stars*, of *that which is poisonous or good* in nature, and of the *effects of the spirit* in nature and mind; in other words, concerning *philosophy, astronomy, alchemy,* and *virtues*. These in turn correspond to the *labor sophiae* (in which the elements or "mothers" are perfected), to *sulphur* as fire (associated with the divine Father, perhaps with the God of the Old Testament who appeared before Moses in a burning bush), to *salt*, as that which is fixed (the reborn body, the transformed substance, or the "work" of the hands in the Eucharist), and to *mercury*, as that which flows or wafts (as does the spirit, as an agent of mediation and as a transformation by the power of faith and imagination).

It is the cumulative force of these parallels that militates against the old medicine, when in the *Opus Paramirum* disease is attributed to a *substantiae ens*. The four humors are rejected in favor of what are here called the three "humors," salt, mercury, and sulphur (I,9:51). The reference to the nonhumoral principles as "humors" is either a slip, one of many inconsistencies; or it is a deliberate displacement of the old term by the new: what counts is above all the identification of the dynamic triad, and the affirmation that a "substance" or entity is indeed at the root of both disease and health. The physician acquires his knowledge of this through experience with the alchemist's fire:

> The first [kind of experience needed by the physician] is that which he acquires from the fire by means of which he pursues the vulcanic art in transmutation, fixation, exaltation, reduction, perfection and other things related thereto. In this experience, the three substances are found whose species and nature and quality is [found] in the entire world, comprised in all natures.
>
> *die erst ist die so er aus dem feuer nimpt, in dem so er die vulcanische kunst treibt in der transmutirung, fixirung, exaltirung, reducirung, perficirung und andern anhangenden dingen disen zugehörig. in diser erfarung werden die drei substanzen erfunden, was art und was natur und eigenschaft so in der ganzen welt ist, begriffen in allen naturen.* (I,9:43)

In some writings, the unity of the three is tantamount to life itself; in the *Opus Paramirum* the three are more like a carved figure that is subsequently "painted over" with life: "Thus is life too. We are carved by God and composed in three substances, [and] thereupon painted over with life" (*also ist das leben auch. ein mal sind wir geschnizlet von got und gesezt in die drei substanzen, nachfolgend ubermalet mit dem leben . . .*—I,9:61). Inconsistencies result here from an imperfect synthesis of the terms of likeness and making: Paracelsus wants to see creation both as action and as process; the former in accordance with his biblicism, and the latter in conformity with his laboratory work. But in the mixture, biblicism is preponderant, so that, where he seems to be most attuned to process, he is in fact most biblical, as in his account of the origin of human life in a watery matrix:

> The world has been born from the matrix, the human being too, and therefore all in all what exists as a creature is from the matrix. Hence, it is necessary to describe what the matrix is. Matrix is that from which the human being grows and subsists. Thus, everything must be in it invisibly, that is in the four elements. In the same way as the world is the matrix of all things that grow, thus too, is there [a] matrix in the body, which has the same anatomy. Before heavens and earth were created, the spirit of God hovered upon the water and was sustained by it. This water was matrix; for in the water heaven and earth were created and in no other matrix. In it, the spirit of God was carried, which is the spirit that is in the human being, which all other creatures do not have.

> *die welt ist aus der matrix geboren, der mensch auch und also für und für, was da ist ein creatur, daselbe alles ist aus der matrix. darauf ist not, was matrix sei zu beschreiben. nun ist matrix die, aus welcher der mensch wachst und ist. darumb so müssen da unsichtig sein, alles das da ist in den vier elementen. zu gleicher weise wie die welt matrix ist aller wachsenden dingen, also ist auch matrix im leibe dieselbig mit gleicher anatomei zuhalten. vor dem und himel und erden beschaffen ward, da schwebet der geist gottes auf dem wasser und ward ob im tragen. dis wasser war matrix; dan in dem wasser ward beschafen himel und erden und in keiner andern matrix nicht. in deren ward der geist gottes tragen, das ist der geist gottes der im menschen ist, den alle andere creaturen nicht haben.* (I,9:190–191)

The notion that the world and man ultimately both emerge from the matrix of the water leads us to expect a naturalistic hypothesis; but what follows is entirely predicated on the literal authority of the first verses of Genesis, in the best medieval tradition: the dark water that was separated by the firmament contained the *Spiritus Creator* and, with the spirit, all invisible prototypes of everything in the world. As hypothetical nature, this would provide us no grounds for asserting the uniqueness of the human creature. Yet Christian doctrine requires it. Hence, it is forcibly adduced from the imagined schema of *creatio ex aqua vel matrice*. Paracelsus remained serenely confident that his theory accorded with Christian doctrine.

By the year 1531, his early hopes of establishing himself in an episcopal or imperial city with the patronage or at least the recognition of an important ruler or citizen had been dashed. The publication of his books on syphilis had been halted in Nuremberg. Even in a minor place on home ground, Sankt Gallen in Switzerland, the site of an extended sojourn in 1531, he was unsuccessful in his overtures to Joachim Watt (Vadianus), the physician and Humanist to whom the third draft of *Opus Paramirum* is dedicated. The author was indeed luckless. However, by now the outlines of his speculative theories were complete. He was increasingly inclined to see the outer failure of his career as a testimony to the intrinsic validity of his theory.

The Book of Knowledge (*Das Buch der Erkanntnus*) is a small and unusual tract which is thought by Goldammer to have resulted from Paracelsus's contact with Sebastian Franck around this time.[157] The little work indeed displays Franck's sense of paradox and his characteristic mixture of defiance and resignation. It begins: "Better is rest than unrest, *sanctissimi mortalium mortales*, more useful, however, [is] unrest than rest . . ." (*Besser ist rue / dann unrue / sanctissimi mortalium mortales / nutzerß aber unrue / dann rue . . .*).[158] The German *rue* and *unrue* can be translated as harmony and discord or war and peace, as well. All conflicts and frustrations are sublimated in a divine plan. Ultimately the more perfect shall govern the less perfect. This is the dictum of a man convinced that his ideas will prevail against adversity, certain even that adversity vouchsafes their truth.

Paracelsus's other writings are not more consistent than the *Opus Paramirum*: it is a deliberately conceived work that attempts to present his central medical-philosophical theories, as founded upon the experience of nature. No palpable proofs of experience in our sense of this term are offered in support of his assertion that all diseases arise from the dynamic three, any more than proof is offered for his opposing claim that all diseases stem from the stars. We cannot arrive at what is characteristic and consistent in the thought of Paracelsus by seizing upon his loose and contradictory statements of causality. We must look instead for the legitimizing patterns of his discourse. These are thrown into clearer relief when his writing is examined in reference to the doctrinal crises of the period. Paracelsus overtly alludes to the controversies over the claims of faith against works, and over the invisible presence of a divine power or substance in the sacraments and throughout the created world. We have seen that the focal point of his theory is the notion of the *image*: the three primary things, plus the elements and *sophia*, are an image of the extended trinity; the pillars of medical knowledge are a kind of afterimage of the quaternary deity, as delineated in his Salzburg theological writing. The authority of the physician-theorist in recognizing the invisible from the visible mirrors the authority imparted by Christ as the God made visible. Just as God is invisibly present for the believer, notably within the sacraments, so also the arcane forces and virtues are invisibly present in nature for the physician. Moreover, the virtues are increasingly acknowledged by Paracelsus to be manifestations of the invisible God. Just as faith and the sacraments exercise a transforming power for Luther, they do so as well for Paracelsus, who takes the further step of discussing the natural power of the imagination as akin to the transforming power of faith. What distinguishes the two so decisively is of course Paracelsus's extension of the trope of the divine image from the first human creature to all of creation, with the corollary elevation of the imagination as a kind of creation by picturing.

These distinctions between Luther and Paracelsus are sharp precisely because of their shared mentality and common ground. Luther's hidden God cannot be compared to what is in this world. Hence, his theology cannot offer detailed blueprints for nature (though his sense of nature as a testimony to the wisdom of the Creator may have been hardly less keen and lyrical than Paracelsus's). One can find in Luther's early lectures or casual utterances in the *Table Talks* notions similar to those that motivated

Paracelsus's theories of nature.[159] Yet for the most part, Luther's nature retains only a lesser significance as a source of contemplation and exhortation, of homiletic metaphors and rhetorical figures. Paracelsus, by contrast, assimilates nature to the mysteries of faith: by carrying over the mysteries of faith into nature.

7 ■ The Illumination of Theory

The Paracelsus who wandered during the 1530s, always in the shadow of his Basel fiasco, forever generalizing the profile of his academic detractors and struggling to assert the theoretical defenses of his medicine, might resemble a contemporary academic intellectual who became convinced of his reforming mission during the Sixties, got caught up in the excitement of unfolding events, and found himself transported by the conditions of the moment into some high but tenuous academic position, only to encounter humiliation and defeat. Radicalized by his rejection and isolated in the climate of retrenching orthodoxy, his overt struggle for reform and personal recognition becomes sublimated in an increasingly elaborate exposition of theory. Paracelsian theory serves as the weapon of last resort, wielded to undercut the conceptual-metaphysical foundations of his opponents.

Paracelsian theory drew on contrasting sources of biblicism and dissenting Spiritualism: the former literalistic, the latter proclaiming spirit over letter. Both were recourses of religious outcasts in his time. He subsumed them with the ascetic ethos of a Franciscan mendicant. Monklike in his celibacy and apostolic self-characterizations, he can seem in the writings of his nadir period almost like a desert anchorite, beset by garish visionary terrors reminiscent of those in Matthias Grünewald's painting of the "Temptation of St. Anthony." Beset by the terrors of night, this solitary pilgrim without an itinerary refocused the power of a speculative faith, vested in the intelligibility of a universe of signs, revealed by the divine illumination of his theory.

Something of the forlorn circumstances that inspired several works of this period pervades his *Books on the Invisible Diseases* of 1531–1532 (*Die Bücher von den unsichtbaren Krankheiten*). The invisible diseases are those that are visible in their symptoms, but caused and cured by the invisible faith or imagination of the temporal or spiritual human creature:

If the works are visible and that from which they come invisible, be advised that they are not invisible for any other reason than that we do not walk in the light which makes such things visible. And it is just as it is when in dark night we hear a bell: we cannot see it, and yet the work of the bell we do see, that is, we hear it.

sind die werk sichtbar und das davon sie komen unsichtbar, so wissent das sie nit anders unsichtbar sind, dan das wir im selbigen liecht nicht wandelen, welches dasselbige sichtbar macht. und ist gleich als wen wir bei der finstern nacht ein glocken hörten, die mögen wir nicht sehen und doch das werk der glocken sehen wir wol, das ist wir hörens. (I,9:253)

One can imagine the wanderer along perilous pathways, hearing in the dark of night the church bells that announced the presence of some invisible town: to walk in the light that makes such things visible was for the traveler a matter of faith in God, but it was also a matter of confidence in his theory of the behavior of the invisible spirits that operated at night. In lending credence to these spirits, the wanderer between cities and worlds expressly rejected the common late-medieval folk piety that accorded to the fourteen auxiliary saints the power to heal, and even to inflict, specific maladies. In the sixteenth century, the popular pious superstitions of the saints were being replaced by Paracelsus, Agrippa, and others with a more reflective, less personalized teaching of magic. Paracelsus's theory of magic considered the effect of imagining illicit sex with a woman: the power of the imagination could give rise to real incubi and succubi from an unchaste sperm carried "by the spirits which wander at night" (*durch die geist, die zu nacht wandeln*):

They carry it to destinations and places where it can be hatched out, as for example among the worms, toads, and similar impure animals. For there there occurs an *actus* of the night spirits with this sperm, involving such animals, as well as with witches, from which many strange monsters are born, of which there is no number, yet they are frightful for our eyes to countenance. . . . Truly, if a human being considers it in himself, [considers] more than I want to write here of this sperm, who would not want to swear an oath to become married?

die tragen in an end und an örter, da er ausgebrütet mag werden,
als unter die würm, krötten und dergleichen unreine tier. dan do
geschicht ein actus von den nachtgeistern mit diser sperma an
solchen tieren, auch mit hexen, daraus dan vil seltzamer monstra
geboren werden deren kein zal seind, aber doch erschreckenlich
im angesicht unserer augen. . . . fürwar so es ein mensch in im
selbst betrachtete, mer dan ich hieher schreib von diseer sperma,
wer wolt ein eid schweren nicht elich zu werden? (I,9:300–301)

Continuing, Paracelsus makes it clear that the monsters born from
the imagination retain the potency of the imagination, and with it
the power to kill:

> Now, take note also of the nature of such monsters. Insofar as
> they derive their origin from the strong imagination, such imag-
> ination also informs these monsters. Therefore, you should
> know this indicates the origin of the basilisk whose true form
> and shape no one can really know. . . . For death follows so quick-
> ly from the sight of it, that no one has time to describe it. For
> such a fierce imagination, which it bears so ferociously full of
> poison in its eyes, arises from the birth of incubuses and suc-
> cubuses.

> *Nun merket auch auf die art solcher monstrorum. dieweil sie aus*
> *der starken imagination iren ursprung nemen, so hangt solche*
> *imagination auch eingebilt denselbien monstris. darauf ir wissen*
> *sollen, das gar nahend hie der ursprung des basilisken ist, des*
> *form und gestalt niemants grüntlich wissen mag. . . . dan so*
> *schnel folgt der tot durch sein gesicht, das nimants der weile hat*
> *in zubeschreiben. dan die heftig imagination, die er so heftig mit*
> *vollem gift in seinen augen hat, nimpt sich aus der geburt* incu-
> bi *und* succubi. . . . (I,9:301)

The basilisk that cannot be confronted without the death of the
beholder is a medieval superstition revived by speculation. In terms
that echo the necessity of faith in the invisible powers of God,
Paracelsus admonishes the reader that human beings truly can be
possessed by a spirit—though, as a physician, he is cautious about
equating the possessed with the devil (I,9:256). At his most rational, Paracelsus could point out that the superstitions that resulted

in women being accused as witches were in reality even more prevalent in the Roman Catholic Church itself (*so doch die superstitiones in der römischen kirchen mer sind, dan bei allen disen frauen und hexen*—I,14:142). However, it would be mistaken to conclude from this that Paracelsus was on the side of reason against superstitious credulousness. In confident moods, he boasted of his knowledge of the generation of artificial life by means of a *kunst spagirica* (I,11:316–317). In reconfirming the existence of legendary giants and elemental spirits, he conflated faith and credulity by arguing that those who refuse to believe in such creatures by the same token refuse to believe in Christ:

> The giants are too powerful and strange for us . . . therefore we don't want to give credence to them and [instead] make a ghost of them. As we likewise do to Christ, [who] is too powerful for us, we also want to do to the giants, so that there should be no one against us whom we should fear.
>
> *die risen sind uns zu stark und zu seltsam . . . drumb wollen wir sie nichts lassen gelten und ein gespenst draus machen. also wollen wir auch Christo tun, ist uns auch zu stark, wollen im auch also wie den risen tun, domit niemants sei der uns zuwider stande oder den wir förchten dörften.* (I,14:143–144)

To doubt the unseen creatures of nature is therefore like denying a Christ whose works and omnipresent powers are also unseen.

The theory of the invisible diseases has been praised as an anticipation of modern psychiatry. This is an estimation that should only merit acceptance when one considers the abuses of the concept of the unconscious—which, at worst, may indeed represent something too close for comfort to the intention represented by Paracelsus's invisible diseases: a *carte blanche* for the powers of discernment and council claimed by the physician-therapist, as well as a pretext for assertions about the inner life of others, and a catch-all excuse for blaming the failure of therapy on the patient rather than the therapist.

It would be difficult to neatly characterize Paracelsus with respect to the rational understanding of the human psyche. While he sometimes rejects old Catholic superstitions, he replaces them with new or revised superstitions of his own. Though he does not share Luther's proclivity to ascribe every spirit except the Holy Spirit to the cohorts of Satan, the physician, like the doctor of Holy Scripture, insists on faith in Christ as the touchstone of truth. If Paracelsus handles this touchstone differently, this is because, for him, creation is not only the ruined Paradise or the kingdom of Lucifer. As we have seen, nature is, to a greater degree than for Luther, a gloss on the Scriptures, a continuous translation of the invisible things of God into the visible ones of creation. For Paracelsus, the light of nature reveals a far more differentiated landscape than it could for the author of the doctrine of the two kingdoms. The dichotomous worlds of doctrine are as if further broken down by Paracelsus into sundry twilight realms of spirit. In his thought, intermediate zones buffer the boundary between the denizens of evil spirits on the one hand and the inner sanctums of divine forces and virtues on the other. The ambivalent power of the imagination and faith is balanced between the two sides. Luther's childhood ambiance of popular beliefs concerning witches and magic spells was no doubt akin to Paracelsus's experience of the reality of the unseen.[160] The mature Luther did not discard such notions in pursuing his central concerns with Scripture and the doctrines derived from it. The rank undergrowth of spirits and witches survived—as it obviously does in the imagination of many religious and secular minds even today. If, for Luther, it persisted in the shadows of the dichotomy of God and Satan, for Paracelsus, at least in his better moments, this twilight sphere could be countenanced without damning it as satanic, as when he reflects that corals have the virtue of warding off *phantasma*, which are "night-spirits," some of which are good and some bad, that haunt and obsess people (I,2:41). His readiness to regard such things earned him ill-repute as a sorcerer in his century, and equally undeserved adulation as a daring explorer of psychic depths in ours.

A powerful theoretical corollary of Paracelsus's understanding of the forces and virtues in nature is his characteristic concept of the signature. The signature is the outward, visible sign or appearance that bespeaks the inner, invisible property or virtue of the thing:

Nature designates every plant that proceeds from it for that to which it is good. Hence, if one wants to learn what nature has designated, one should recognize it by the sign for the virtues that are in the things. For every physician should know that all the forces that are in the natural things are recognized by the signs; from which it follows then that the physiognomy and chiromancy of natural things should be understood to the highest degree by the physician.

Die natur zeichnet ein ietlichs gewechs so von ir ausgêt zu dem, darzu es gut ist. darumb wan man erfaren wil, was die natur gezeichnet hat, so sol mans an dem zeichen erkennen, was tugent im selbigen sind. wan das sol ein ietlicher arzt wissen, das alle kreft, so in den natürlichen dingen sind, durch die zeichen erkant werden, daraus dan folgt, das die physionomei und chiromancei der natürlichen dingen zum höchsten sollent durch ein ietlichen arzt verstanden werden. (I,2:86)

It might appear from this that the author has in mind only plants and that his theorizing pertains to the occult sciences; but this is not the case. The signatures mark everything in nature, including everything that pertains to the human creature: "for nothing is without a sign. . . . and nothing is so secret in the human being that it does not have an outward sign" (*dan nichts ist on ein zeichen. . . . und nichts ist so heimlichs im menschen, das nit ein auswendig zeichen an im hat*—I,2:86). "The same [doctrine of the] signature has gone quite out of custom and has been very much forgotten, from which many errors follow" (*die selbig signatur ist gar aus dem brauch komen und ir gar vergessen worden, aus dem dan groß irsal folget*—I,2:86). Like every other truth, that of the signature comes ultimately from God: "Nature has been so highly qualified by God, that not by hearing, but by the light of nature, all this has to be experienced . . ." (*die natur ist so hoch begabt von got, das nit mit hören, sonder mit dem liecht der natur das alles muß erfaren werden . . .*—I,2:87). There were undoubtedly superstitious folk sources for the notion of the signature; but in the context of Paracelsus's philosophy as a whole, it is simply another variant of the central notion of creation as an image production: "Thus the works themselves give the sign [for] what they are, as a painted picture gives its sign that it is a painting . . ." (*Also geben die werk das zeichen was es ist, wie ein gemalts bilt gibt sein zeichen, das ein gemelt ist . . .*—I,1:79). "Thus the signs that themselves tell what it is, teach the physician what he should be" (*also die zeichen, die sich selbs anzeigen was es ist, lernen den arzt, was er auch sein sol.*—I,1:79). The self-characterizing things can instruct the physician about what his character ought to be, because the God who first created the natural macrocosm last of all crafted the human microcosm so that this final creature should learn the secrets of the world from all that came into creation beforehand (I,1:79). The work of the physician therefore fulfills the divine plan of revelation.

Luther's pious admiration for nature as a testimony to the power and wisdom of God might have been compatible with this doctrine of the signatures and signs made by the Maker. But the strict division of the two kingdoms and the focus on the word of Scripture as an exclusive road to truth were not. Just as the ambiguous spirits and demons of Paracelsus were to be assigned to the camp of Satan in the thinking of orthodox Protestants, the signatures of things were to become a source of inspiration—not so much for the orthodox as for the dissenters, Protestant mystics, poets, Spiritualists, and Pietists, whose contemplative Christianity led them to seek signs not only in Scripture but in all of experience, and above all in the "Book of Nature." Paracelsus eloquently summarized both his affinity with and his distance from Lutheranism when he inquired: "For just as Christ speaks, *perscrutamini scripturas*, why should I not say of this as well: *perscrutamini naturas rerum?*" (*dan so Christus spricht, perscrutamini scripturas, warumb wolt ich nicht auch sagen darvon: perscrutamini naturas rerum?*—I,11:130). What others called the Book of Nature was added to Holy Scripture as a source of truth, added, however, upon the authority of Christ and as a parallel to the Bible, and in a context that presupposed the immediacy and individualism encouraged by the Reformation.

In his later career, the "science of signs or signatures" (*scientia signata*) allows Paracelsus to unite the features of his thought that juxtapose it with the principles of the Reformation. Whether in plants, in the heavens, in the depths of the earth, or in the human nature and character, the signature invariably makes the hidden manifest; it reveals the inner in the outer and holds the key to nature as a divine language (I,12:172–180). Even in a context in which nature, as distinct from "the hand of God," is called the *signator* (I,12:173), the signatory revelation carries out the divine will and intention:

Thus nature has ordained that the outer signs indicate the inner works and virtues, thus it has pleased God that nothing should remain concealed, but rather what lies in all creatures should be revealed through the sciences.

Also hat die natur verordnet, das die eußern zeichen die innern werk und tugent anzeigent, also hat es got gefallen, das nichts verborgen bleibe, sonder das durch die scientias geoffenbart würde, was in allen geschöpfen ligt. (I,12:177)

This plan of creation is predicated by the subject of medicine, by the human body:

> Many people might be bewildered as to why God has ordained such a thing as that the human being should learn of that which is concealed by means of the arts. There is no other reason except that the human body has its use, or the like, and [one should therefore] learn of that which God has created and incorporated spiritually into the body. Thus, [God] has not ordained that science should remain unknown, but rather that all secrets are in it and all virtues are under the reign of the sciences through which is to be discovered what lies spiritually in all things.

> *es möcht manchen verwundern, warumb got solches verordnet hat, das der mensch durch die kunst das verborgene sol erfaren? so ist es doch alein die ursach, das der leib des menschen sein ubung habe oder dergleichen, und das erfare, was got in die körper spiritualisch gelegt und verschaffen hat. darumb hat er nicht geordnet, das die scientia unerkantlich sei, sonder alle heimlikeit seind in ir und alle tugent seind den scientiis underworfen in der erkantnus, durch sie zu erfaren was spiritualisch in allen dingen ligt.* (I,12:177)

What follows, then, in order to illustrate the meaning of the "signature" is Paracelsus's usual reasoning that before a craftsman can build a house, he must first have an image of the house "in his imagination" (*ein zimerman, der ein haus bauet, der hats am ersten in seiner imagination, und wie dieselbig ist, also wird das haus—* I,12:177). Just as the house reveals the latent intention of the craftsman, the things of creation reveal through their "form and figure" (*form und figur*) the concealed virtues in nature (I,12:178). The signature ultimately coincides with the created thing itself, insofar as it is understood as part of the divine plan and purpose of creation. As Paracelsus had written apropos the malady of colic: "For what is the entire world but a sign that it is of God, and that God has made it?" (*dan was ist die ganz welt als ein zeichen das sie gottes ist und das sie got gemacht hat?*—I,1:80) As sign or signature, each thing in nature has an outer and an inner, a visible and an invisible aspect; and these aspects correspond to the persons of trinitarian Father and Son in the plan of revelation, or to the aspects of the elemental substance and of concealed divinity in the eucharistic host. The inner virtue of the thing correspends to the Holy Spirit. As the *Labyrinth of Errant Physicians* declares, the true "science" lies within the things themselves. The true knowledge of nature, the knowledge founded on the four pillars of medicine, brings out the inner structure of things, and, in so doing, imitates the divine being. This is why Paracelsus in the depths of his despair could triumphantly proclaim that all disciplines merge in medicine, as all roads lead to Rome; and it is why he could pronounce that the knowledge of the physician is an apostolic gift.

As we have seen, the theoretical core of ideas, which was deeply felt and believed by Paracelsus, had crystallized for him by the early 1530s, forming itself in his writing during the same years in which the confessions were splitting apart and taking on new shapes around reconceived centers of authority. During this interval of crisis, the issues of faith against works, of letter against spirit, and of the real divine presence in the sacrament against the mere token or remembrance, were fomenting turmoils of contested allegiance and redefining the loyalties of territorial entities throughout the Empire. Such conflicts are either echoed or subsumed in Paracelsian theory. Doctrinally, he falls between the hardening positions: by emphasizing works as well as faith, by supplementing the Bible with a nature crafted in the image of the Creator, by recognizing beneath the outer "letters" of nature the concealed divine spirit, and by upholding the divine presence in a sense that differed from that of the Lutherans or Catholics. The great continental shift of the early Reformation was breaking up into distinct masses, divided by the authority of the literal word of the Bible, of Humanistic studies, of the inner word and spirit, or of Catholic hierarchy and tradition. Paracelsus had found his own ground in nature as divine revelation, in a segment of medieval authority that, by force of his theories, began to give rise to a new tradition of manifestations.

Although the term *theorica* as such does not play as central a role as the term *bild* with its variants, *theorica* is certainly important and symptomatic of the direction of his thought after Basel. In his earliest medical-theoretical work, *theorica* has no special significance of its own. The *Volumen Paramirum* declares that every "faculty" (that is, each one of the five "sects" of medicine) has its own adequate *theoric, practic und physic*: each is capable of theorizing about, as well as of curing, diseases in one of the five ways embraced in the inclusive, syncretic tone of this early tract (I,1:165). Here, and indeed throughout much of Paracelsus's writing, *theorica* is enumerated along with *practica* and often accompanied by *philosophia, physica,* and other such terms. The enumeration places no special emphasis: *theory* is just one kind of study or activity among others in the writings on syphilis or in the *Hospital Book* (I,7:328, 356, 408). In contrast to this, his "German Commentaries on the Aphorisms of Hippocrates," thought to be of the Basel period, render the term *theorica medica* problematical in a way that places it atop the pillars of his medicine, with the implication that medical theory crowns or subsumes the entire structure of his thought. The commentary on the Hippocratic aphorism *experimentum fallax* indicates that the author is not only echoing the commonplace rejection of the so-called "empirics" in medicine (whose hit-or-miss approach knows nothing of reasons), but that he is thereby pointing up his medical theory as the necessary completion of all such inadequate "experience":

Thus medicine stood in the beginning, which was not [a] theory, but only a matter of experience: this has a laxative effect, this constipates; but *what, how*—that was still hidden. Hence one [patient] was ruined, the other got healthy. Now, however, that theory exists, it is no longer that way. Knowledge advances and is no longer a fallible experimentation. This is the result of medical theory, which stands in the four pillars: philosophy, astronomy, alchemy, and *physica* [the latter is equivalent to our archaic *physic*, i.e., the art or practice of medical healing].

Also ist die arznei im anfang gestanden, das kein theorica gewesen ist, alein ein erfarenheit: das laxirt, das constipirt; was aber, wie aber, ist verborgen gewesen. darumb ist einer verderbt, der ander gesund worden. so aber iez theorica da ist, so ist es nimer also. scietia get für und ist nimer experimentum fallax. das macht die theorica medica, die in vier seulen stehet: philosophia, astronomia, alchimia und physica. (I,4:497)

Typically, medical history is divided into two great epochs: then was bad, now is good. Why? Because of the arrival of a "medical theory," encompassing the four pillars. Here, there is a variant fourth pillar—*physica*, "physic," instead of *tugent*—suggestive of an all-encompassing, theoretically integrated practice and art of medicine.

In order for the Paracelsian *theorica* to acquire its fullest significance, it must not only be made to encompass the pillars of medicine, as it does in the above example; its relationship to *practica* must also be rendered problematical. This occurs most explicitly in the draft of a work on "the falling ailment of the mother"—interpreted by Sudhoff as "hysteria": *Von hinfallenden Siechtagen der Mutter (De Caduco matricis)*, in volume eight of the first division. A work of the immediate post-Basel period, *De Caduco* is one variant of a work in progress: a draft that appears provisional and rough, yet extends itself beyond the usual fragment length to constitute a full tract of fifty pages. Its position in the thematic development of the period is relatively clear: *De Caduco* alludes to some previous treatise; presumably one of the *Eleven Treatises* of the same title *(Vom fallend)*. This was the treatise in which the author had proclaimed the qualifications of *ein lector und professor ordinarius* and railed against the Humanistic orientation of his opponents. The subsequent draft of *De Caduco* under discussion here heightens this polemic by further exploring the division of "falling illness," thereby contending that, in addition to the specific forms of disease demonstrated elsewhere against the generalities of Galenic medicine, the "falling illness" itself has a specifically female form. Its elucidation is apparently to be offered as a test case for the entire Paracelsian orientation toward specific diseases. Despite its roughness, the draft *De Caduco* parallels the *Opus Paramirum* in distinguishing a female pathology; in so doing, the author seizes the occasion to adumbrate the problematic relationship of theory and practice and to explicate his theory in its broad metaphysical ramifications.

In treating of the falling illness of the matrix, the author begins by asserting that the human being is an entire anatomy of the great world (I,8:325). He proceeds to the disease itself: it is a kind of fainting and convulsion, resembling epilepsy in the cramping or extending of the limbs and foaming of the mouth *(mit der glidmaß auszudenen mit dem krampf, mit dem gesicht, mit dem schaum vor dem mund*—I,8:326). Of paramount importance is the fact that this disease occurs only in women: this authorizes a discussion of the matrix or womb which places it in the context of Paracelsian theory as a whole. Nature is a whole, reflected variously at different levels or in different spheres: "For in all things are [sic] one operation [or force]" (*Dan in allen dingen sind eine wirkung*—I,8:328). But the operation that is insensate in plants is conscious in animals. This may be said to confirm that, since all things are in all, an unconscious process is unfolding in the womb or matrix, like the tree, which "drinks" without sensation. In any event, the great and small worlds—the cosmos, the human cosmos, and the matrix from which the human is born—are related not only by analogies, but also by paternal and maternal relations. And of course, "the three, sulphur, mercury, and salt" (I,8:329–330), have many essences that are effected by the (paternal) action of the stars.

Oddly, no clear conclusion concerning the disease itself is drawn, though at the end some specific recipes for treatment are offered. What is more spectacular in *De Caduco* is the handling of the terms *theory* and *practice*, which are problematized and pondered over throughout. The thrust of the draft is an appeal to the existence of a woman's version of what was presumably a general category of ailment. This thrust is in turn understood as the validation of a distinctive, female-specific theory and practice. By a further implication, this acceptance of a female theory and practice acts as a rationale for the free speculation of Paracelsian theory itself when he asserts, in a statement debatable for him: "theory proceeds from practice and practice not from theory" (*dan die theorik gehet aus der praktik und die praktik nit aus der theorik*. . .—I,8:357). However, "theory" must also be anchored in higher truth, in the stars and in the divine being. *De Caduco* engages in a digressive speculation on the theory and practice of the historiographer (*geschichtschreiber*), whose description must have a double aspect: there is a kind of astral prefiguration of great men such as Alexander. This is their "theory"; and their earthly existence is its "practice" (I,8:339–340). The digression alludes to his notion of prophecy. It was the period in which Paracelsus was writing of his interpretations of meteorological portents or of the Nuremberg images of the popes. Astrological projection seems an odd analog for medical theory and practice, until one considers that prophecy is linked to medical theory by virtue of the concept of the *image* as a prototype or creator: the author vows to write unremittingly of "philosophical and astronomical things of nature" (*philosophische und astronomische naturalia*): "For they prefigure the entire human being, [they] teach and give him to be understood" (*dan sie fürbilden den ganzen menschen, lernen und geben in zu erkennen*). This pursuit pertains to the high purpose of "the great theory" (*der großen theorik*), which he is committed to continue elucidating as he has begun (I,8:339). Astrology is thus an important pillar of Paracelsian medicine.

The *Opus Paramirum* (*Paramiri liber quartus de matrice*) contains similar speculations on the special diseases of women, on their metaphysical context, and on the consequent necessity of arriving at a two-track explanation, which, taken altogether, renders theory whole and complete against the inadequacies of his competitors: "that results in formulating a new theory of women (*das ursacht ein neue theoricam zu machen von der frauen* . . .—I,9:201); "That is a just theory that proceeds from the light of nature and not from the whimsical heads of people . . ." (*Das ist ein rechtschaffene theorica, so aus dem liecht der natur gehet und nicht aus den erdichten köpfen* . . .—I,9:214). Gender theory is, however, only one aspect of a whole that encompasses creation theory: "Know thus that all things must be regarded by the doctor in their first beginning" (*also wissent, das alle ding in dem ersten anfang müssen vom arzt betract werden*— I,9:219). Creation theory has as its corollary the hierarchy of created spheres and pathogenic causes: there are diseases that arise from the special created nature of woman (I,9:202, 205); there are those, such as jaundice (*gelsucht*), that are imparted by man's nature to woman's nature (I,8:214); and finally those, such as pestilence (*pestis*), that are imparted by the heavens, which are above the nature of the man (I,8:219). Just as the creation of the cosmos entailed an act of separation, the two bodies, male and female, are created separate. The male is body as spirit, the female body corporeal (I,9:215). This may seem suggestive of Gnosticism; however, the defining context has been set by references to Genesis 1:1-3, where the spirit hovers upon the waters prior to creation. The separation of waters by the firmament parallels the separation of the female from the male body. The crafting of the creature is after the image of the Creator—who *is* the spirit hovering over the primal waters, comparable to the male seed of procreation upon the waters of the matrix (I,9:194). The very terms microcosm and macrocosm appear more comprehensible if it is borne in mind that their cosmic closure is eschatological: their separation is their "firmament"; their organism circumscribed by creation and destruction. Circumspection regarding the confining limits of the hierarchical spheres of creation is the prudence of the physician:

> Thus is to be considered first of all the heavens of the lower sphere, then the upper and lower together as one heaven, then the type, as the body, then as the mother in herself: now the theory is complete in the things, and a similar modality is to be sought in medicine.

> *also ist vom ersten zubetrachten der himel der undern sphaer, darnach die obern und undern zusamen als ein himel, darnach die art, als dan der leib, als dan die mutter an ir selbst; iezt in den dingen ist die theorica ganz, und eine solche art ist auch in der arznei zu suchen.* (I,9:224)

Thus gender theory of a sort liberates or legitimates the autonomy of Paracelsus's theoretical speculation; however, his speculations are anchored in his hypertrophied biblicism which construes the images of Creator and creation in each creature.

By no means does such speculation lead always to the same results. Another interesting fragment is *Von den podagrischen Krankheiten und was in anhängig ist (On the diseases of gout and what is pertinent to them)*, fragment B in volume one of the first division, one of several *Podagra* pieces included in that volume. Its uncommonly vitriolic rancor again conveys the impression of the immediate post-Basel period, as does the question, posed also in the *Hospital Book* of 1529, "What is the help of medicine other than love? *(was ist die hülf der arznei anderst als die liebe?*—I,1:349). There are several diatribes against distinct kinds of medical thought that are most likely to have been encountered in Strasbourg and Basel. There is a warning against the universal peril: "Will no one consider with what a great vice the cunning of the physicians is galloping through Europe?" *(Wil niemants betrachten, mit was großem laster die listikeit der arzt lauft durch Europam?*—I,1:348) A signal distinction is drawn between the light of nature and the improvisation of those who rely on experimentation: "For where the light of nature is not at work in a physician, but rather [knowledge] is collected piecemeal, what is such [a physician] but an experimenter, from whom no physician can ever be be born" *(dan wo nicht das liecht der natur in einem arzt wirkt sonder das flikwerk hinun-*

der gesamlet, was ist ein solcher anderst dan ein experimentator, aus dem kein arzt nimermer mag geborn werden—I,1:353). The fragment also takes aim at anatomy, but does so, as usual, by taking over the term and giving it a different meaning, which is here connected, among other things, with palm reading.

What is of salient interest in this and other fragments is the speculative progression. He begins by evoking the general crisis of confidence in medicine, presented both in terms of his personal conflict with his opponents and in terms of the balance of theory and practice. His opponents are inexperienced, and his theory superior both in point of philosophy and in point of the practice from which it emanates. As to gout, the theme of the fragment, the reader should not be perturbed that he proposes to heal it without the help of the codexes of his detractors. Nor should the reader "be dismayed with him, that they say I was in prison three times, and went through many wars and have fought much, frivolously, and the like" (*noch weniger laß dich entsezen ab mir, das sie sagen, ich sei dreimal im gefengniß gelegen, ich hab vil krieg durchlaufen, ich habe vil freventlich geschlagen, etc. und anders mer*—I,1:349–350). He begins, then, by detailing all the sites in the body where *podagra* can occur, all the joints or bones that are susceptible to this ailment that he also refers to as rheumatism (*rheuma*—I,1:352). The body's susceptibility in its pains to the powers of the heavens should come as no surprise to us (*ir schmerzen ligt im gewalt des himels* . . .); a comparison drawn with torture (*gleich wie das renken am folterseil*—I,1:352) reminds us of the all-round severity of life.

When the disquisition on the *loca podagrae* comes to an end after discussing manifestations in the inner body, the physician tells the reader that this is the ground on which he will reveal the "strange cause, origin and issuance of the disease" (*von der seltsamen ursach, ursprung und herkomen der selbigen krankheit*—I,1:353). But before doing so, he and all concerned must first consider "the mother of medicine" (*mir und euch allen gebürt am ersten von der muter der arznei zu reden*—I,1:353). This leads him to his quarrel with the advocates of experimentation: "The experiments don't make a physician, the light of nature makes a physician" (*die experimenten machen kein arzt; das liecht der natur macht ein arzt*—I,1:354). What is needed is a "science" (*scienz*), which the physician acquires, as a child requires a father and mother to be born (I,1:354). Here, contrary to his earlier and later usage, he

speaks of "four philosophies" and of "four astronomies" which together constitute the "eight mothers" of true medical knowledge
(I,1:354).

> The book of medicine is nature; and in the same manner as you
> see yourself in a mirror, you must also see in nature all your sci-
> ence, and do so just as certainly and as little mendaciously as
> you have yourself in the mirror in person.

> *das buch der arznei ist die natur und zu gleicher weis, wie du*
> *dich selbs im spiegel sichst, also mußt du auch in der natur all*
> *deine scientias sehen und das als gewiß und als wenig*
> *betrüglich, als du dich im spiegel persönlich hast.* (I,1:354–355)

Medical knowledge is a mirror image of ourselves in the mirror of
nature. This reformulates the microcosm-macrocosm relationship
centered upon the pivotal notion of image: here the image caught in
the mirror. An image made is an entity or creature, an image *seen*
knowledge. The seemingly wild digressions that follow are attempts
to bring the image postulations into mutual focus.

The author next proceeds to explain the "eight mothers" in connection with the great and small worlds. Presumably they are the
two sets of four elements: we are born of them in our human mother and also in our macrocosmic mother. This brings him to the concept that unites these—the *limbus*: "for the human being is nothing
other than the limbus. Though, however, there are two of them, so
that the small [one] is made from the great" (*das der mensch nichts*
anders ist dan der limbus. wiewol aber der selbigen zwen seind so ist
der klein aus dem großen gemacht—I,1:355). The limbus equates
nature and creature by asserting that all have grown from the same
ground and seed, although the ground of the seed is revealed here
as nothing less than the divine Word (cf. John 1:1):

> Limbus in itself is the seed from which all creatures grow and
> have proceeded, just as from a little seed a tree grows. Though
> it is different in the respect that the limbus had its earth in the
> Word of God, which in the other seed gives [disposes] through a
> mean to the end of its fruit.

> *limbus an im selbs ist der sam, daraus alle creaturen wachsen*
> *und gangen sind, zu gleicher weis wie aus einem semlin ein*

baum wechst. wiewol es ist mit solcher underscheidt geschiden,
das limbus sein erden hat gehabt in dem wort gottes, welchs in
dem andern samen durch ein mittel zum ende seiner frucht gibt.
(I,1:355)

The reference to the creation through the Word, as proclaimed by
John 1:1, can serve as a reminder that, despite the connections of
Paracelsus's view of the informed predispositions of organic entities
and of the outer signatures of things with non-Christian superstitions,[161] to Paracelsus himself all the divine forces and signs appear
to be perfectly harmonious with biblical teachings. The doctrine of
the limbus makes it possible to assert the likeness of the human
being with the mirror image of nature. It is a likeness of paternity:

Now the *limbus major* is the seed, from which have proceeded
all creatures. *Limbus minor* is the last creature into which the
great limbus goes. For as the human being has been made from
the limbus from which has been taken everything that the creatures have been, and the same [limbus], taken in the manner as
a sperm is taken, which then is the small limbus. As a son is
born from his father, in the same way has the [small] limbus
been taken from the greater [limbus]. And just as the son has
in him all the body parts of the father, so, too, the human being
bears all creatures within him.

Nun ist limbus maior der sam, aus dem gangen seind alle crea-
turen. limbus minor ist die lezte creatur in die der groß limbus
gehet. dan wie der mensch aus dem limbo gemacht ist, do ist
genomen alles das, so die creatur gewesen seind, und aus den sel-
bigen zu gleicher weis als ein sperma genomen, der dan ist der
klein limbus. wie ein son von seim vater geboren wird, also ist der
limbus aus dem großeren genommen. und wie der sohn des
vaters alle glitmaßen an im tregt, also tregt auch der mensch alle
creaturen in im. (I,1:355)

The idea here is that the one being as an indivisible whole gives rise
to the other being; accordingly, the one must have contained the
other latent in it. The last must therefore contain all that went
before it, the son the father; the human being the whole of nature.
Limbus is a term of transformation, it is the mystery of becoming in
its natural form. This is a visionary thought. But what immediate

purpose does it serve, if not to ward off the idea that what is actually inside a human being is precisely what one would find if one were to open up and dissect the human body? As the author says near the end of the fragment, apropos chiromancy, which he extends from palmistry to all the lines of the body:

> that we know from without the inner chiromancy, how the same stands in the entire body. If we know as much and the same [person] dies and we bring him into the anatomy, we will find within what we have seen and shown without. Therefore it is necessary to know that; for the diseases lie concealed in themselves.

> *das wir von außen wissen die inner chiromancei, wie die selbige stant im ganzen leib. so wir das wissen und der selbig stirbet und wir füren in in die anatomei, so finden wir innen was wir außen gesehen haben und angezeigt. drumb ist von nöten das zu wissen; dan verborgen ligen die krankheiten in in selber.* (I,1:371)

What is visible without is an image of what is invisible within. The human creature contains all previous creatures, because man was created last by God. The image-correspondences only serve to evade the sort of thesis that confronted Paracelsus in opponents such as Vendelinus Hock, the Strasbourg competitor who championed anatomical dissection and whose challenge to Paracelsus was one of the taunts in the satirical poem by the Basel students, *Manes Galeni*.[162] The system of correspondences and the metaphysical grandeur of the limbus are proposed to obviate a materialism that explains the body by the body.

In the fragment on *Podagra*, the pivotal term of the image is employed in order to suggest a theory of disease. In opposition to the positivism of the body, Paracelsus asserts that only man and woman together constitute a whole human being (*und beide machen ein ganzen menschen das ist ein menschen*—I,1:362). This of course makes good sense, but he goes on to state that this does not mean one entity, but rather one "image" (*als frau und mann nit alein* ein *ding seind sonder ein bilt*—I,1:362); and—what makes no sense at all—a single "anatomy" (*dan* eine *anatomei ist mann und frau*— I,1:363). (The thesis of the androgyny later developed by Jacob Boehme is peripheral and negative in Paracelsus.[163]) But we can expect here an extension of the conceptual parity of male and female; and it comes in the assertion that disease longs for its woman, that is, its medicine (*nun folgt dorauf das die krankheit begert ir frauen, das ist die arznei*—I,363). Despite the grammatical gender of *krankheit* that dictates the female pronoun, disease is male and medicine female. Under the heading of *Physionomia*, he goes on to make disease into an invisible microcosm, a shadow person: "At the start, and before I discuss physiognomy, be advised first of all that each disease is an entire human being (*ein ganzer mensch*), and has an invisible body and is *corpus microcosmi* and is also [a] microcosm" (*Im anfang vor dem ich die physionomei fürhalt, so wissen am ersten, das ein igliche krankheit ein ganzer mensch ist und hat ein unsichtigen corpus und ist ein corpus microcosmi und ist auch microcosmus*—I,1:365). The qualities of the disease microcosm which invisibly occupies the body determine the centers of disease or pain. One of many Paracelsian constructs to depict disease, the disease microcosm again conveys his extreme aversion to acknowledging the divisibility of organic entities, let alone the validity of what can only be ascertained by dissecting them. Instead of empirical experience, Paracelsus conjures with ever-new constructions of macrocosm and microcosm, with his pivotal concept of the image, with his equations of outer and inner and visible and invisible. The resultant theories seem to rise like wraiths, evolving into new forms, all intangible and inscrutable in their relation to reality as we know it. The variations are not contingent upon his evaluation of any new evidence. At least for this layman, it is difficult to imagine any systematic approach to healing at the root of his variants.

However, this is only one way of looking at such discourse. When one begins to recollect and analyze the existential feeling of a debilitating disease, the notion of being possesed by a body of disease, an invisible microcosm, makes good sense. The notion that medicine is a feminine entitity with which the virulent male disease is united to be calmed, and in order to engender a reborn being of health—this is as strikingly poetic a depiction as that of Zwingli's *Prayer Song in Time of Plague*. Like the Lutheran theology of the cross, Paracelsian theory could address the whole man or woman, diagnosing illness in visionary terms and aiming to heal the inner as well as the outer being. In its suggestive appeal both to the spiritual and the physical creature, his theory anticipated the Pietistic dramatization of the travails of the soul.

In this sense, his theory stood on an experience more or less closed to academic medicine, then as now. A more scientific procedure would identify and weigh its objects. Paracelsus weighs his, after his own fashion, on the scale of the image: disease and health as male and female interprets the process of illness and reconvalescence—though this tells us nothing whatsoever about gout or rheumatism as such.

This kind of medicine rests on a form of thought that is contemplative rather than causal or analytic, an intuition that takes in the whole of a phenomenon and interprets its meaning in reference to other whole beings and, ultimately, in reference to the divine Author. In tendency, then, Paracelsus's "experience" suggests something altogether different from and very nearly the opposite of the quantifying empirical analysis and experiment of the scientist. Typically, the programmatic later treatise, *Labyrinthus Medicorum Errantium* (1538), begins with the usual rejection of Galen, Avicenna, and traditional medieval medicine. The author then extols what he calls the first book of all science and medicine: the divine being and wisdom. From this source alone, "the light of nature" proceeds. In pursuing the light of nature, the physician follows in the footsteps of the apostles, who did not preach Christ by their own authority, but rather "through the one that had spoken with fiery tongues within them" (*durch den der mit feurigen zungen in inen geret hat*—I,11:164). This of course refers to the Holy Spirit, who was their schoolmaster. The errant physicians, by contrast, seek an immanent experience of that which is in and of this world. They are said to wander to and fro as misguided pilgrims, conducting countless "experiments," only to discover lost in their labyrinth what would appear to be the vanity of vanities: the "experiments of experiments and all mad labyrinths (*experimenta experimentorum und alle tollen labyrinthen*—I,11:166). These misguided doctors of tradition and experimentation mistakenly trust in a human wit and understanding. Yet, as in all other matters: "the greater the wit, the greater the error! For human understanding does not exist." (*ie mer wiz ie mer irgangen. dan des menschen verstant gibts nit.*—I,11:168).

Rhetorically, this is exceptionally well done for an author whose formulations are often quite clumsy. The abysmal labyrinth of tradition and experimentation is a successful adaptation from classical mythology. The proverb-like paradox of wit and error is close to the style of the *Two-Hundred and Eighty Paradoxes* of Sebastian

Franck, the dissenting Protestant Spiritualist mystic who crossed paths with Paracelsus in Nuremberg. There is a tone of prophetic insinuation, an eschatological highlighting of the errant physicians: they are set against "the new ones" about whom the author paraphrases Matthew 19:30—"The last, however, shall be the best" (*die lezten werden aber die besten*—I,11:168).

In what follows, it becomes evident that in Paracelsus's experience the mystical aspect is not merely rhetorical; indeed, it conveys an epistemology of divine illumination. The highest and first book of medicine is "wisdom" (*sapientia*). All things are ruled from within by a divine "knowledge" or "science" (*scientia*) that operates within nature itself (I,11:171, 192). This immanent power is nothing if not the knowledge of him who created all things. Hence, "medicine must flow from the spirit that is within the human being which is from [God] to whom it returns again" (*aus dem dan folgt, das die erznei aus dem geist fließen muß, der im menschen ist, welcher von dem ist, zu dem er wieder gehet*—I,11:172). As part of this mystical *exitus* and *reditus*, knowledge or wisdom—"experience," in the sense of the author—descends from above, as the Epistle of James teaches, and flows from within, as did the spirit that spoke with fiery tongues in the apostles (I,11:172–173). Therefore, true knowledge and valid experience disclose "the secrets and mysteries of nature" (*die secreta und mysteria der natur*—I,11:173). In studying nature, we learn and research "the writing of God which reveals to us all things" (*die geschrift gotes, die uns die ding alle offenbaret*), and this all the more so because we are the image (*biltnus*) of God (I,11:173). This sort of divine experience is contrasted with the mere evidence of the senses: "Unless we are experienced in the same book, we are blind with seeing eyes" (*so wir im selbigen buch nit erfaren sind, so sind wir mit sehenden augen blind*—I,11:173–174). The mystical antithesis of the blind who see and the seeing who are blind underscores the distinction between experiment and experience: "For the eyes indicate only the experiment, but not the experience" (*dan die augen zeigen experimentum an, aber nit experientiam*—I,11:191–192). The true experience also knows of the duality of the world as microcosm and macrocosm and is therefore not deceived by the image given by those eyes that lack understanding (I,11:185). The true "theory" is accordingly like theology: it is inspired by and informed with the correspondences of Creator, creation, and creature. *Theorica* therefore recognizes the underlying coherence of all things. To the true knowledge—which comes from God and indeed is knowledge of God—"theology, practice, and theory" (*theologei, practica und theorica*) cannot be separated (I,11:199). "Thus, medical theory also stems from God" (*so ist nun theorica medica auch von got*—I,11:200). In the same context, Paracelsus compares the "letter" or "paper" of the Gospel with its transcendent spirit: since any mere "letter" is insufficient, the medical theorist must likewise seek "what is learned from above and illuminated" (*das muß von oben herab gelernt werden und erleucht*). In the final analysis, theory is the "illumination which proceeds from the one who is light itself" (*illumination, die da ausgehet von dem, der selbst das liecht ist*—I,11:201). In the end, Paracelsian theory would take leave of all contending "doctrines, phantasies, speculation" (*doctrinen, fantaseien, speculiren*) to secure an authority from above.

It is only an apparent contradition to this illuministic theory, when the concurrent *Book of the Tartaric Diseases* states that the *theoricus medicus* is taught solely by "that which the eyes see and the fingers touch" (*was die augen sehen und was die finger tasten*—I,11:24). When it comes to the meaning of this, as usual no specifics are offered, nothing beyond a general and sweeping claim to have perused the countries of the world as the pages of a book: there is a *theorica nationum* that demonstrates "what sort of bodies of tartarus are in each" (*was in iedlichen für corpora tartari sind*—I,11:27). Without a trace of actual verification, the "diversities" of the world are cited: it is his characteristic, and spectacularly successful, maneuver aimed at turning to his own advantage the "vagrancy" (*lantstreichung*) that would otherwise have been held against him (I,11:27). Here, as is so often the case, Paracelsus appeals not to concrete geographical experience, but rather to the credulousness of people in the age of discovery. A shrewdly crafted mystique balances medicine with religion. In focusing on one or the other, scholars overlook the primacy of his theory—a term with ancient contemplative, as well as modern critical, resonances— delivering instead either a false empiricism, or the pontifications which the conclusion of Gause's theological study classed as fourthrank lay theology.

Conclusion

Common opinion understands Paracelsus as a figure of the Renaissance, Faustian in his challenge to medieval authority and forward-looking in relying on experience and launching progressive innovations in science and medicine. I have presented him here instead as an idiosyncratic creature of the early Reformation, whose notion of experience was tangential to the beginnings of empirical science even in his own time. This conclusion is based on a revisionist dating of his works and on the relative weight of his religious and medical thought, of which the latter appears on close examination at root more religious than scientific. On the whole, his writings present a kind of speculation that is given more to mystical contemplation than to induction from the evidence of the senses. To a significant degree, the "Faustian" reputation of Paracelsus emerged as the projection of a national-cultural myth. It was encouraged by the categories of academic and professional specialization, by premises that highlight the distinctness of *die Neuzeit* and dichotomize science and religion. One would misrepresent the authorial intention of Paracelsus by characterizing his theological writings as extraneous dabblings of a lay theologian, for he asserted much the same authority in divine and in natural matters. It is inconsistent to take his assurances of medical knowledge and achievement at full value, while ignoring or rationalizing away his claims to be a doctor of Holy Scripture. The character of his work as *theory* assists us in overcoming such divisions and in recognizing the inception of his thought under conditions of social and religious controversy. This point of origin is attested to by the attendant circumstances of Paracelsus's career, by the pervasive role within his writings of defenses, diatribes, and self-legitimations, and by the centrality of his notion of the *image*, the key term that extends the articulation of divine authority from Scripture to created nature.

It can be objected that we commit a willful anachronism in applying to Paracelsus the contemporary usage *theory*, with its connotations of a critical thinking that endeavors to surmount the conventions and limitations of traditional academic studies. Certainly, a different *Zeitgeist*, worlds apart from ours, gave rise to and defined his *theorica*. However, the anachronism of declaring his work *theory* (as opposed to philosophy, medicine, lay theology, or some varying combination of all the above) is instrumentally useful, for it casts a different light on some of his representative writings. Their content is not really medicine, nor systematic philosophy, nor, strictly speaking, theology. This is true not only of many of his fragments and drafts, but also of the works regarded as his most mature and systematic. One obfuscates the real content of his *Labyrinthus Medicorum Errantium* rather more with the terms *philosophy* or *medicine* than with the term *theory*. His *Astronomia Magna* assaults rival constructions of authority and erects its burgeoning terms and distinctions by extrapolating from the canonical accounts of the creation in Genesis ("In the beginning God created the heavens and the earth") and John ("In the beginning was the Word"). A free speculation devolving from these biblical passages generates numerous anthropological and naturalistic notions, concerning the duality of the human being, the role of the firmament, the letter-like, signifying meaning of the created things of nature, and the divine image that makes the human being distinct. There are resonances with Neoplatonism and with dissenting sects of his time. However, the guiding idea of this, his "entire religion of all creatures" (*die ganze religion aller creaturen*—I,12:3) is "Holy Scripture" as the "cornerstone" of all divine and worldly wisdom (I,12:32). In passing over the words of Paracelsus in pursuit of some deeper or more titillating source, interpreters have sometimes proceeded like unrestrained archeologists, smashing through intact structures in order to dig out an artifact of their own preconception.

Other terms than theory might be applicable to Paracelsus's free speculation based on the biblical accounts of creation. But *theorica* is found in his own writing as a complement of *practica*. The fact that it outstrips "practice" and takes on a life of its own is not necessarily what distinguishes it from modern critical theory. Paracelsian *theorica* is characterized by its movement across the boundaries of academic divisions, by its capacity to generate terms and concepts, and by its concern with particular phenomena such as the unclassified female disease, the shifting terrain of pathology, or the purported diversities of lands and peoples. Such phenomena are cited to secure the legitimacy of his recasting of all disciplines and categories. In a movement that only appears to contrast with the quest for the particular, *theory* is also an impulse to ascend, abruptly and vertically, as it were, from the particular to the metaphysical or the divine object—the supreme individual whose hidden, transcendent nature illuminates the pattern of all other natures. Paracelsian theory is contemplative and mystical.

Theory as dissent is essential to the seventeenth-century reception of Paracelsus by dissenters, mystics, and poets. This was natural enough, given that a religious center of authority was already present in his writings, programmed as they were with an alternative interpretation of the project of reformation. Here, it seemed, was a reform that adhered to the individualism and egalitarianism of the early Reformation, by conceding to the inspired individual a direct, intuitive access to divine truths, a reform that could claim to go beyond Luther in addressing the needs of earthly existence, the health of the individual and the commonweal of the community. It was a reform with an alternate pathway to knowledge, one supplementing the Bible: the light of nature. Paracelsian doctrine instructed that it was possible to penetrate beneath the outer appearances of elemental nature in the same way that the Spiritualist dissenters of the sixteenth century taught that one could penetrate the tyrannical scriptural letter of orthodoxy to discern the spirit or the inner word.

Among Protestant dissenters, Valentin Weigel (1533–1588) was the most receptive and critical conduit for Paracelsism. Toward the end of the sixteenth century, this liberal-minded Lutheran pastor in the Saxon town of Zschopau wrote a number of treatises critical of the repressiveness of Lutheran orthodoxy. Weigel was repelled by what he saw as the narrowness of religious life and the hypocricy of its representatives. He attempted to get to the heart of the malaise by criticizing the underlying foundations of an authority that had once again come to be vested in an academic hierarchy: the new Protestant scholasticism which angered Weigel as the university establishment had enraged Paracelsus. Weigel embraced the inner word of the mystics, arguing that knowledge depends quite as much on the knowing subject as on the object of knowledge. He also incorporated into his theories the authority of external nature as a revelation of the divine will. His writings circulated, especially after his death, as did numerous imitations.

On the eve of the Thirty Years' War in Germany, Weigelian or pseudo-Weigelian writings were joined by those of the shoemaker and mystic Jacob Boehme (1575–1624). Equally critical of the new orthodoxy, Boehme synthesized many elements in his speculation, including key notions from the Paracelsian writings. The latter were being collected, circulated, and edited in his region. The first attempt at a complete edition of Paracelsus was published in 1587 by Johannes Huser. Though the edition did not include the religious writings, they were studied, or at least present, in Boehme's city of Görlitz.

Boehme's first book, *Aurora* (1612), speculated on the image-correspondences of macrocosm and microcosm in order to explicate the hidden God in nature. *Aurora* followed Luther and Paracelsus in conceiving of God as ubiquitous within the created world. In subsequent books, Boehme progressed from the statically conceived relations of creation and creature to the more dynamic conception of a universal divine process informing all of life, nature, and history. He interpreted the parallel triads of sulfur, mercury, and salt and of soul, spirit, and body in *The Three Principles of Divine Being* (1618), and spiritualized the Paracelsian signature in *Signatura Rerum* (1621). His later writings equated faith with a magical, transforming power of the imagination. *Theory* was not his term; however, Boehme rivaled Paracelsus in his speculative virtuosity and in his exaltation of the particularity of things, which he likewise related to the divine apex of all knowledge. The writings of Weigel and Boehme, which circulated widely among dissenters during the Thirty Years' War, helped to create an ethos of antiauthoritarian protest and opposition. Less radical than Weigel and Boehme, but nonetheless also receptive to many of the same impulses of reflective mysticism and nature philosophy, the Lutheran pastor and devotional author, Johann Arndt (1555–1621), produced one of the greatest sources for German Pietism with his four books *On True Christianity*.

The clarion call for a "reformation of the whole wide world" in the first of the Rosicrucian manifestoes (published in 1614, four years prior to the Thirty Years' War) set the tone for the social or political appropriation of Paracelsus, the tendency that Frances Yates labeled *The Rosicrucian Enlightenment,* in her book of that title.[164] A complete reconstitution of social, political, spiritual, cultural, and civic life was envisaged in the utopia of Johann Valentin Andreae's *Christianopolis*, first published in Strasbourg in 1619. Often associated with the Paracelsian legacy, these seventeenth-century utopian projections of a fundamental transformation of life can be characterized by means of the term *reconfiguration*. Whereas the Lutheran orthodox legacy of the Protestant Reformation had settled on a concept of imputed justification, the dissenting voices sought a substantial renewal and improvement of human life in both its individual and communal manifestations.

Weigel and Boehme are too complex to be treated merely as conduits of Paracelsism. Elsewhere, I have written on their traditional sources and historical origins. Much has also been written of Paracelsus's influence on literature and philosophy. In two studies that contrast interestingly, Joachim Telle has documented the low esteem in which the style of Paracelsus was held by many early German commentators; and Karl-Heinz Weimann the fascination of the Paracelsian legend and ideas for literary writers from the sixteenth to the twentieth century, in Germany, England, and France.[165] Prior to the twentieth century, the most avid period of the reception of Paracelsus and Boehme was that of German Romanticism. The entire tenor, orientation, and free movement of Paracelsian speculative theory were intimately akin to the German Romantics' ambivalence toward systematic philosophy and their penchant for mystical religiosity.

Paracelsian theory survived as an organic thinking, merging anthropology, nature philosophy, and mysticism. But there was also a different, pointed reaction which was willing to consider his initiatives as an alchemical physician, without accepting his writings and theories as a whole. Even Galenist physicians and the scholars such as Conrad Gesner, who disliked Paracelsus on principle, were stimulated by the prospect of new discoveries in alchemy or herbal medicine. As previously noted, it was Gesner who associated Paracelsus with Dr. Faust and with the pagan lore of ancient Druids; but Gessner also collected as much information as possible about Paracelsus, related his reputation for treating ailments, and hoped to discover more about the curative powers of simple medications.[166]

In contrast to the reception of Paracelsus in the twentieth century, which has portrayed him as ahead of his time and therefore subject to the persecution of reactionaries, the assessments of skeptical minds in his century were more differentiated. For example, the Nuremberg official city physician Georg Palma (1543–1591) studied him, writing out excerpts in a notebook and jotting commentaries in the margins of Paracelsus's works. In the preparation of medications, Palma gave credit to the man who had once excoriated the Nuremberg physicians and apothecaries. Palma was sufficiently interested in this aspect of Paracelsus that he catalogued and indexed his chemical formulas. Otherwise, however, the city physician of Nuremberg penned more than a few criticisms of Paracelsus's mystifications, absurdities, and rank terminological inventions: *"Opiniones sunt tua omnia, rationes nullae."* Pointedly, Palma recognized a gross disregard for the methods of the exact sciences, including mathematics and geometry, that were of potential service to anatomy.[167] Obviously, then, the early reaction to Paracelsus was not necessarily an all-or-nothing option between the medieval and the progressive.

The opinions recorded by the Basel physician Theodor Zwinger are equally valuable in forestalling any budding impression that the obscurities of Paracelsus were simply the way people commonly thought in the sixteenth century.[168] Born in 1533, Zwinger was a nephew of Oporinus, whose youthful four-year stint as amanuensis to Paracelsus had been followed by the staid life of a professor of Greek in Basel. Oporinus was also the printer whose immortal achievement was the publication of Vesalius's great anatomical work *De Humani Corporis Fabrica,* in 1543. To Zwinger, Oporinus had recounted Paracelsus's characteristic boast that too much fuss was being made over the writings of Luther and Zwingli; and that when he, Paracelsus, began to write, he would send these two, along with the pope, back to grammar school. Like Gesner and Palma, Zwinger was sufficiently intrigued by the Paracelsian allure to invest some effort in researching his life and work. Interestingly for us, Zwinger recorded the view held by some that Paracelsus had received his teaching of the three primary things either from a fifteenth-century alchemist or from an ancient work named after the trinity (presumably the *Book of the Holy Trinity* of 1415).[169] Like Palma, Zwinger was intrigued by the prospect of discovering the healing powers hidden in things; but no less like his Nuremberg colleague, he took Paracelsus to task for an ignorance of anatomy which had led to absurd statments about the body and its organs.[170] Gesner, Palma, and Zwinger are but three among many who responded to Paracelsism in the sixteenth century, but their reactions suggest that a more differentiating response—in contrast to the later choice between adulation and condemnation—was initially not uncommon.

There are elements within Paracelsian theory that make it attractive to the critics of modern life: its sanctification of nature, its incorporation of the feminine into the understanding of God and the world, its attempt to encompass the two truths of science and religion in a single truth with human dimensions, and its quest for a more thorough reform of life than any envisaged by the orthodox. But in concluding this account of Paracelsian theory, I want to submit a word of caution against the temptation to revive his ideas and employ them for modern ends. No matter how vital the modern ends may be, the effort to render Paracelsus relevant to their advancement only obscures the actual contents of his writings, making a straw man into a revered predecessor of contemporary aspirations. This serves neither the understanding of Paracelsus nor the advancement of the modern ends. Who is to say, for example, that modern ecologists are any more his linear descendents than a chemical-pharmaceutical industry that might point with some justification to the prophetic myth of *Elias Artista*, presaging the miraculous powers of a future alchemy?[171] And why shouldn't a modern technology which produces clones and test-tube babies pride itself in realizing the dream of creating the *homunculus*? Those who turn a blind eye to the destruction of entire species might cite Paracelsus to justify the subordination of animal life to human in the divine plan— just as effectively as others can cite him to argue the sanctity of the unique forms of nature.[172] Intellectual historians should perhaps be wary of the impulse to discover the noble savage on every dark continent of the past, to uncover the protofeminist as a disguised subverter of patriarchy, or the proto-Marxist, masquerading as a religious sectarian. The supposed subversive who courageously transgressed all conventions may have been abstrusely devoted to the narrowest creed. Religious sectarians may have anticipated some aspects of a later secular culture, but they most definitely anticipated the culture of contemporary religious sectarians. Sixteenth-century dissenters therefore cannot be transfigured into revolutionary socialists by waving a dialectic wand and mumbling *mutatis mutandis*. There is something particularly disconcerting in watching

Paracelsus don one costume after another, first the Romantic
Faustian trappings, then the staid vest of the positivistic scientist,
then the brown khakis of a Storm Trooper ranting about folk and
race, then the somber cloth of an Evangelical missionary for
Christian ethics, and at last the green sweatshirt of an ecological
activist and advocate of homeopathic medicine. We learn more by
recognizing him for what he was: neither the Faustian hero nor the
precursor of modern progress. It is possible that Goethe came close
to the truth in Faust's memory of his father as a *dunkler
Ehrenmann,* who worked steadfastly against plague but whose poisons killed more souls than the epidemic itself. In all events, intellectual history ought to be on guard, as much as medicine, against
well-intentioned remedies that are actually panaceas or poisons.

If Paracelsus was not exemplary and if it is senseless to claim
him as a precursor of present-day values or ideas, what, the reader
might ask, is the good of studying him. Aside from his inherent fascination, I would hope that the discussion has stimulated or reconfirmed the reader's awareness that prevalent terms for periods such
as *Renaissance* or *Reformation* cannot be understood as measured
intervals of history or closed systems of thought, but only as centers
of authority around which various beliefs and theories revolve, some
circling nearer the center and others orbiting in a remote darkness
of past or even future time. To regard Paracelsus as our forerunner
is to allocate him to the one-dimensional direction of historical
progress. To examine the centered coherence and incoherence of his
thought is to shift the encounter from the diachronic dimension of
progress to a synchronic one of theoretical positions, to an inner
realm in which a different relevance to current thinking should
become apparent. Paracelsian theory reacted to a critical imbalance
of authority in which one discipline and one material of study—theology and the exegesis of Scripture in his time—seemed to over-
shadow the progress of the others, notably of medicine, in much the
same way as the experimental sciences now outstrip the humanities, creating an imbalance, a loss of authority that has elicited over-
arching speculative theories in the humanities. This is why the *scientia signata* seems to resemble the logic and outlook of contemporary critical theory. (The two expressions of "theory" are in any case
close enough that Foucault could retail the Paracelsian signature
approvingly.[173]) Like a contemporary theory that is rooted in the

semiology of de Saussure and the structuralism of Lévi-Strauss, the Paracelsian *scientia signata* and *ars signatoria* undertook to encompass various arts and sciences within a theoretically posited universe of signs and images. Paracelsus rejected Scholasticism along with the ancient authority of Galen and the new anatomy; and he was as suspicious of empirical experimentation as contemporary critical theorists are hostile toward positivism. Like them, Paracelsus hoped to leap from the particular to the universal, though in his case the universal touched the divine source of truth, theory emerged as mystical illumination.

In his hour, the areas of learning that were achieving life-transforming successes were, in the broadest sense of the term, literary and interpretive, as was biblical exegesis. The healing pursuits of medicine limped far behind. A Humanistic medicine could only trail along in the footsteps of the arts by recovering ancient medical writings. In our own time, the relationship is exactly reversed: the natural sciences are revolutionizing the world for better or worse, while literary studies are trailing along far from the beaten path, struggling to discover a vantage point, like Paracelsus's *scientia signata*, from which more than their circumscribed focus of study might be surveyed, from which the findings of the exact scientists might be encompassed as just another *theory*, perhaps even as a sort of fiction, narrative, or myth—intelligible only within some larger, meaningful scheme of reality, accessible to the unaided intuition. In the sixteenth century, a universal reform of life was intimated by Luther's *Letter to the Christian Nobility*. But this promised universal reform was frustrated, for Paracelsus, by the sluggish gait of medicine—overshadowed, as it seemed, by a theology that could heal the soul, and by the liberal arts, with their recovery of ancient texts. Medicine could offer no comparable breakthroughs in healing the body or discovering the causes of disease. The Paracelsian *theorica*, predicated on the universal homologies of nature as image and sign, was an individualistic, Faustian-heroic response to the disparity. For us, a critical theory schooled in literary studies and in the human and social sciences offers the new access to meaning—the only alternative, it seems, to the depersonalized knowledge industry of the exact sciences.

It should be acknowledged that there are reasons why we are taken with the Faustian-Paracelsian myth: he represents the lone, bare-handed researcher, the fearless delver into secrets. We can respond to his myth, because for us even the most intimate self-knowledge, that of our vital or psychic processes, comes mediated by a vast, technical, knowledge-manufacturing division of labor. A bureaucratized knowledge industry dispels the mystery of life, without answering its ultimate questions. By comparison, the Faustian-Paracelsian hero appears to have dwelt in a condition of archaic simplicity and freedom. The arresting terminologies of the *arcana*, *magnalia*, and *quintessentiae* radiate the iridescences of the alchemist's laboratory, where colors and shapes glow in alembics, arousing a sense of awe and promise. Paracelsus as a mythic type evokes this heroic pursuit of knowledge. Jorge Luis Borges only gave our vicarious urge to see his quest succeed its most beautiful and ironic expression in *The Rose of Paracelsus*:[174] after the aging magician Paracelsus has steadfastly refused to show off his alchemical prowess by restoring an incinerated rose in order to gain a pupil in the quest for the Philosopher's Stone, the magician casually effects the transformation after the young man has gone from him in disappointment.

Paracelsian theory aspired to encompass the whole, to see it in a new light, and to comprehend it by a measure both human and divine: this is expressed in the tenet that mind can recognize a philosophical mirror image in nature as clearly as a reflection in a mirror. The nemesis of this article of faith is embodied in the basilisk, the monster whose gaze kills and whose poison is the deadliest of all poisons, *ein imaginirt gift* (I,11:315), an "imagined poison," or poison of the imagination. The basilisk is the minotaur in the Paracelsian labyrinth of errors. The nemesis of the engendering imagination that magically creates without material action is the gaze poisoned by malignant reflection.

All the defects of Paracelsian theory can be summarized in a single error: it claims to yield a practice-oriented medicine and medical philosophy, but it is in fact closer to contemplative and speculative mysticism. Where medicine is about causes and cures, mysticism, including that of Paracelsus, contemplates the being of what is. Borrowing from traditions it aims to overcome, his theory not only presupposes the miraculous, which most thinkers of his age would have done; it encourages a heightened degree of credulousness. Scholarly admirers have sifted through the mass of medical formulas and pronouncements in his writings in order to find the handful that can be used to vindicate his reputation as a scientist. But even scholars favorably disposed to him have failed to demonstrate that his acceptable formulas or assertions arose through a rational or methodical procedure. Scholars have scarcely even attempted to establish that his reflections are *on balance* meaningful with reference to a rational understanding of the etiology, prevention, or cure of diseases.

However, the appeal of Paracelsian theory is related to its flaws. It lies in an unsurpassable evocation of the engendering power of imagination and desire, a power raised to the level of a religious conviction. Paracelsian theory refuses to accept death on its ancient terms. To refute the contingent materiality of human life, it labors to construct elaborate schemes in which the divine, natural, and human can be understood reciprocally. The divine and human image makes things what they are and secures the authority of the theorist. This notion of image only sheds its abstractness and becomes expressive when applied to *processes*. Perhaps this is so because, unlike objects in space, processes can possess a triadic structure in a time centered in the *now* of the contemplative observer. In any case, Paracelsus's theory is only marginally about matters of causality. The heart of his speculative theory contemplates the meanings of processes rather than their causes. If his terms can still touch a responsive chord, it is because an awarness of the unique particularity and intrinsic significance of nature is being reformulated for us by the possibility of its destruction, a destruction already well underway.

Notes

1. Unless otherwise noted, citations of Paracelsus refer either to 1. the edition of Karl Sudhoff: *Theophrast von Hohenheim, genannt Paracelsus, Sämtliche Werke. Abteilung 1. Die medizinischen, naturwissenschaftlichen und naturphilosophischen Schriften* (Munich: Barth, subsequently, Munich and Berlin: Oldenbourg, 1922f.), also referred to as division one; or 2. to the second division edited by Kurt Goldammer, *Sämtliche Werke. Abteilung 2. Theologische und religionsphilosophische Schriften.* (Stuttgart, formerly Wiesbaden: Steiner Verlag, 1955f.) Parenthetical citations in the text refer to division, volume, and page. The first citation is to division one, volume eight, pages 43 and 47 (I,8:43, 47).

2. See Paracelsus (I,8:33): "About all of which [the originality of the author], my secretaries will testify that such [things as I write] proceed from [my] mouth . . ." (*uber das alles meine secretarii bezeugen, das solches vom mund get . . .*). Cf. the account of Oporinus cited in Karl Sudhoff, *Paracelsus. Ein deutsches Lebensbild aus den Tagen der Renaissance* (Leipzig: Bibliographisches Institut, 1936), 46–9.

3. Sudhoff (*Paracelsus*, 46ff.) sternly disapproved of the account of Oporinus, but offered nothing to disprove it. The same has to be said of Sepp Domandl's censorious investigation of "Weyer, Oporin, Paracelsus. Die Hintergründe des Pamphlets von 1555," *Salzburger Beiträge zur Paracelsusforschung* 13 (1975): 53-70. In fact, while taking the spuriousness of the letter for granted, Domandl appears rather to strengthen the case for Oporinus, whose integrity and courage as the publisher of Vesalius lends added crediblity to the memoir of his younger days. On the manuscript tradition and variants of the letter, see Udo Benzenhöfer, "Zum Brief des Johannes Oporinus über Paracelsus," in *Sudhoffs Archiv* 73:1 (1989): 55-63.

4. On the classical literary origin of Paracelsus's motto in the fable of the foolish frogs that ask Jupiter for a king and receive a wicked water snake as their ruler, see Robert-Henri Blaser, "Die Quelle des Paracelsischen 'Alterius non sit,'" in *Paracelsus in Basel. Sieben Studien über Werk, Wirkung und Nachwirkung des Paracelsus in Basel* (Festschrift for Blaser) (Basel: Muttenz, 1979).

5.   Walter Pagel accepted the credentials but noted the meagerness of the evidence, "Paracelsus probably studied at various Italian universities, perhaps including Ferrara. It is not certain that he received the doctorate; the only documentation would seem to be a personal deposition made before a magistrate in Basel. (This deposition was accepted in lieu of an oath by a witness in a lawsuit between two Strasbourg burghers, one of whom had been a patient of Paracelsus.)" "Paracelsus," in *Dictionary of Scientific Biography*, 304.

6.   Bernhard Milt, "Paracelsus und Zürich," *Vierteljahresschrift der naturforschenden Gesellschaft in Zürich* 86 (1941): 321–54, esp. 322.

7.   Hartmut Rudolph, "Einige Gesichtspunkte zum Thema 'Paracelsus und Luther'," *Archiv für Reformationsgeschichte* 72 (1981): 34–53.

8.   Robert-Henri Blaser, "'Ulrich Gyger, sin diener.' Versuch einer biographischen Rekonstruktion," in *Kreatur und Kosmos. Internationale Beiträge zur Paracelsusforschung (Kurt Goldammer zum 65. Geburtstag),* ed. Rosemarie Dilg-Frank (Stuttgart: Fischer, 1981).

9.   See Austin Patterson Evans, *An Episode in the Struggle for Religious Freedom: The Sectaries of Nuremberg, 1524–1528* (New York: Columbia University Press, 1924), esp. 149, 167ff.; cf. Nikolaus Paulus, *Protestantismus und Toleranz im 16. Jahrhundert* (Freiburg/Breisgau: Herder, 1911), 32–61; Joseph Lecler, *Toleration and Reformation*, vol. 1 (New York: Association Press, 1960).

10.   See Dietrich Georg Kieser, "Entwurf einer philosophischen Geschichte der Medizin," the Introduction to his *System der Medicin, zum Gebrauche bei akademischen Vorlesungen und für praktische Ärzte,* 1 (Halle: Hemmerde und Schwetschke, 1817), 43–7. Kieser's Hegelian reflections indicate the sense of epoch that prevailed in estimations of Paracelsus and his times prior to the clouding of issues by the subsequent mystique of the Renaissance understood as an intellectual tendency divorced from or opposed to the Reformation: *Mit Luther, dem Reformator in der Religion, erschien nun gleichfalls von der Zeit gefordert Paracelsus. Da wir alle Erscheinungen in der Geschichte als im Gange der Ausbildung des Menschengeschlechtes notwendig bedingt annehmen müssen, so ist es auch Paracelsus Reformation in der Medicin. Um das Alte, Unbrauchbare zu zerstören, bedurfte es einer gewaltsamen Revolution* (43). For other nineteenth-century estimations, see Michael Benedict Lessing, *Paracelsus, sein Leben und Denken* (Berlin: Reimer, 1839).

11.   See Hartmut Rudolph, "Schriftauslegung und Schriftverständnis bei Paracelsus," in Rosemarie Dilg-Frank (ed.), *Kreatur und Kosmos.*

Internationale Beiträge zur Paracelsus-Forschung (Stuttgart: Fischer Verlag, 1981), 102–24, esp. 101.

12. See Introduction by Kurt Goldammer to Paracelsus, *Auslegung des Psalters Davids* I, (II,4:xxviii).

13. Kurt Goldammer, *Paracelsus. Natur und Offenbarung* (Hannover: Oppermann, 1953), 18.

14. Hartmut Rudolph, "Paracelsus' Laientheologie in traditions-geschichtlicher Sicht und in ihrer Zuordnung zu Reformation und katholischer Reform," *Sudhoffs Archiv* 85:31 (1993): 79–97.

15. Goldammer, *Paracelsus. Natur und Offenbarung*, 68; cf. Hartmut Rudolph, "Paracelsus' Laientheologie," 86 (*Die theologischen Anfänge Hohenheims liegen nicht—wie gewöhnlich dargelegt—in der ersten Salzburger Zeit, also 1524/25, sondern fallen mit dem Beginn seiner schriftstellerischen Tätigkeit überhaupt zusammen*). Rudolph is, in my opinion, correct in stating that from the very beginning of his career as an author, Paracelsus was concerned with theology; however, as I attempt to demonstrate in ch. 1, he is mistaken in endorsing the view that this "beginning" was prior to Salzburg; as he puts it: *nach bisheriger Annahme ja um 1520, also irgendwo auf seiner Wanderung durch Europa . . .*" (86).

16. Hans J. Hillerbrand, *The Protestant Reformation* (New York: Harper, 1968), xxv.

17. Oberman, "Headwaters of the Reformation: *Initia Lutheri - Initia Reformationis*," in *The Dawn of the Reformation: Essays in Late Medieval and Early Reformation Thought* (Edinburgh: Clark, 1986), 45.

18. See Ferdinand Seibt, "Johannes Hergot. Die Reformation des 'Armen Mannes'"; and Barbara Bettina Gerber, "Sebastian Lotzer. Ein gelehrter Laie im Streit um das Göttliche Recht," in *Radikale Reformatoren*, ed. Hans-Jürgen Goertz (Munich: C.H. Beck, 1978).

19. Heiko Oberman, "Headwaters of the Reformation," 41–2.

20. Kurt Goldammer, in *Paracelsus. Natur und Offenbarung*, 84, seems to indicate that Paracelsus professed the absolute reality of the presence of Christ in the Eucharist—although this meant the spirit-body of Christ, the *limbus aeternus*. (*Sie* [i.e., *die Eucharistie*] *gibt uns die Gewalt, "ein Sohn Gottes zu werden." Sie gliedert ein in dem Auferstehungsleben Christi, sie nährt das Fleisch der Glorie. Auf dieser Grundlage kann die absolute Realität der Gegenwart Christi im Abendmahle vorgetragen werden, ohne daß man in eine dinglich-materielle Auffassung des Sakraments verfällt . . .*). That the

healing powers vested in the *arcana* are divine, uncreated, eternal forces in nature has been recognized by Walter Pagel in *Das medizinische Weltbild des Paracelsus. Seine Zusammenhänge mit Neuplatonismus und Gnosis* (Kosmosophie I) (Wiesbaden: Steiner, 1962), 50; and elsewhere, as well as by Goldammer, in *Der göttliche Magier und die Magierin Natur. Religion, Naturmagie und die Anfänge der Naturwissenschaft vom Spätmittelalter bis zur Renaissance, mit Beiträgen zum Magie-Verständnis des Paracelsus* (Stuttgart: Steiner, 1991), 79.

21. I accept as authentic the work dated in Villach, 1537, *Die neun Bücher de Natura Rerum* in the eleventh volume of the first division. Despite the misgivings of Sudhoff, it seems to contain almost nothing but the most common Paracelsian motifs in his characteristic style. It is quite characteristic of the Paracelsian "cosmography" as a whole when this writing states that, just as nature consists of three alchemistic principles, ". . . thus too is the entire realm of the earth divided, as Europe, Asia, and Africa has been divided, which is a prefiguration of the three principles" (*und also ist das ganz ertrich der welt in drei teil gescheiden, als da ist der dreien principiorum. . .*—I,11:362). Cf. *Von hinfallenden Siechtagen der Mutter*, where the three "parts" of the world are again distinguished as *Europa, Asia*, and *Africa* (I,8:364-5).

22. See Gisela von Boehm-Bezing, *Stil und Syntax bei Paracelsus* (Wiesbaden: Steiner, 1966), 87–8 (*P. überrascht den Leser des öfteren mit sprachlicher Farbigkeit und Frische, wo er bestimmte Verhältnisse seiner Umwelt verächtlich macht. Ironische und metonymische Einkleidungen treten oft dicht gedrängt in den Schimpftiraden auf*).

23. Cited by Milt, 335; also in Sergius Golowin, *Paracelsus. Mediziner—Heiler—Philosoph* (Munich: Goldmann, 1993), 24 (Gesner writes to his friend Crato in 1560: *Dieser Paracelsus war unseres Wissens ein Magier, ein merkwürdiger Mensch. Verschiedene meiner Freunde kannten ihn. ... daß er bei den Dämonen in die Schule gegangen sei, wie dies früher unsere Druiden taten. ... Aus dieser Schule gingen die sogenannten fahrenden Scholaren hervor, unter welchen ein gewisser Faust, der erst unlängst gestorben ist, besonders berühmt war.*).

24. Kurt Goldammer, *Paracelsus in der deutschen Romantik* (Vienna: Verband der wissenschaftlichen Gesellschaften Österreichs, 1980), 17ff.

25. C. G. Jung, *The Spirit in Man, Art, and Literature*, trans. R. F. C. Hull (London: Routledge and Kegan Paul, 1966), 15.

26. Walter Pagel, *Paracelsus: An Introduction to Philosophical Medicine in the Era of the Renaissance* (Basel: Karger, 1958), 40–1

("Paracelsus stood for religious and intellectual freedom. . . . He sought eternal bliss in deeds of self-denial rather than in mere belief and divine grace, factors withdrawn from the sphere of human influence and understanding. Luther on the other hand forged a new religious dogmatism based on the rejection of human activity and free will in favour of mystical belief and the doctrine of election. . . . A deep gulf thus divorces Paracelsus from Luther.").

27. Cf. Walter Pagel, "Paracelsus als 'Naturmystiker,'" in Antoine Faivre and Rolf Christian Zimmermann (ed.), *Epochen der Naturmystik. Hermetische Tradition im wissenschaftlichen Fortschritt* (Berlin: Erich Schmidt Verlag, 1979), 52–104.

28. Allen G. Debus, *The French Paracelsians: The Chemical Challenge to Medical and Scientific Tradition in Early Modern France* (Cambridge: Cambridge University Press, 1991), 6, xv.

29. Friedrich Mook, *Theophrastus Paracelsus. Eine kritische Studie* (Würzburg: Staudinger'sche Buchhandlung, 1876); Karl Sudhoff, *Versuch einer Kritik der Echtheit der Paracelsischen Schriften. Part 1. Bibliographica Paracelsica.* (Berlin: Verlag Riemer, 1894; reprinted Graz: Akdademische Druck- und Verlagsanstalt, 1958); Part 2. *Paracelsus-Handschriften* (Berlin: Riemer, 1899); "Ein Rückblick auf die Paracelsus-Jahrhundertfeier," *Monatshefte der Comenius Gesellschaft* 4 (1895): 115–22; reprinted in Udo Benzenhöfer (ed.), *Paracelsus* (Darmstadt: Wissenschaftliche Buchgesellschaft, 1993).

30. Agnes Bartscherer, *Paracelsus, Paracelsisten und Goethes Faust. Eine Quellenstudie* (Dortmund: Ruhfus, 1911), 160.

31. I am indebted to observations made by my colleague James Van Der Laan for this perspective on Goethe's *Faust*.

32. Friedrich Gundolf, Paracelsus (Berlin: Bondi, 1927), 18–9 (*Wir spüren den makrokosmischen Eifer in solchen Sätzen: er ist Hohenheims eigenste Gesinnung damals, ganz neu, ganz fremd den scholastischen wie den evangelischen, den humanistischen bürgerlichen wie den mystischen Erdempfindungen, und in dieser Frische des Aufbruchs und Einbruchs vielleicht erst wieder bei dem Goethe des Urfaust zu finden. Denn die vielsuchende und sammelnde Neugier der drei oder vier folgenden Naturforschergenerationen, die wir mit den Namen Conrad Geßner, Sebastian Münster, Georg Agricola, Kepler, Leibniz, Haller andeuten, sind weit mehr als Paracelsus wieder den Büchern, den mystischen Weltkonstruktionen oder der grüblerischen Innenschau zugekehrt, bald mehr den einzelnen Stoffen, bald mehr den allgemeinen Zusammenfassungen*).

33. Erwin Guido Kolbenheyer, *Die Kindheit des Paracelsus, Das Gestirn des Paracelsus, Das dritte Reich des Paracelsus* (Munich: Müller, 1917, 1921, 1925).

34. *Das Gestirn des Paracelsus*, 192–211.

35. The breadth and character of the Paracelsus cult during the years of National Socialist ascendancy and rule can be gauged from the burgeoning entries in Karl-Heinz Weimann's *Paracelsus-Bibliographie, 1932–1960* (Wiesbaden: Steiner, 1963).

36. Franz Spunda, *Das Weltbild des Paracelsus* (Vienna: Andermann, 1941), 7.

37. Spunda, 11.

38. Spunda, 15.

39. See the charmingly written biography of the emigrant from Germany Henry M. Pachter, *Paracelsus: Magic into Science* (New York: Schuman, 1951).

40. Several assertions about Paracelsus's originality are exaggerated: 1. Galenic medicine knew specific external causes of disease; if not the term *specificum*. Cf. Georg Sticker, "Entwicklungsgeschichte der spezifischen Therapie," *Janus* 33 (1929): 131–190. 2. Paracelsus was by no means the first to employ alchemy for medicinal purposes, nor to analyze healing waters (on the prior work of Michael Savonarola, see Lynn Thorndike, *A History of Magic and Experimental Science*, vol. 4 (New York: Columbia University Press, 1934), 208ff. 3. His chemical advancements are uncertain. Thus, his use of the term *zinc* is no guarantee that he grasped anything about the properties of this metal, according to the assessment of W. P. D. Wightman's *Science in a Renaissance Society* (London: Hutchinson, 1972). 4. Many of Paracelsus's supposed innovations in creating a German medical language have been rejected by Gerhard Eis, "Zum deutschen Wortschatz des Paracelsus," in *Vor und nach Paracelsus* (Stuttgart: Gustav Fischer, 1965). Many other claims have been challenged, too. However, the point is not to quibble over specifics, but to examine the experiential foundation on which his real or reputed achievements were based.

41. One attempt at comparing alternate versions of Paracelsus's writings in order to ascertain the relationship of the drafts and determine whether variations reveal a development (perhaps toward greater reliance on empirical results) has been undertaken in the recent Master's Thesis of M. Ann Jorgensen, *Paracelsus and the Process of Authorship: An*

Examination of the Two Versions of the Eleven Tractates (Normal, Illinois: M.A. Thesis in German at Illinois State University, 1994). The versions studied proved to be not copies (they contain no identical passages), but rather one is a version composed or dictated with the prior variant in mind. Differences of style and tone are evident. The author concludes that, "Diagnoses seldom differ, but causes and cures vary widely between the first versions and the second versions" (83).

42. Walter Pagel, *Paracelsus. An Introduction to Philosophical Medicine in the Era of the Renaissance* (Basel: Karger, 1958), 347.

43. J. K. Proksch, *Paracelsus als medizinischer Schriftsteller. Eine Studie* (Vienna and Leipzing: Safar, 1911); *Zur Paracelsus-Forschung. Eine Antwort auf die in den "Mitteilungen zur Geschichte der Medizin" erschienene Rezension des Prof. Karl Sudhoff* (Vienna and Leipzig: Safar, 1912).

44. Georg Agricola, *Die Pest. Drei Bücher* (1554), in *Ausgewählte Werke* 6 (Berlin: VEB Deutscher Verlag der Wissenschaften, 1961), 254ff.

45. Proksch, Paracelsus, 20, 27.

46. Nancy G. Siraisi, *Medieval and Early Renaissance Medicine: An Introduction to Knowledge and Practice* (Chicago: University of Chicago Press, 1990), 32–3.

47. Siraisi, 33 (Nicholas seems to have stood in an ambivalent relationship to traditional authority: according to recent scholarship his recommendations were probably inspired less by folk medicine than by academic interest in theriac, which had as its main ingredient viper's flesh).

48. See Proksch, *Paracelsus*, 30. The critic denies that there is even any clear evidence that Paracelsus so much as carried out a surgical operation, much less achieved any success in so doing. (. . . *so findet sich doch in allen seinen Schriften, so voll von überschwenglichem Eigenlob sie immer sind, nirgends der kleinste Anhaltspunkt dafür, daß er je irgend eine chirurgische Operation selbst ausgeführt oder durch eine derselben den mindesten Erfolg erzielt hat*).

49. Michael Servetus, *A Translation of his Geographical, Medical and Astrological Writings*, trans. O'Malley, C. D. (Philadelphia: American Philosophical Society, 1953), 202ff.

50. Cf. Jung, *The Spirit in Man*, 16.

51. Goldammer, *Paracelsus. Natur und Offenbarung*, 59 (*Paracelsus ist noch völlig im Mittelalter verankert, denkt als mittelalterlicher Mensch*); 62 (*Mittelalterlich ist die Gegenüberstellung Makrokosmos-Mikrokosmos. Sie*

gehört ihm genau so wie den Scholastikern, den mittelalterlichen, arabis-
chen und jüdischen Magiern und spekulativen Mystikern).

52. Ernst Heinrich Reclam, *Die Gestalt des Paracelsus in der Dichtung.*
Studien zu Kolbenheyers Trilogie (Leipzig: Reclam, 1938), 66.

53. See Goldammer, *Paracelsus. Natur und Offenbarung,* 14.

54. Theophrast von Hohenheim, genannt Paracelsus, *Theologische und*
religionsphilosophische Schriften 1, ed. Wilhelm Matthießen (Munich:
Barth, 1923).

55. Franz Hartmann, *Paracelsus* (New York: Lovell, 1891); Rudolf
Steiner, *Mysticism at the Dawn of the Modern Age* [based on lectures given
in 1900] (Engelwood, N.J.: Rudolf Steiner Publications, 1960); Karl Joël, *Der*
Ursprung der Naturphilosophie aus dem Geiste der Mystik (Jena: Diederichs,
1906).

56. Wilhelm Matthießen, *Die Form des religiösen Verhaltens bei*
Theophrast von Hohenheim, genannt Paracelsus (Bonn: Inaugural
Dissertation, 1917). A large part of Matthießen's dissertation is reproduced
in Udo Benzenhöfer (ed.), *Paracelsus* (Darmstadt: Wissenschaftliche
Buchgesellschaft, 1993), 156–219. Matthießen draws distinctions that are
of importance for further research in the religious work (the distinction of
the "light of nature" and the "light of the spirit"). However, on the whole his
study is entirely in the spirit of Sudhoff's emphasis on the supposed
"empiricism" of Hohenheim. There are pretentious denials of "mysticism"
and disassociations of Paracelsus from "ecstatic" mysticism of a kind in
vogue among some intellectuals of this period.

57. Bodo Sartorius Freiherr von Waltershausen, *Paracelsus. Am*
Eingang der deutschen Bildungsgeschichte (Leipzig: Meiner, 1935), 194, 14.

58. Franz Strunz, *Theophrastus Paracelsus. Idee und Problem seiner*
Weltanschauung (Salzburg-Leipzig: Pustet, 1937), 73.

59. Wilhelm Ganzenmüller, "Paracelsus und die Alchemie des
Mittelalters," "Alchemie und Religion im Mittelalter," in *Beiträge zur*
Geschichte der Technologie und der Alchemie (Weinheim/Bergstraße: Verlag
Chemie: 1956).

60. Michael Bunners, *Die Abendmahlsschriften und das medizinische*
Werk des Paracelsus (Inaugural Dissertation, Humboldt University Berlin,
1961); Stephan Török, *Die Religionsphilosophie des Paracelsus und ihr zeit-*
geschichtlicher Hintergrund (Inaugural Dissertation, University of Vienna,
1946).

61. See the textually well-informed book by Kilian Blümlein, *Naturerfahrung und Welterkenntnis. Der Beitrag des Paracelsus zur Entwicklung des neuzeitlichen naturwissenschaftlichen Denkens* (Frankfurt/Main: Peter Lang, 1986), 23 (*Schon in seiner ersten Schrift, den "Elf Traktat" von 1520 stellt Paracelsus fest. . .*). Cf. the otherwise superbly informed Hartmut Rudolph, "Paracelsus' Laientheologie in traditionsgeschichtlicher Sicht," 86 (*Eine genaue Analyse der genannten Schriften* [including *Elf Traktat*], *die Hohenheim nach bisheriger Annahme ja um 1520, also irgendwo auf seiner Wanderung durch Europa, abgefaßt haben muß. . .*). Gause, privileged to consult with Rudolph and Goldammer, builds her view of the early theological evolution on 1520 as point of departure—*Paracelsus. Genese und Entfaltung der frühen Theologie* (Tübingen: Mohr, 1993), 85, 95.

62. Karl Sudhoff, *Geschichte der Medizin (3. und 4. Auflage von J.L. Pagels "Einführung in die Geschichte der Medizin"* (Berlin: Karger, 1922), 248.

63. Sudhoff, *Paracelsus*, 20.

64. Sudhoff, *Paracelsus*, 19–20.

65. Harold J. Grimm, *Lazarus Spengler: A Lay Leader of the Reformation* (Columbus: Ohio University Press, 1978), 47 ("In March 1521, when Spengler still hoped that Pirckheimer and he would receive fair treatment by the papal legeate Aleander at the Diet of Worms and that the pope would approach the problems associated with the evangelical movement with an open mind, there was published anonymously the clever *Dialogue at the Apothecary Shop*. In it the author, believed by some to have been Spengler, portrays God as a person in charge of an apothecary shop, the Christian Church; the papacy is the *Unguentum apostolicum*, or apostolic ointment, represented in Worms by Archbishop Albert of Mainz; the priesthood as the *Unguenta*, or anointed; and those who support Luther as the *Radices*, or roots, claiming that Luther's doctrines are rooted in the *Angelica*, or the Gospel. During the verbal battle that the apothecary overhears, the *Herbae*, or herbs, seek to act as mediators, claiming that they are qualified to do so because they came from the roots and are the source of the ointments. When the *Apostolicum* states that Luther's works are to be condemned and burned, the *Herbae* answer that these works should not be destroyed without a fair hearing because they are rooted in the *Angelica*. . . . But the dialogue ends on a happy note, with the pope's acceptance of the evangelical doctrine of the Lord's Supper.").

66. R. Hooykaas, "Die Elementenlehre des Paracelsus," *Janus* 39 (1935): 175–87, esp. 177.

67. Kurt Goldammer, "Introduction," *Auslegung des Psalters Davids I, Theologische und religionsphilosophische Schriften,* 4 (1955), XLV; cf. Paracelsus, "Eingang zum leser sein gruß," *Auslegung des Psalters Davids II, Schriften* 5 (1957), 125.

68. Goldammer's tendency has been to expand the religious periods without casting them aside. His study of 1953 knew a distinct theological interlude: 1531–35 (*Dann entschwand er der großen Welt und durchzog, rastlos und heimatlos, mit theologischen Problemen beschäftigt und von der religiösen Gärung der Zeit erfaßt, das Appenzellerland.—Paracelsus,* 24); the introduction to volume 3 retains it less exclusively (1986, xxxi). Gause's *Paracelsus* assigns religious writing even to medical-scientific years such as 1527 (61).

69. Cited from Sudhoff, *Paracelsus,* 21.

70. Martin Luther, *Werke* 18 (Weimar: Böhlau, 1908), 37ff.

71. Luther, *Werke* 18, 72.

72. Luther, *Werke* 18, 47.

73. Wolfgang Kühn, "Paracelsus und die Fugger," *Die Medizinische* 47 (1952): 1506–8.

74. See Philip Ziegler, *The Black Death* (New York: John Day, 1969); Daniel Williams (ed.), *The Black Death: The Impact of the Fourteenth-Century Plague* (Papers of the Eleventh Annual Conference of the Center for Medieval and Early Renaissance Studies), intro. Nancy Siraisi (Binghamton: Center for Medieval and Early Renaissance Studies, 1982); especially useful is the collection, *The Black Death: A Turning Point in History?*, ed. William M. Bowsky (New York: Holt, Rinehart and Winston, 1971).

75. See Gerald Strauss, *Nuremberg in the Sixteenth Century* (New York: Wiley and Sons, 1966), 123; cf. Friedrich Lütge, "Germany: The Black Death and a Structural Revolution in Socioeconomic History," in Bowsky (ed.), *The Black Death;* Ernst Kelter, "Das deutsche Wirtschaftsleben des vierzehnten und fünfzehnten Jahrhunderts im Schatten der Pestepidemie," in *Jahrbuch für Nationalökonomie und Statistik* 165 (1953): 161–208.

76. Robert S. Gottfried, *The Black Death: Natural and Human Disaster in Medieval Europe* (New York: Macmillan, 1983), 156 ("The second plague pandemic reached an etiological turning point in the late fifteenth century, which began Europe's transition to a new disease era. . . . early sixteenth-century epidemics ranked in virulence with the most severe plagues of the fifteenth century.").

77. Cited from J. R. Hale, *Renaissance Europe: Individual and Society, 1480–1520* (Berkeley: University of California Press, 1971), 25.

78. Martin Haas, *Huldrych Zwingli und seine Zeit. Leben und Werk des Zürcher Reformators* (Zurich: Zwingli Verlag, 1969), 85.

79. I have discussed the role of the plague in the Görlitz reform in Andrew Weeks, *Boehme: An Intellectual Biography of the Seventeenth-Century Philosopher and Mystic* (Albany: State University of New York Press, 1991), 18–9; cf. Otto Kämmel, "Johannes Hass, Stadtschreiber zu Görlitz," *Das Neue Lausitzische Magazin* 51 (1874): 1–246, esp. 117–41; and Alfred Zobel, "Untersuchungen über die Anfänge der Reformation in der preußischen Oberlausitz," parts 1 and 2, *Das neue Lausitzische Magazin* 101, 102 (1925, 1926): 133–88, 126–251.

80. Martin Luther, "Should Ministers Flee in Time of Pestilence?" in *Table Talk, Works* 54, (Philadelphia: Fortress, 1967), p. 434 (No. 5503 in the Weimar Ausgabe).

81. Lynn Thorndike, *A History of Magic and Experimental Science*, 5, 128 (Thorndike refers to an account of August Prost, *Corneille Agrippa: sa vie et ses oeuvres*, published in two volumes in Paris in 1881, 1882.).

82. Andreas Osiander d.Ä., *Gesamtausgabe* 5 (*Schriften und Briefe, 1533 bis 1534*), ed. Gerhard Müller and Gottfried Seebaß (Gütersloh: Mohn, 1983), 384–411.

83. Osiander, 39.

84. Leona Baumbgartner and John F. Fulton, *A Bibliography of the Poem "Syphilis sive Morbus Gallicus" by Girolamo Fracastoro of Verona* (New Haven: Yale University Press, 1935), 35.

85. Fracastor[o], Girolamo, *La Syphilis* (1530), trans. and intro. Alfred Fournier (Paris: Delahaye, 1869), 11.

86. Gerhard Eis, *Medizinische Fachprosa des späten Mittelalters und der frühen Neuzeit* (Amsterdam: Rodopi, 1982), 248.

87. Thorndike, *A History of Magic and Experimental Science* 4, 357ff., 378–9.

88. Dennis E. Rhodes, "Medical Incunabula," in Alain Besson (ed.), *Thornton's Medical Books, Libraries and Collectors: A Study of Bibliography and the Book Trade in Relation to the Medical Sciences* (Aldershot: Gower

House, 1990), 30–42, esp. 31; see on herbals: Yvonne Hibbot, "Medical Books of the Sixteenth Century," *Thornton's*, 43–83; and Charles Singer, *A Short History of Medicine* (New York: Oxford University Press, 1928).

89. Fielding H. Garrison, *An Introduction to the History of Medicine* (London: Saunders, 1913), 198.

90. Gerhard Eis, *Medizinische Fachprosa des späten Mittelalters und der frühen Neuzeit* (Amsterdam: Rodopi, 1982), 248.

91. Rhodes, 30.

92. Thorndike, *The History of Magic and Experimental Science* 5, 431–2.

93. Karl Sudhoff, "Pestschriften aus den ersten 150 Jahren nach der Epidemie des 'schwarzen Todes' 1348," in *Archiv für die Geschichte der Medizin (Sudhoffs Archiv)* 4 (1911): 191–221; 4:6 (1911): 389–423; 6:5 (1913): 313–378; 7:2 (1913): 57–114; 8:1 (1914): 175–215; 8:4 (1915): 236–89; 9 (1916): 53–78; 9:3 (1916): 117–67; 17:1–3 (1925): 12–139; 17:5–6 (1925): 241–91.

94. Anna Montgomery Campbell, *The Black Death and Men of Learning* (New York: AMS Press, 1966).

95. Pagel, *Paracelsus: An Introduction to Philosophical Medicine in the Era of the Renaissance*, 174ff.

96. Pagel, *Paracelsus: An Introduction to Philosophical Medicine in the Era of the Renaissance*, 223.

97. Kurt Goldammer, *Der göttliche Magier und die Magierin Natur. Religion, Naturmagie und die Anfänge der Naturwissenschaft vom Spätmittelalter bis zur Renaissance. Mit Beiträgen zum Magie-Verständnis des Paracelsus. (Kosmosophie* 5) (Stuttgart: Steiner, 1991), 48.

98. See Gerhard Eis, especially: "Zum deutschen Wortschatz des Paracelsus," "Hans Suff von Göppingen," and "Kultische Keuschheit in der mittelalterlichen Wundarznei," in *Vor und nach Paracelsus. Untersuchungen über Hohenheims Traditionsverbundenheit und Nachrichten über seine Anhänger* (Stuttgart: Gustav Fischer, 1965).

99. On Paracelsus's relationship to medieval medical alchemy, see Pagel, *Paracelsus: An Introduction to Philosophical Medicine in the Era of the Renaissance*, 258–73.

100. Marie-Louise Portmann, "Paracelsus im Urteil von Theodor Zwinger," *Nova Acta Paracelsica. Beiträge zur Paracelsus-Forschung. Neue Folge* 2 (1987): 20 (note 30).

101. Wilhelm Ganzenmüller, *Beiträge zur Geschichte der Technologie und der Alchemie* (Weinheim/Bergstraße: Verlag Chemie, 1956), 231–72. Ganzenmüller quotes from the work: *Dy medicinen sult ir gerne enphahen, der vom tod ist auferstanden ihesus cristus, der das ewige leben ist* (346). On the history of the interpretations of the three principle things, see Willem Frans Daems, "'Sal-Merkur-Sulfur' bei Paracelsus und das 'Buch der Heiligen Dreifaltigkeit,'" *Nova Acta Paracelsica* (1982): 189–207. Daems was able to confirm that one figure within Paracelsus's circle of associates owned this work which circulated in handwritten copies (203).

102. Montaigne's travel through German lands lasted for one month (September 29–October 27, 1580) and included stops in towns of importance in the life of Paracelsus, including Basel, Augsburg, Innsbruck, and Sterzing. Since Montaigne was concerned during this period about his health, visiting spas during his journey, and since he also knew the reputation of Paracelsus and met with learned men in Basel, including Theodor Zwinger, it is certainly possible that he could have found an occasion to inquire about the ongoing controversies over Paracelsism. I am indebted to my colleague Dr. Chris Michaelides for calling my attention to the relevance of Montaigne's travel journal as a record of life on the road in sixteenth-century Switzerland.

103. Anna Montgomery Campbell, *The Black Plague and Men of Learning* (New York: AMS Press, 1966), 120–1.

104. For an excellent discussion of the origin, extent of impact during the Renaissance, and subsequent life of this notion, see Antoine Faivre, "L'imagination créatrice," *Revue de Allemagne* 13:2 (April–June 1981): 355–90).

105. See Campbell, among the examples that can be cited: the prestige of astrological plague theory was associated with the University of Paris (37–8); the combination of astrological, humoral, and miasmic theories (40–1, 48); infection as distinct from corrupt air (56, 60); a supernatural malignant spirit (61); the spiritual causation of "accidents of the soul," involving anger or intemperate emotions (77).

106. Campbell, 62.

107. Pagel, *Paracelsus: An Introduction to Philosophical Medicine in the Era of the Renaissance*, 172–82; cf. Pagel, "Paracelsus als Naturmystiker," in Antoine Faivre and Rolf Christian Zimmermann, *Epochen der Naturmystik* (Berlin: Schmidt Verlag, 1979), 77–8.

108. Sudhoff, "Pestschriften," *Archiv für die Geschichte der Medizin* 7:2 (1913): 96, 98 (*Auch die "ymaginacio" und die Ansteckungsfurcht mache die Menschen pestkrank . . .*).

109. Leoniceno's comment in his *Booklet on the Epidemic Commonly Known as the French Disease*, is quoted by W. P. D. Wightman in *Science in a Renaissance Society* (London: Hutchinson, 1972), 84.

110. Kurt Goldammer, "Vorwort des Herausgebers," Paracelsus, *Sämtliche Werke* II:3 (Wiesbaden: Steiner, 1986), X.

111. Of particular interest is a dissertation written under the Vienna historian Heinrich Ritter von Srbik and published in three parts: Albert Hollaender, "Die vierundzwanzig Artikel gemeiner Landschaft Salzburg, 1525," "Studien zum Salzburger Bauernkrieg 1525 mit besonderer Berücksichtigung der reichsfürstlichen Politik," parts 1 and 2, *Mitteilungen der Gesellschaft für Salzburger Landeskunde* 71, 72, 73 (1931, 1932, 1933): 65–88, 1–44, 39–108; Karl Bittel, "Paracelsus im Bauernkrieg? Eine Korrektur zu seiner Biographie," *Propyläen* 39 (1942): 74; Herbert Klein, "Paracelsus und der Bauernkrieg," *Mitteilungen der Salzburger Landeskunde* 9 (1951): 176–78; Karl Pisa, *Paracelsus in Österreich. Eine Spurensuche* (Vienna: Niederösterreichisches Pressehaus, 1991), 55ff.

112. See Klein, 176.

113. Hollaender, "Salzburger Bauernkrieg," part 1 (1932), 18 (*Nur muß ausdrücklich bemerkt werden, daß in keiner südostdeutschen [Klageschrift] so völlig alles auf das religiös-biblische Moment zurückgeführt wird, wie etwa in den Vierundzwanzig Artikeln*), 24 (*So beginnt nun das mächtige Ringen um Glauben und Recht—göttliches und altes werden hier eins, das Evangelium zur sozialen Heilslehre*").

114. Katharina Biegger, "*De invocatione Beatae Mariae Virginis.*" *Paracelsus und die Marienverehrung* (Stuttgart: Steiner, 1990), 201.

115. See George Hunston Williams, *The Radical Reformation* (Philadelphia: Westminster, 1962); and Gause's *Paracelsus* on the medieval mystical origins of the divinization of Maria (70-2) and its clash with Reformation doctrine (32, 48).

116. Biegger, *"De invocatione Beatae Mariae Virginis"*, 9 (*Die Eigenart seiner Religiösität zwischen den Konfessionen tritt darin unverkennbar zutage. In die reformatorische Kritik am Kult der Heiligen stimmte Paracelsus schon früh ein. Gleichzeitig verehrte er bis an sein Lebensende Maria als himmlische Gestalt, und von der Existenz heiliger Menschen, die sich durch Wunder zu erkennen geben, war er tief überzeugt*).

117. Biegger, *"De invocatione Beatae Mariae Virginis,"* 203.

118. See I,3:241 (Goldammer's footnote *a*), 262 (Goldammer's footnote *w*).

119. Paul Oskar Kristeller, *Renaissance Thought: The Classic, Scholastic and Humanist Strains* (New York: Harper, 1955), 44.

120. Edward Grant, *Studies in Medieval Science and Natural Philosophy* (London: Variorum, 1981), 270.

121. This distinction corresponds to a characteristically negative view of animals as worthy of subjugation and domination. See Maria Suutala, *Tier und Mensch im Denken der deutschen Renaissance* (Helsinki: Societas Historica Finlandiae, 1990).

122. In one of the Paracelsus Salzburg manuscripts, Paracelsus writes to his forensic opponents that he has lost out in a debate because of his stuttering. (*Darum, daß ich euch euer Maulgeschrei unbeantwortet gelassen hab, und mich gering geschätzt. Darum daß ich etwas reulich abgezogen bin, ist das die mehrer Ursach, daß ich dreien euch Gelehrten mit meiner stammleten Zungen nicht folgen mag, als ihr denn mich erkennt von Jugend auf, daß ich die allemal stammlet getragen hab.—Sudhoff, Paracelsus-Handschriften*, 296), cited from Karl Bittel (ed.), *Paracelsus. Leben und Lebensweisheit in Selbstzeugnissen* (Stuttgart: Reclam, 1944), 33.

123. Hartut Rudolph, "Einige Gesichtspunkte zum Thema 'Paracelsus und Luther," *Archiv für Reformationsgeschichte* 72 (1981): 34–54.

124. Sudhoff, *Paracelsus*, 18.

125. Sudhoff, *Paracelsus*, 22.

126. Sudhoff, *Paracelsus*, 22.

127. Sudhoff, *Paracelsus*, 43.

128. Miriam Usher Chrisman, *Strasbourg and the Reform: A Study in the Process of Change* (New Haven: Yale University Press, 1967), 45–67.

129. Thomas A. Brady, Jr., *Ruling Class, Regime and Reformation at Strasbourg, 1520–1555* (Leiden: Brill, 1978); Brady, *Turning Swiss: Cities and Empire, 1450–1550*; Lorna Jane Abray, *The People's Reformation: Magistrates, Clergy, and Commons in Strasbourg, 1500–1598* (Ithaca: Cornell University Press, 1985).

130. Peter G. Bietenholz, *Basle and France in the Sixteenth Century: The Basle Humanists and Printers in Their Contacts with Francophone Culture* (Toronto: University of Toronto Press, 1971), 90–2.

131. Robert-Henri Blaser, "Neue Erkenntnisse zur Basler Zeit des Paracelsus," in *Paracelsus in Basel*, 22, 28–9.

132. Blaser, "'Manus Galeni adversus Theophrastum'. Ein Beitrag zur Deutung des Basler Pasquills gegen Paracelsus," in *Paracelus in Basel*; cf. Sudhoff, *Paracelsus*, 38–9.

133. See R. Hooykaas, "Die Elementenlehre des Paracelsus," *Janus* 39 (1935): 175–87.

134. I am indebted to the expert discussion of Hartmut Rudolph, "Kosmosspekulation und Trinitätslehre," in *Paracelsus in der Tradition* (*Salzburger Beiträge zur Paracelsusforschung*, 21 (Vienna: Verband der wissenschaftlichen Gesellschaften Österreichs, 1980), 32–47. However, I cannot agree that it is possible, or rather even conceptually meaningful, to ascertain with respect to a citation such as Paracelsus's "All things have come from the trinity—like a shadow on the wall . . . copied from the same as its likeness" (*Alle ding seindt kommen aus der trinitet—wie ein schatten an der wand . . . abconterfet von denselbigen auf ir gleichnus*—from Rudolph, p. 34), that this is a Platonic—as opposed to biblical—conception. For us, insofar as we regard the entire Paracelsian scheme of correspondences as of purely historical interest, it may seem meaningful to inquire after specific sources. But for Paracelsus the very resemblance of two such sources would have indicated that they were not two but one and divine. As to which authority Paracelsus names more often, there can be absolutely no doubt that the Bible outweighs any authority accorded to Plato or Neoplatonism.

135. Ernst Wilhelm Kämmerer, *Das Leib-Seele-Geist-Problem bei Paracelsus und einigen Autoren des 17. Jahrhunderts* (Wiesbaden: Steiner, 1971).

136. Regin Prenter, *Spiritus Creator: Luther's Concept of the Holy Spirit* (Philadelphia: Fortress, 1953), 184.

137. For a discussion of the theories derived from the triad as gunpowder, see Lawrence M. Principe and Andrew Weeks, "Jacob Boehme's Divine Substance *Salitter*: Its Nature, Origin, and Relationship to Seventeenth-Century Scientific Theories," in *British Journal of the History of Science* 22 (1989): 52–61.

138. Cited from Friedrich Ohly, "Vom geistigen Sinn des Wortes im Mittelalter," *Schriften zur mittelalterlichen Bedeutungsforschung* (Darmstadt: Wissenschaftliche Buchgesellschaft, 1977), 12 (cf. *Patrologia Latina* 177, 375C; Hugo of St. Victor, *Eruditio didascalia* V,3).

139. Ohly, "Vom geistigen Sinn," 14–15.

140. Cited from Hartmut Rudolf, "Einige Geschichtspunkte zum Thema 'Paracelsus und Luther,' " 51, note 66.

141. Andrew Weeks, *German Mysticism From Hildegard of Bingen to Ludwig Wittgenstein: A Literary and Intellectual History* (Albany: State University of New York Press, 1993), 133.

142. See Karl-Heinz Weimann, *Paracelsus-Bibliographie 1932–1960* (Wiesbaden: Steiner, 1963), 52 (the lecture was held at the Charles University in June 1944).

143. Cf. Udo Benzenhöfer und Wolfgang U. Eckhart (eds.), *Medizin im Spielfilm des Nationalsozialismus* (Hannoversche Abhandlungen zur Geschichte der Medizin und der Naturwissenschaften, 1) (Tecklenburg, 1990).

144. For the forgotten Nazi utilization of Paracelsus's antisemitism, see for example Erich Otto, "Aus der Geschichte der Medizin: Paracelsus und die Juden. Ein Beitrag zur Paracelsus-Forschung," *Hippokrates* 13:41 (October 8, 1942): 777–80.

It is noteworthy that Paracelsus's post-Basel antisemitism seems to arise in part as an identification with the persecuted Christ, whose rejection by the Jews is evoked more and more luridly (I,8:37, 137, 157). However, his thrust is by no means directed only against figurative "Jews" but also against real Jewish competitors who claim superiority but practice deception, and who are to be denied any sort of knowledge, since even their Kabbalah is of non-Jewish origin (I,12:156–7; cf. 270, 355, 373).

145. See Kurt Goldammer, "Friedensidee und Toleranzgedanke bei Paracelsus," *Archiv für Reformationsgeschichte* 46 (1955): 20–46; also in *Paracelsus in neuen Horizonten* (Vienna: Verband der Wissenschaftlichen Gesellschaften Österreichs, 1986). Unfortunately, the argument for

Paracelsus's humanity has been set forth without even an acknowledgment of his other side. A particularly venomous attack on Jewish medicine from the author's preface to *Labyrinthus medicorum errantium* (I,11:167) is turned into a bracketed reference ("Folgt eine Auseinandersetzung über die traditionelle Schulmedizin und über die Rolle der jüdischen, arabischen und griechischen Ärzte") in the Reclam edition of the work edited by Goldammer. See *Vom Licht der Natur und des Geistes* (Stuttgart: Reclam, 1960, 1984), 37.

146. See Goldammer, "Paracelsische Eschatologie," in *Paracelsus in neuen Horizonten*.

147. Gerald Strauss, *Nuremberg in the Sixteenth Century* (New York: Wiley and Sons, 1966).

148. Cited from Sudhoff, *Paracelsus*, 68–9.

149. Antoine Faivre, "L'imagination créatrice (fonction magique et fondement mythique de la image)," in *Revue d'Allemagne* 13:2 (April–June 1981):355–90.

150. Theophrastus Paracelsus von Hohenheim, *Das Mahl des Herrn und Auslegung des Vaterunsers*, ed., trans., and comment. by Gerhard J. Deggeller (Dornach-Basel: Hybernia Verlag, 1950).

151. *Das Mahl des Herrn*, 13–4.

152. Johannes Hemleben, *Paracelsus. Revolutionär, Arzt und Christ* (Stuttgart: Verlag Huber, 1973), 171.

153. Ernst Sommerlath, *Der Sinn des Abendmahls nach Luthers Gedanken über das Abendmahl, 1527–1529* (Leipzig: Dörffling & Franke, 1930), 83.

154. Sommerlath, 117–20.

155. *Das Mahl des Herrn*, 45.

156. Clemens Stoll, "Paracelsus in Beratzhausen/Oberpfalz," *Nova Acta Paracelsica*, Neue Folge 2 (1987): 33–9.

157. Kurt Goldammer, *Das Buch der Erkanntnus des Theophrast von Hohenheim, gen. Paracelsus*, ed. and intro. Kurt Goldammer (Berlin: Schmidt Verlag, 1964), 11ff.

158. *Das Buch der Erkanntnus*, 20.

159. See Norman E. Nagel, in "Martinus: 'Heresy, Doctor Luther, Heresy!'," in *Seven-Headed Luther: Essays in Commemoration of a Quincentenary, 1483–1983*, ed. Peter Newman Brooks (Oxford: Clarendon Press, 1983). Nagel effectively summarizes Luther's early, traditional characterization of the works of creation as divine messages: "Every creature is a work which is to be heeded as a speech of God. Yet they are only signs and not the substance; only God is that [reference to Luther's Weimar Edition, 3:560.35]" (35–6). Along with his expressions of the concealment of God, there are pronouncements in Luther's *Table Talks* that seem to see in nature a revelation of God (see, for example, talks 2005 or 6530 in the Weimar Edition).

160. Heiko A. Oberman, *Luther: Man Between God and the Devil*, trans. Eileen Walliser-Schwarzbart (New York: Doubleday, 1992), 102–3.

161. On non-Christian sources of the doctrine of the signatures, see Edmund O. von Lippmann, *Entstehung und Ausbreitung der Alchemie*, 3 (Weinheim/Bergstraße: Verlag Chemie, 1954), 124.

162. Sudhoff, *Paracelsus*, 43.

163. See Weeks, *Boehme*, 114–21. Cf. Paracelsus, I,11: 375. The "androgyne" is here equivalent to the hermaphrodite: "Thus know here that many people are born who bear monstrous signs with them into the world. . . . Thus also are born hermaphrodites and androgynes, that bear two concealed signs . . ." (*Also wissen hie, das vil menschen geboren werden, die mit inen monstrosische zeichen auf die welt bringen. . . . also werden auch oft geboren hermaphroditae und androgyni, das sind menschen die da haben zwei heimliche zeichen . . .*).

164. Frances A. Yates, *The Rosicrucian Enlightenment* (New York: Routledge & Kegan Paul, 1972).

165. Joachim Telle, "Die Schreibart des Paracelsus im Urteil deutscher Fachschriftsteller des 16. und 17. Jahrhunderts," Karl-Heinz Weimann, "Paracelsus in der Weltliteratur," in Udo Benzenhöfer (ed.), *Paracelsus* (Darmstadt: Wissenschaftliche Buchgesellschaft, 1993).

166. Milt, "Paracelsus und Zürich," 321–54, esp. 333.

167. Klaus G. König, *Der Nürnberger Stadtarzt Dr. Georg Palma (1543–1591)* (Stuttgart: Gustav Fischer Verlag, 1961), 78–85.

168. Marie-Louise Portmann, "Paracelsus im Urteil von Theodor Zwinger," *Nova Acta Paracelsica*, Neue Folge 2 (1987): 15–32.

169. Portmann, "Paracelsus im Urteil von Theodor Zwinger," 20–1.

170. Portmann, 22–3; cf. König, *Palma*, 82–3.

171. Walter Pagel, "The Paracelsian Elias Artista and the Alchemical Tradition," in Rosemarie Dilg-Frank (ed.), *Kreatur und Kosmos. Internationale Beiträge zur Paracelsus-Forschung* (Stuttgart: Fischer Verlag, 1981), 6 ("To Paracelsus Helias represents various features of an ideal through which enlightenment and happiness will descend upon future generations and lift the veil of obscurity which still blinds him and his age. Helias is the perfect adept to come.").

172. For an interesting account of Paracelsus's negative notions of animals, characteristic for his Renaissance naturalism which was constrained to uphold the uniqueness of the human creature, even while seeing the human being as part of nature, see Suutala, *Tier und Mensch im Denken der deutschen Renaissance*.

173. Michel Foucault, *Les mots et les choses: une archéologie des sciences humaines* (Paris: Gallimard, 1966).

174. Jorge Luis Borges, *La rosa de Paracelso y Tigres azules* (Madrid: Editorial Swan, 1986).

Select Bibliography ─────────────

I have included here the standard edition of Paracelsus. It presents the reader with the following classifications: 1. the completed medical, philosophical, or scientific division edited by Karl Sudhoff; and 2. the division edited by Kurt Goldammer, reserved for the religious, religio-philosophical, and social-ethical writings, an edition now about half complete. The two journals devoted to Paracelsus scholarship appear irregularly and present a mix of academic and well-informed amateur scholarship, along with some pure adulation and a good deal of organizational and local-interest contributions. They are *Nova Acta Paracelsica* (originally the yearbook of the Swiss Paracelsus Society, after 1987 continued in reduced format as *Neue Folge*; vol. 1ff. in Einsiedeln, 1944ff.; after 1991, Bern, Verlag Peter Lang) and *Salzburger Beiträge zur Paracelsusforschung* (published by the International Paracelsus Society in Salzburg). For a general introduction to Paracelsus scholarship and its perennial and current questions, the most valuable collections are those edited by Benzenhöfer; Dilg and Rudolph; Dilg-Frank; Braun; and Telle. The collected essays of Blaser, Eis, and above all of Goldammer (*Paracelsus in neuen Horizonten*) are of foundational importance.

The remainder of this select bibliography is intended to offer material relevant to issues discussed in this book. The recent popular accounts by Gerek and Rueb should suggest current tendencies of positive and negative reception.

Anrich, Elsmarie. *Groß göttlich Ordnung: Thomas von Aquin, Paracelsus, Novalis und die Astrologie*. Tübingen: Matthiesen, 1951.

Artelt, Walter. "Wandlungen des Paracelsusbildes in der Medizingeschichte." *Nova Acta Paracelsus* 8 (1957): 33–38.

Baron, Frank. "Der historische Faustus, Paracelsus und der Teufel." In *Salzburger Beiträge zur Paracelsusforschung*. Vienna: Verband der Wissenschaftlichen Gesellschaften Österreichs, 1978.

Bartscherer, Agnes. *Paracelsus, Paracelsisten und Goethes Faust: Eine Quellenstudie.* Dortmund: Ruhfus, 1911.

Benzenhöfer, Udo (Ed.). *Paracelsus.* Darmstadt: Wissenschaftliche Buchgesellschaft, 1993. (Without a doubt, this is the best introductory collection of critical materials on Paracelsus.)

———. "Leben—Werk—Aspekte der Wirkung." In Benzenhöfer (Ed.), *Paracelsus.*

Bernouilli, René. "Montaigne und Paracelsus. Ein Essay." In *Gesnerus* 49 (1992): 311–22.

Betschart, Ildefons. "Der Begriff 'Imagination' bei Paracelsus," *Nova Acta Paracelsica* 6 (1952): 52–67.

———. "Zwei unveröffentliche Arbeiten aus seinem Nachlaß": "Die Signaturenlehre des Paracelsus," "Paracelsus und der faustische Mensch bei Goethe," *Nova Acta Paracelsica* 9 (1977): 164–79; 180–9.

Biegger, Katharina. *"De invocatione Beatae Mariae Virginis." Paracelcus und die Marienverehrung (Kosmosophie* 6) Stuttgart, formerly Wiesbaden: Steiner, 1990.

Bittel, Karl (Ed.). *Paracelsus. Leben und Lebensweisheit in Selbstzeugnissen.* Leipzig: Reclam, 1944.

Blaser, Robert-Henri. "Hutten und Paracelsus, zwei Schicksale der deutschen Renaissance." *Nova Acta Paracelsica* 9 (1977): 69–96.

———. *Paracelsus in Basel; Sieben Studien über Werk, Wirkung und Nachwirkung des Paracelsus in Basel.* Basel: St. Arbogast Verlag Muttenz, 1979.

———. "Ulrich Gyger, sin diener; Versuch einer biographischen Rekonstruktion." In *Kreatur und Kosmos*, 53–56.

Blumenberg, Hans. *Die Lesbarkeit der Welt.* Frankfurt/Main: Suhrkamp, 1981.

Blümlein, Kilian. *Naturerfahrung und Welterkenntnis. Der Beitrag des Paracelsus zur Entwicklung des neuzeitlichen naturwissenschaftlichen Denkens.* (This is a systematic discussion of the concepts of Paracelsus, with an extensive bibliography.) Frankfurt/Main: Peter Lang, 1992.

Bornkamm, Heinrich. "Paracelsus." In *Das Jahrhundert der Reformation; Gestalten und Kräfte.* Göttingen: Ruprecht, 1961.

Braun, Lucien. "L'interpretation de la nature chez Paracelse." *Paracelsus, Werk und Wirkung. Festgabe für K. Goldammer zum 60. Geburtsburg.* ed. Sepp Domandl. *Salzburger Beiträge zur Paracelsusforschung.* Vienna: Verband der Wissenschaftlichen Gesellschaften Österreichs, 1975.

——. "Nature et Philosophie." *In Kreatur und Kosmos* (1981).

——. "Paracelsus und die Philosophie. Eine systematische Betrachtung," *Die Internationale Paracelsusgesellschaft in Salzburg.* Vienna: Verlag Notring der Wissenschaftlichen Verbände Österreichs, 1965.

——. *Studia Paracelsica. Grundsätzliche Einführung in Hohenheims Gedankenwelt.* Strasbourg: Association des Publications pres les Universités, 1983.

——. *Paracelsus; Alchimist—Chemiker—Erneuerer der Heilkunde. Eine Bildbiographie.* Zurich: SV International, 1988.

——. "Vorläufige Bemerkungen zu Hohenheims Naturbegriff," *Salzburger Beiträge zur Paracelsusforschung.* Vienna: Verband der Wissenschaftlichen Gesellschaften Österreichs, 1978.

Braun, Lucien, Kurt Goldammer, Pierre Deghaye, Ernst Wilhelm Kämmerer, Bernard Gorceix, and Rosemarie Dilg-Frank. *Paracelse. (Cahiers de l'Hermétisme)* Paris: Albin Michel, 1980.

Bunners, Michael. *Die Abendmahlsschriften und das medizinisch-natur-philosophische Werk des Paracelsus.* Berlin: Humboldt University, Inaugural Dissertation, 1961.

Campbell, Anna Montgomery. *The Black Death and Men of Learning.* New York: AMS Press, 1966.

Chrisman, Miriam Usher. *Strasbourg and the Reform: A Study in the Process of Change.* New Haven and London: Yale University Press, 1967.

Copleston, Fredrick, S.J. *A History of Philosophy: Volume Three, Late Mediaeval and Renaissance Philosophy.* Garden City, N.Y.: Doubleday, 1963.

Daems, Willem Frans. "'Sal-Merkur-Sulfur' bei Paracelsus und das 'Buch von der Heiligen Dreifaltigkeit.'" *Nova Acta Paracelsica* (1982): 189–205.

Darmstaedter, Ernst. *Arznei und Alchemie. Paracelsus-Studien.* Leipzig: Barth, 1931.

Debus, Allen G., and Robert P. Multhauf. *Alchemy and Chemistry in the Seventeenth Century.* Los Angeles: William Andrew Memorial Library, 1966.

Debus, Allen G., and Ingrid Merkel. (Eds.), *Hermetism and the Renaissance: Intellectual History and the Occult in Early Modern Europe.* Folger Shakespeare Library. London: Associated University Presses, 1988.

Debus, Allen G., "The Paracelsian Aerial Niter, *Isis,* 55 (1964): 43–61.

——. *The English Paracelsians.* London: Oldbourne Press, 1965; New York: Franklin Watts, 1966.

———. *The Chemical Dream of the Renaissance.* Churchill College, Cambridge. Overseas Lecture Series, No. 3. Cambridge: Heffer, 1968.

———. "The Paracelsians and the Chemists; The Chemical Dilemma in Renaissance Medicine." *Clio Medica* 7 (1972): 185–99.

———. "Alchemy." *Dictionary of the History of Ideas*, 1, pp. 27–34. 5 vols. Ed. Philip P. Wiener. New York: Charles Scribner's Sons, 1973–4.

———. *The Chemical Philosophy: Paracelsian Science and Medicine in the Sixteenth and Seventeenth Centuries.* New York: Science History Publications, 1977.

———. *The French Paracelsians; The Chemical Challenge to Medical and Scientific Tradition in Early Modern France.* Cambridge: Cambridge University Press, 1991.

———. *Man and Nature in the Renaissance.* Cambridge University Press, 1978.

———. *Chemistry, Alchemy and the New Philosophy, 1550–1700.* London: Variorum Reprints, 1987.

———. "Iatrochemistry and the Chemical Revolution." In: *Alchemy Revisited: Proceedings of the International Conference on the History of Alchemy at the University of Groningen 17–19 April 1989*, pp. 51–66. Ed.by Z.R.W.M. von Martels. Leiden, New York, Copenhagen, Cologne, 1990.

Decker-Hauff, Hans Martin. "Die Vorfahren des Paracelsus," *Salzburger Beiträge zur Paracelsusforschung.* Vienna: Verband der Wissenschaftlichen Gesellschaften Österreichs, 1978.

Deggeller, Gerhard J. (Ed. and Trans.). *Theophrastus Paracelsus von Hohenheim: Das Mahl des Herrn und Auslegung des Vaterunsers.* Basel: Hybernia-Verlag, 1950.

Deichmann, W. B., Henschler, D., Holmstedt, B., Keil, G. "What is there that is not poison?" In *Archives of Toxicology* 59 (1986): 207-13.

Delumeau, Jean. *Angst im Abendland. Die Geschichte kollektiver Ängst im Europa des 14. bis 18. Jahrhunderts.* Trans. Monika Hübner. Reinbeck/Hamburg: Rowolt, 1985.

Dilg, Peter, und Hartmut Rudolph (Eds.). *Resultate und Desiderata der Paracelsusforschung.* (*Sudhoffs Archiv.* Beiheft 31) Stuttgart: Steiner, 1993.

Dilg, Peter. "Resultate und Desiderata der Paracelsusforschung." (In the above).

Dilg-Frank, Rosemarie. "Zu Begriff und Bedeutung von "pestis/pestilentia" und ihrer Verwendung bei Paracelsus," *Salzburger Beiträge zur*

Paracelsusforschung. Vienna: Verband der Wissenschaftlichen Gesellschaften Österreichs, 1978.

———. (Ed.). *Kreatur und Kosmos: Internationale Beiträge zur Paracelsus-forschung. Kurt Goldammer zum 65. Geburtstag.* Stuttgart: Fischer, 1981.

Domandl, Sepp. "Paracelsus, Weyer, Oporin: die Hintergründe des Pamphlets von 1555." *Paracelsus; Werk und Wirkung. Festgabe für Kurt Goldammer zum 60. Geburtstag*; ed. Sepp Domandl. Vienna: Verband der Wissenschaftlichen Gesellschaften Österreichs 1975 (*Salzburger Beiträge zur Paracelsusforaschung*, 13), 53–70 and 391–392.

Dyk, Anton. "Scientia und Experientia bei Paracelsus im Rahmen der abendländischen Naturwissenschaft," *Salzburger Beiträge zur Paracelsusforschung.* Vienna: Verband der Wissenschaftlichen Gesellschaften Österreichs, 1978.

Eis, Gerhard. *Vor und nach Paracelsus: Untersuchungen über Hohenheims Traditionsverbundenheit und Nachrichten über seine Anhänger.* Stuttgart: Gustav Fischer Verlag, 1965.

Fussler, Jean-Pierre. *Les idées ethiques, sociales et politiques de Paracelse (1493–1541) et leur fondement.* Strasbourg: Association des Publications près Universités, 1986.

Ganzenmüller, Wilhelm. *Die Alchemie im Mittelalter.* Paderborn: Bonifacius, 1938. Reprinted by Hildesheim: Olms, 1967.

———. *Beiträge zur Geschichte der Technologie und der Alchemie.* Weinheim/Bergstraße: Verlag Chemie, 1956.

Gause, Ute. *Paracelsus. Genese und Entfaltung seiner frühen Theologie. Spätmittelalter und Reformation*, Neue Reihe 4. Tübingen: Mohr, 1993.

Gerek, Frank. *Paracelsus—Arzt unserer Zeit. Leben, Werk und Wirkungsgeschichte des Theophrastus von Hohenheim.* Zurich: Benziger, 1992.

Goertz, Hans-Jürgen (Ed.). *Radikale Reformatoren: 21 biographische Skizzen von Thomas Müntzer bis Paracelsus.* Munich: C.H. Beck, 1978.

Goldammer, Kurt. "Aus den Anfängen evangelischen Missiondenkens," in *Paracelsus in neuen Horizonten: gesammelte Aufsätze. Salzburger Beiträge zur Paracelsusforschung.* Vienna: Verband der Wissenschaftlichen Gesellschaften Österreichs, 1986.

———. "Arbeit und Arbeitsruhe in der Sicht des Reformers Paracelsus," in *Paracelsus in neuen Horizonten.*

———. "Die Astrologie im ärztlichen Denken des Paracelsus," in *Paracelsus in neuen Horizonten.*

————. "Der Beitrag des Paracelsus zur neuen wissenschaftlichen Methodologie und zur Erkenntnislehre," in *Paracelsus in neuen Horizonten.*

————. "Bemerkungen zur Struktur des Kosmos und der Materie bei Paracelsus," in *Paracelsus in neuen Horizonten.*

————. (Ed. and Intro.). *Das Buch der Erkanntnus des Theophrast von Hohenheim, genannt Paracelsus, aus der Handschrift mit einer Einleitung von Kurt Goldammer.* Berlin: Schmidt Verlag, 1964.

————. "Der cholerische Kriegsmann und der melancholische Ketzer" in *Paracelsus in neuen Horizonten.*

————. "Friedensidee und Toleranzgedanke bei Paracelsus," in *Paracelsus in neuen Horizonten.*

————. "Die geistlichen Lehrer des Theophrastus Paracelsus," in *Paracelsus in neuen Horizonten.*

————. *Der göttliche Magier und die Magierin Natur.* Stuttgart: Steiner, 1991 (*Kosmosophie* 5).

————. "Humor bei Paracelsus," in *Paracelsus in neuen Horizonten.*

————. "Magie bei Paracelsus," in *Paracelsus in neuen Horizonten.*

————. "Das Menschenbild des Paracelsus zwischen theologischer Tradition, Methologie und Naturwissenschift," in *Paracelsus in neuen Horizonten.*

————. "Neues zur Lebensgeschichte und Persönlichkeit des Theophrastus Paracelsus," in *Paracelsus in neuen Horizonten.*

————. "Paracelsische Eschatalogie," in *Paracelsus in neuen Horizonten.*

————. "Die Paracelsische Kosmologie und Materietheorie in ihrer wissenschaftsgeschichtlichen Stellung und Eigenart," in *Paracelsus in neuen Horizonten.*

————. *Paracelsus: Humanisten und Humanismus. Ein Beitrag zur kultur- und geistesgeschichtlichen Stellung Hohenheims.* In *Salzburger Beiträge zur Paracelsusforschung* 4. Vienna: Verband der Wissenschaftlichen Gesellschaften Österreichs, 1964

————. *Paracelsus in der deutschen Romantik, Salzburger Beiträge zur Paracelsusforschung. Salzburger Beiträge zur Paracelsusforschung* 20. Vienna: Verband der Wissenschaftlichen Gesellschaften Österreichs, 1980.

————. *Paracelsus in neuen Horizonten. Gesammelte Aufsätze. Salzburger Beiträge zur Paracelsforschung* 24. Vienna: Verband der Wissenschaftlichen Gesellschaften Österreichs, 1986.

————. *Paracelsus; Natur und Offenbarung.* Hannover: Theodor Oppermann Verlag, 1953.

———. "Zur philosophischen und religiösen Sinngebung von Heilung und Heilmittel bei Paracelsus," in *Paracelsus in neuen Horizonten*.

Grabner, Elfriede. "Der Zauberer Paracelsus. Theophrastus von Hohenheim im Lichte volkstümlicher Überlieferung." In: *Antaios* 11 (1970) 380–92.

Grant, Edward. *Studies in Medieval Science and Natural Philosophy*. London: Variorum, 1981.

Gundolf, Friedrich. *Paracelsus*. Berlin: Georg Bondi, 1927.

Hacking, Ian. *The Emergence of Probability*. (Chapter 5, "Signs") Cambridge: Cambridge University Press, 1975.

Hale, J. R. *Renaissance Europe: Individual and Society, 1480–1520*. Berkeley: University of California Press, 1971.

Helmrich, Hermann Ernst. *Das Herz im Kosmos und die Pharmakologie des Herzens bei Paracelsus*. Heidelberg: Haug Verlag, 1986.

Hemleben, Johannes. *Paracelsus. Revolutionär, Arzt und Christ*. Stuttgart: Hubner, 1973.

Hollaender, Albert. (Based on a dissertation written for Heinrich Ritter von Srbik, Vienna): "Die vierundzwangzig Artikel gemeiner Landschaft Salzburg, 1525," "Studien zum Salzburger Bauernkrieg 1525 mit besonderer Berücksichtigung der reichsfürstlichen Politik," parts 1 and 2, *Mitteilungen der Gesellschaft für Salzburger Landeskunde* 71, 72, 73 (1931, 1932, 1933): 65–88, 1–44, 39–108.

Hooykaas, Reijer. "Die chemische Verbindung bei Paracelsus," *Sudhoffs Archiv für die Geschichte der Medizin und Naturwissenschaft* 32:3 (1939): 166–75.

———. "Die Elementenlehre des Paracelsus," *Janus* 39 (1935): 175–87.

Joël, Karl. *Der Ursprung der Naturphilosophie aus dem Geiste der Mystik*. Jena: Diederichs, 1906.

Jung, Carl Gustav. *Alchemical Studies*. Trans. R. F. C. Hull. London: Routledge and Kegan Paul, 1967.

———. "Paracelsus the Physician," in Jung, *The Spirit in Man, Art, and Literature*. Trans. R. F. C. Hull. London: Routledge and Kegan Paul, 1966.

Kaiser, Ernst. *Paracelsus in Selbstzeugnissen und Bilddokumenten*. Reinbek/Hamburg: Rowohlt, 1969.

Kämmerer, Ernst Wilhelm. *Das Leib-Seele-Geist-Problem bei Paracelsus und einigen Autoren des 17. Jahrhunderts*. Wiesbaden: Steiner Verlag, 1971.

Karcher, J. "Thomas Erastus (1524–1583), der unversöhnliche Gegner des Theophrastus Paracelsus" *Gesnerus* 14 (1957): 1–13.

Keil, Gundolf, and Willem Frans Daems. "Paracelsus und die 'Franzosen.'" *Nova Acta Paracelsica* 9 (1977): 99–151.

Kerner, Dieter. "Ein Brief des Paracelsus an Erasmus von Rotterdam." *Die Waage* 1 (1959): 146–9.

Klein, Herbert. "Paracelsus und der Bauernkrieg," *Mitteilungen der Salzburger Landeskunde* 9 (1951): 176–8.

Kolbenheyer, Erwin Guido. *Paracelsus-Trilogie (Die Kindheit des Paracelsus, Das Gestirn des Paracelsus, Das dritte Reich des Paracelsus).* Munich: Müller, 1917, 1921, 1925.

Kopp, Hermann. *Die Alchemie in älterer und neuerer Zeit. Ein Beitrag zur Kulturgeschichte.* Reprinted by Hildesheim: Olms, 1962.

Koyré, Alexandre. *Mystiques, spirituels, alchimistes du XVIe siècle allemande.* Paris: Gallimard, 1971.

Kühn, Wolfgang. "Paracelsus und die Fugger. Ein Beitrag zur Geschichte des Guajakhandels," Parts 1 and 2. *Die Medizinische* 44, 47 (1952): 1404–6, 1506–8.

Lemper, Ernst-Heinz. "Görlitz und der Paracelsismus." In: *Deutsche Zeitschrift für Philosophie* 18 (1970): 347–360.

Lippmann, Edmund O. von. *Entstehung und Ausbreitung der Alchemie. Ein Lese- und Nachschlage-Buch.* Weinheim/Bergstraße: Verlag Chemie, 1954.

Magnus, Hugo. *Paracelsus, der Überarzt. Eine kritische Studie.* Breslau: Kern, 1906.

Matthießen, Wilhelm. *Die Form des religiösen Verhaltens bei Theophrast von Hohenheim, genannt Paracelsus.* Inaugural Dissertation Bonn, 1917; also partially published, Düsseldorf: Jumpertz, 1917; reprinted in Benzenhöfer (Ed.), *Paracelsus.*

Metzke, Erwin. *Coincidentia Oppositorum. Gesammelte Studien zur Philosophiegeschichte.* Witten: Luther-Verlag, 1961.

Midelfort, H. C. Erik. "The Anthropological Roots of Paracelsus' Psychiatry." In *Kreatur und Kosmos.*

Miller-Guinsburg, Arlene. "Die Ideenwelt des Paracelsus und seiner Anhänger in Hinsicht auf das Thema des christlichen Magus und dessen Wirken." *Von Paracelsus zu Goethe und Wilhelm von Humboldt. Salzburger Beiträge zur Paracelsusforschung* 22. Vienna: Verband der Wissenschaftlichen Gesellschaften Österreichs 1981.

———. "Paracelsian Magic and Theology: A Case Study of the Matthew Commentaries. In *Kreatur und Kosmos* (1981): 125–39.

———. "Von Paracelsus zu Böhme: Auf dem Wege zu neuen Bestandsaufnahmen in der Beeinflussung Böhmes durch

Paracelsus," *Salzburger Beiträge zur Paracelsusforschung*. Vienna: Verband der Wissenschaftlichen Gesellschaften Österreichs, 1978.

Milt, Bernhard. "Conrad Gesner und Paracelsus." In: *Schweizerische medizinische Wochenschrift* 59 (1929) Nr. 18, 486–8 and 506–9.

———. "Paracelsus und Zürich." In: *Vierteljahresschrift der naturforschenden Gesellschaft Zürich* 86 (1941): 321–54.

———. *Mad Princes of Renaissance Germany*. Charlottesville: University Press of Virginia, 1994.

Mook, Friedrich. *Theophrastus Paracelsus. Eine kritische Studie*. Würzburg: Staudinger'sche Buchhandlung, 1876.

Müller, Martin. *Registerband zu Sudhoffs Paracelsus-Gesamtausgabe (medizinische, naturwissenschaftliche, philosophische Schriften)*. *(Nova Acta Paracelsica. Supplementum)* Einsiedeln: Eberle, 1960.

Müller-Jahncke, Wolf-Dieter. "Der Paracelsische Weg zu Astrologie und Magie." In Benzenhöfer (Ed.), *Paracelsus*.

Müller-Salzburg, Leopold. "Faust und Paracelsus. Ein Vortrag," *Nova Acta Paracelsica* 10 (1982): 128–46.

Oberman, Heiko A. *Luther: Man Between God and the Devil*. Trans. Eileen Walliser-Schwarzbart. New York: Doubleday, 1992.

Otto, Erich. "Paracelsus und die Juden. Ein Beitrag zur Paracelsus-Forschung." *Hippokrates* 41 (8 October 1942): 777–80.

Ozment, Steven E. *The Reformation in the Cities: The Appeal of Protestantism to Sixteenth-Century Germany and Switzerland*. New Haven and London: Yale University Press, 1975.

Pachter, Henry M. *Paracelsus: Magic into Science*. New York: Henry Schuman, 1951.

Pagel, Walter. "Gedanken zur Paracelsus-Forschung und zu van Helmont," *Salzburger Beiträge zur Paracelsusforschung*. Vienna: Verband der Wissenschaftlichen Gesellschaften Österreichs, 1978.

———. *From Paracelsus to Van Helmont: Studies in Renaissance Medicine and Science*. London: Variorum Reprints, 1986.

———. "J. B. Van Helmont's Reformation of the Galenic Doctrine of Digestion—and Paracelsus." *Bulletin of the History of Medicine* 29 (1955): 563–8.

———. *Das medizinische Weltbild des Paracelsus: seine Zusämmenhänge mit Neuplatonismus und Gnosis*. Wiesbaden: Steiner, 1962.

———. *Paracelsus. An Introduction to Philosophical Medicine in the Era of the Renaissance*. Basel: S. Karger, 1958, 1982.

————. "Paracelsus als Naturmystiker." In: Antoine Faivre und Rolf Christian Zimmermann (eds.), *Epochen der Naturmystik; Hermetische Tradition im Wissenschaftlichen Fortschritt*. Berlin: Erich Schmidt, 1979.

————. "Prognosis and Diagnosis: A Comparison of Ancient and Modern Medicine," *Journal of the Warburg Institute* 2 (1939): 382–98.

————. *The Smiling Spleen: Paracelsianism in Storm and Stress*. Basel: Karger, 1984.

Paracelsus. *Sämtliche Werke*. 1. Abteilung [division one]: *Medizinische, naturwissenschaftliche und philosophische Schriften*. Ed. Karl Sudhoff. Munich (Berlin): Barth (Oldenbourg), 1922–1933. (The last volume, fourteen, contains a table of contents for the division that is cross-referenced with the Huser edition.)

————. *Sämtliche Werke*. 2. Abteilung [division two]: *Theologische und religionsphilosophische Schriften*. Ed. Kurt Goldammer. Wiesbaden (Stuttgart): Steiner, 1955ff. Initially planned to comprise fourteen volumes, the second division undertaken with the initial cooperation of Daniel Achelis, Heinrich Bornkamm, Donald Brinkmann, Paul Diepgen, Gerhard Eis, Erwin Metzke, and Walter Mitzka, is now about half finished. The volumes that are either in print, in preparation, or planned, according to the catalog furnished by the Franz Steiner Verlag, comprise the following titles:

1. *Allgemeines zum "Seligen Leben." Gott, Christus, Kirche.* (In preparation.)

2. *Ethische, soziale und politische Schriften. Schriften über Ehe, Taufe, Buße und Beichte.* 1965.

3. *Dogmatische und polemische Einzelschriften.* 1986.

4. *Auslegung des Psalters Davids, Teil I: Kommentar zu den Psalmen 75 (76) bis 102 (103).* 1955.

5. *Auslegung des Psalters Davids, Teil II: Kommentar zu den Psalmen 103 (104) bis 117 (118).* 1957.

6. *Auslegung des Psalters Davids, Teil III: Kommentar zu den Psalmen 118 (119) bis 137 (138).* 1959.

7. *Auslegung des Psalters Davids, Teil IV: Kommentar zu den Psalmen 138 (139) bis 150. Auslegung über die Zehn Gebote Gottes. Fragmentarische Entwürfe zu den Zehn Geboten. Jesajakommentar. Danielkommentar.* 1961.
Register der Wörter, Sachen, Namen und Bibelstellen in den Bänden 4–7: Auslegungen zum Alten Testament. Ed. Kurt Goldammer in cooperation with Rudolf Mohr, Karl-Heinz Weimann, *i.a.* 1995.

Planned:
8./9. *Evangelienkommentare und Kommentare zu den neutestamentlichen Briefen.*
10. *Abendmahlschriften.*
11. *Sermones.*
12. *Marienschriften.*
———. *Selected Writings*, ed. and intro. Jolande Jacobi. Princeton: Princeton University Press, 1958.

Peuckert, Will-Erich. *Die große Wende.* Hamburg: Claassen & Goverts, 1948.

Pisa, Karl. *Paracelsus in Österreich. Eine Spurensuche.* St. Pölten, Vienna: Verlag Niederösterreichisches Pressehaus, 1991.

Pfefferl, Horst. "Valentin Weigel und Paracelsus." *Paracelsus und sein dämonengläubiges Jahrhundert*, ed. Sepp Domandl. Vienna: Verband der Wissenschaftlichen Gesellschaften Österreichs, *Salzburger Beiträge zur Paracelsusforschung*, 26 (1988): 77–95.

Portmann, Marie-Louise. "Paracelsus im Urteil von Theodor Zwinger. *Nova Acta Paraselsica* Neue Folge 2 (1987): 15–32.

Reclam, Ernst Heinrich. *Die Gestalt des Paracelsus in der Dichtung. Studien zu Kolbenheyers Trilogie.* Leipzig: Reclam, 1938.

Rees, Graham. "Francis Bacon's Semi-Paracelsian Cosmology," *Ambix* 22:2 (July 1975): 81–101; 22:3 (November 1975): 161–73.

Rosner, Edwin. "Hohenheims Bergsuchtmonographie." In *Kreatur und Kosmos.*

Rothlin, Ernst. "Über Grundgedanken der ärztlichen Erziehung und der Behandlungsweise von Kranken bei Paracelsus," *Paracelsus-Schriftenreihe der Stadt Villach*, ed. Gotbert Moro. Klagenfurt: Landesmuseum für Kärnten, 1958.

Rudolph, Hartmut. "Einige Gesichtspunkte zum Thema 'Paracelsus und Luther'." *Archiv für Reformationsgeschichte* 72 (1981): 34–53.

———. "Fragen zum sogenannten Vita beata-Schrifttum des Paracelsus; Untersuchungen aus der Marburger Paracelsus-Edition." (Mit einer ergänzenden Nachbemerkung von Kurt Goldammer). In *Nova Acta Paraselsica* 9 (1977) 193–204.

———. "Individuum und Obrigkeit bei Paracelsus." In *Nova Acta Paraselsica*, NF 3 (1988) 69–76.

———. "Kosmosspekulaton und Trinitätslehre. Ein Beitrag zur Beziehung zwischen Weltbild und Theologie bei Paracelsus," *Salzburger Beiträge zur Paracelsusforschung.* Vienna: Verband der Wissenschaftlichen Gesellschaften Österreichs, 1978.

————. "Paracelsus' Laientheologie in traditionsgeschichtlicher Sicht und in ihrer Zuordnung zu Reformation und katholischer Reform." In Dilg, Peter (Ed.). *Resultate und Desiderata der Paracelsusforschung.*

————. "Schriftauslegung und Schriftverständnis bei Paracelsus." *Kreatur und Kosmos.* Ed. Rosemarie Dilg-Frank (1981): 101–124.

————. "Theophrast von Hohenheim (Paracelsus); Arzt und Apostel der neuen Kreatur." Hans Jürgen Goertz (Ed.), *Radikale Reformatoren. 21 biographische Skizzen von Thomas Müntzer bis Paracelsus.*

Rueb, Franz. *Mythos Paracelsus. Werk und Leben von Philippus Aureolus Theophrastus Bombastus von Hohenheim.* Berlin: Quintessenz, 1995.

Sartorius Bodo, Freiherr von Waltershausen: *Paracelsus am Eingang der deutschen Bildungsgeschichte.* Leipzig: Felix Meiner, 1936.

Schipperges, Heinrich. *Paracelsus. Der Mensch im Licht der Natur.* Stuttgart, 1974.

————. *Die Entienlehre des Paracelsus. Aufbau und Umriß seiner Theoretischen Pathologie.* Berlin: Springer, 1988.

Schlegel, Emil. *Paracelsus in seiner Bedeutung für unsere Zeit, Heilkunde, Forschungsprinzipien, Religion.* Munich: Verlag der Ärztlichen Rundschau, 1907.

Schmitt, Charles B. *Studies in Renaissance Philosophy and Science.* London: Variorum, 1981.

Schneider, Wolfgang. "Die deutschen Pharmakopöen des 16. Jahrhunderts und Paracelsus." *Pharmazeutische Zeitung* 106 (1961): 1141–5.

————. "Der Wandel des Arzneischatzes im 17. Jahrhundert und Paracelsus." In Benzenhöfer (Ed.), *Paracelsus.*

————. "Über den Liber praeparationum des Paracelsus," *Salzburger Beiträge zur Paracelsusforschung.* Vienna: Verband der Wissenschaftlichen Gesellschaften Österreichs, 1978.

Scholz-Williams, Gerhild. "Die dritte Kreatur: das Frauenbild in den Schriften von Paracelsus." In Ingrid Bennewitz (Ed.). *Der frauen buoch. Versuch zu einer feministischen Mediävistik.* Göppingen: Kümmerle Verlag, 1989.

————. "Frühmoderne Transgressionen: Sex und Magie in der *Melusine* und bei Paracelsus." *Daphnis* 20:1 (1991): 80–102.

Schneller, Klaus. "Paracelsus. Von den Hexen und ihren Werken." In: Becker, G., Bovenschen, G., Brackert, H. u.a.: *Aus der Zeit der Verzweiflung. Zur Genese und Aktualität des Hexenbildes.* Frankfurt/M.: Suhrkamp, 1977.

Schubert, Eduard, and Karl Sudhoff. *Paracelsus-Forschungen.* 1. Heft: *"Inwiefern ist unser Wissen über Theophrastus von Hohenheim durch Friedrich Mook und seinen Kritiker Heinrich Rohlfs gefördert worden?"* 2. Heft: *"Handschriftliche Dokumente zur Lebensgeschichte Theophrastus von Hohenheim."* Frankfurt/M.: Reitz und Koehler, 1887 and 1889.

Sigerist, Henry. "Laudanum in the Works of Paracelsus," *Bulletin of the History of Medicine* 9 (1941): 530–44.

Singer, Charles. *A Short History of Medicine. Introducing Medical Principles to Students and Non-Medical Readers.* New York: Oxford University Press, 1928.

Siraisi, Nancy G. *Medieval and Early Renaissance Medicine: An Introduction to Knowledge and Practice.* Chicago and London: University of Chicago Press, 1990.

Smith, Pamela H. "Paracelsus as Emblem." *Bulletin of the History of Medicine* 68 (1994): 314–22.

Spunda, Franz. *Das Weltbild des Paracelsus.* Vienna: Wilhelm Andermann Verlag, 1941.

Stanelli, Rudolf. *Die Zukunfts-Philosophie des Paracelsus als Grundlage einer Reformation für Medicin und Naturwissenschaft.* Vienna: Gerold's Sohn, 1884.

Stoll, Clemens. "Paracelsus in Beratzhausen/Oberpfalz." In *Nova Acta Paracelsica* Neue Folge 2 (1987): 33–9.

Strauss, Gerald. *Nuremberg in the Sixteenth Century.* New York: Wiley and Sons, 1966.

Strunz, Franz. *Theophrastus Paracelsus. Idee und Problem seiner Weltanschauung.* Salzburg-Leipzig: Pustet, 1937.

Sudhoff, Karl. *Bibliographia Paracelsica: Besprechung der unter Hohenheims namen 1527–1893 erschienenen Druckschriften.* Graz: Akademische Druck- und Verlagsanstalt, 1958.

———. *Kurzes Handbuch der Geschichte der Medizin.* [3. und 4. Auflage von J. L. Pagels "Einführung in die Geschichte der Medizin," 1898] Berlin: Karger, 1922.

———. "Ein Rückblick auf die Paracelsus-Jahrhundertfeier (1895)." In Benzenhöfer (Ed.), *Paracelsus.*

———. *Paracelsus; ein deutsches Lebensbild aus den Tagen der Renaissance.* Leipzig: Bibliographisches Institut 1936.

———. *Versuch einer Kritik der Echtheit der Paracelsischen Schriften. 1.Teil: Bibliographia Paraselsica; Besprechung der unter*

Hohenheims Namen 1537–1893 erschienenen Druckschiften. Berlin: Georg Reimer, 1894.

Suutala, Maria. *Tier und Mensch im Denken der deutschen Renaissance*. Helsinki: Societas Historica Finlandiae, 1990.

Telle, Joachim. "Paracelsus im Gedicht; Materialien zur Wirkungsgeschichte Theophrastus von Hohenheim im 16. und 17. Jahrhundert." In *Fachprosa-Studien. Beiträge zur mittelalterlichen Wissenschafts- und Geistesgeschichte*, ed. Gundolf Keil. Berlin: Erich Schmidt, 1982.

———. (Ed.) *Parerga Paracelsica. Paracelsus in Vergangenheit und Gegenwart*. Stuttgart: Steiner Verlag. 1991.

———. "Die Schreibart des Paracelsus im Urteil deutscher Fachschriftsteller des 16. und 17. Jahrhunderts." In Benzenhöfer (ed.), *Paracelsus*.

Temkin, Owsei. *Galenism: Rise and Decline of a Medical Philosophy*. Ithaca and London: Cornell University Press, 1973.

Thorndike, Lynn. *A History of Magic and Experimental Science*. (Volumes five and six: The Sixteenth Century). New York: Columbia University Press, 1941.

Török, Stephan. *Die Religionsphilosophie des Paracelsus und ihr zeitgeschichtlicher Hintergrund*. (Inaug. Diss. theol.) 2. Teile. Vienna (Typescript), 1946.

Trillitzsch, Winfried. "Paracelsus bei den Basler Humanisten." In: *Klio* 68 (1986): 542–51.

Vogler, Werner. "Ein Dokument zum Aufenthalt von Paracelsus in St. Gallen im Jahre 1533." In: *Nova Acta Paracelsica* Neue Folge 3 (1988): 26–7.

Vogt, Alfred. *Theophrastus Paracelsus als Arzt und Philosoph*. Stuttgart: Hippokrates-Verlag 1956.

Walker, D. P. *Spiritual and Demonic Magic from Ficino to Campanella*. London: Warburg Institute, 1958.

Webster, Charles. *From Paracelsus to Newton: Magic and the Making of Modern Science*. (Eddington Memorial Lecture) Cambridge: Cambridge University Press, 1982.

Weeks, Andrew. *Boehme: An Intellectual Biography of the Seventeenth-Century Philosopher and Mystic*. Albany: State University of New York Press, 1991.

———. *German Mysticism from Hildegard of Bingen to Ludwig Wittgenstein*. Albany: State University of New York, 1993.

Wegener, Christoph. *Der Code der Welt. Das Prinzip der Ähnlichkeit in seiner Bedeutung und Funktion für die paracelsische Naturphilosophie und Erkenntnislehre.* Bern: Peter Lang, 1988.

Weimann, Karl-Heinz. "Auswahl-Bibliographie der neueren Paracelsus-Literatur," *Salzburger Beiträge zur Paracelsusforschung* 3 (1961): 11–20.

———. "Paracelsus in der Weltliteratur." In *Germanisch-romanische Monatsschrift* 42 Neue Folge 11 (1961): 241–74. Reprinted in Benzenhöfer (ed.), *Paracelsus.*

———. "Paracelsus-Lexikographie in vier Jahrhunderten." In *Kreatur und Kosmos.*

———. *Paracelsus-Bibliographie 1932–1960, mit einem Verzeichnis neu entdeckter Paracelsus-Handschriften (1900–1960).* Wiesbaden: Steiner, 1963.

Wightman, W. P. D. *Science in a Renaissance Society.* London: Hutchinson, 1972.

Yates, Frances A. *Giordano Bruno and the Hermetic Tradition.* Chicago: University of Chicago Press, 1964.

———. *The Rosicrucian Enlightenment.* London: Routledge and Kegan Paul, 1972.

Zanier, Giancarlo. *L'Espressione e l'Immagine. Introduzione a Paracelso.* Triest: Edizione Lint, 1988.

Zekert, Otto. *Paracelsus, Europäer im 16. Jahrhundert.* Stuttgart: Kohlhammer, 1968.

Index